Reputation and Judicial Tactics

This book argues that national and international courts seek to enhance their reputations through the strategic exercise of judicial power. Courts often cannot enforce their judgments and must rely on reputational sanctions to ensure compliance. One way to do this is for courts to improve their reputation for generating compliance with their judgments. When the court's reputation is increased, parties will be expected to comply with its judgments, and the reputational sanction on a party that fails to comply will be higher. This strategy allows national and international courts, which cannot enforce their judgments against states and executives, to improve the likelihood that their judgments will be complied with over time. This book describes the judicial tactics that courts use to shape their judgments in ways that maximize their reputational gains.

DR. SHAI DOTHAN is a senior researcher with the Global Trust Project at Tel Aviv University and an adjunct professor in the faculty of law at the Hebrew University of Jerusalem.

COMPARATIVE CONSTITUTIONAL LAW AND POLICY

Comparative constitutional law is an intellectually vibrant field that encompasses an increasingly broad array of approaches and methodologies. This series collects analytically innovative and empirically grounded work from scholars of comparative constitutionalism across academic disciplines. Books in the series include theoretically informed studies of single constitutional jurisdictions, comparative studies of constitutional law and institutions, and edited collections of original essays that respond to challenging theoretical and empirical questions in the field.

Volumes in the Series

Comparative Constitutional Design edited by Tom Ginsburg (2012)

Consequential Courts: Judicial Roles in Global Perspective edited by Diana Kapiszewski, Gordon Silverstein, and Robert A. Kagan (2013)

Social and Political Foundations of Constitutions edited by Denis J. Galligan and Mila Versteeg (2013)

Presidential Legislation in India: The Law and Practice of Ordinances by Shubhankar Dam (2014)

Constitutions in Authoritarian Regimes edited by Tom Ginsburg and Alberto Simpser (2014)

Social Difference and Constitutionalism in Pan-Asia edited by Susan H. Williams (2014)

Constitutionalism in Asia in the Early Twenty-First Century edited by Albert Chen (2014)

Constitutions and Religious Freedom Frank Cross (2014)

Reputation and Judicial Tactics: A Theory of National and International Courts by Shai Dothan (2015)

Reputation and Judicial Tactics

A Theory of National and International Courts

SHAI DOTHAN

Tel Aviv University, Faculty of Law

CAMBRIDGE
UNIVERSITY PRESS

CAMBRIDGE
UNIVERSITY PRESS

32 Avenue of the Americas, New York, NY 10013-2473, USA

Cambridge University Press is part of the University of Cambridge.

It furthers the University's mission by disseminating knowledge in the pursuit of education, learning, and research at the highest international levels of excellence.

www.cambridge.org
Information on this title: www.cambridge.org/9781107031135

First published 2015

Printed in the United Kingdom by Clays, St Ives plc

A catalog record for this publication is available from the British Library.

Library of Congress Cataloging in Publication Data
Dothan, Shai, author.
Reputation and judicial tactics : a theory of national and international courts / Shai Dothan.
pages cm – (Comparative constitutional law and policy)
ISBN 978-1-107-03113-5 (Hardback)
1. Courts. 2. Judges. 3. Reputation (Law) I. Title.
K2100.D68 2014
347'.01–dc23 2014021012

ISBN 978-1-107-03113-5 Hardback

To my parents

Contents

Acknowledgments

The issues discussed in this book arose while I was writing my PhD dissertation "Reputation and Judicial Strategy – Tactics of National and International Courts" under the guidance of Prof. Eyal Benvenisti at Tel Aviv University Faculty of Law. Parts of this book were written while I was a post-doctoral fellow at the University of Chicago Law School and later at the Hebrew University of Jerusalem Faculty of Law at the Research Group on Effective International Adjudication directed by Prof. Yuval Shany and funded by a European Research Council Starting Grant for Frontier Research. Other parts were written later while I was a senior researcher at Tel Aviv University Faculty of Law at the Global Trust Research Project directed by Eyal Benvenisti and funded by an ERC Advanced Grant. I owe an immense debt of gratitude to Eyal Benvenisti, who invested countless hours in helping me develop my research. I also owe special thanks to Lisa Bernstein, Tom Ginsburg, and Yuval Shany for their guidance, criticism, and support.

This book benefited from the comments of many colleagues: Barak Atiram, Ian Ayres, Patrick Barry, Or Bassok, Rafi Biton, Thorbjorn Bjornsson, Ziv Bohrer, Jianlin Chen, Rishad Chowdhury, Avinoam Cohen, John J. Donohue III, William Eskridge, Jr., Talia Fisher, Courtney Flowers, Olga Frishman, Daniela Gabbay, Rotem Giladi, Alon Gildin, Joe Glasrud, Alon Harel, Simon Hentrei, Sigall Horovitz, Guy Hyman, Neli Iltcheva, Saggi Katz, Michal Lavi, Jonathan Lewy, Adi Leibovitch, James T. Lindgren, Kate Lindgren, Henry Lovat, Lilach Lurie, Tal Mimran, Robin Mordfin, Gilad Noam, Elad Oreg, Victor Peskin, Ariel Porat, Mariana Mota Prado, W. Michael Reisman, Susan Rose-Ackerman, Susan Rosenberg, Moran Sadeh, Sigal Shahav, Yahli Shereshevsky, Sivan Shlomo-Agon, Maxwell L. Stearns, Alex Stein, Maria Varaki, Jason Varuhas, Ingo Venzke, Uri Weiss, Omri Yadlin, and Amotz Zahavi.

Parts of this book draw on two previous publications: Judicial Tactics in the European Court of Human Rights, 12 *Chicago Journal of International Law* 115 (2011); How International Courts Enhance Their Legitimacy, 14 *Theoretical Inquiries in Law* 455 (2013).

Papers based on the theory developed in this book were presented at the Tel Aviv University Law Faculty Doctoral colloquium (2008, 2010), the Tel Aviv University Law and Economics/ IO workshop, the Aspiring Scholars Symposium at Yale Law School, the Fox Fellows Seminar, the Annual Conference of the Israeli Supreme Court clerks, the Siena/Tel-Aviv/Toronto Workshop in Law & Economics

(2010), the European Association of Law and Economics 2010 and 2011 Annual Meetings, the Legal Scholarship Workshop at the University of Chicago Law School, and seminars at the Hebrew University Law School, the Bar Ilan University Law School, the Haifa University Law School and the Tel Aviv University Law School.

I gratefully acknowledge the financial support of Yehuda and Civana Kahani (née Goitein), who donated the scholarship that supported me during my PhD studies in memory of Israeli Supreme Court Justice David Goitein (1900–1961), and of the Fox International Fellowship, which supported me during a research period at Yale University.

My biggest debt of gratitude, in this book as well as in all other endeavors, is to my parents: Yoav and Ilana Dothan. I dedicate this book to them.

1 Introduction

More than sixty years ago, Poland agreed to compensate Polish citizens who had lost their property when the Soviet Union annexed parts of Poland. Yet Poland did not keep this promise and failed to pay. The citizens sued to obtain compensation and won their suits in Polish courts. Yet, even after its national courts ruled that it was obligated to do so, Poland refused to pay. Nonetheless, fifty years after the promise was made, an individual filed a suit at the European Court of Human Rights (ECHR), and the court ruled that Poland had violated its citizens' right to property. Poland responded by enacting legislation to ensure these individuals received proper compensation.[1]

[1] Details from *Broniowski* v. *Poland*, judgment of June 22, 2004, 2004-V EUR. Ct. H.R. 1, discussed at length in Chapter 6.

Why would a country be more willing to comply with the judgments of an international court than with its own domestic courts? After all, when international courts render judgments against states, they have no means of enforcing their judgments. The answer, which this book explores in some detail, lies in the idea that courts, particularly those without enforcement power, actively seek to build reputational capital and to use it in ways that increase the costs to states of failing to comply with their judgments. Reputation helps to explain why some international courts – like the European Court of Human Rights (ECHR) – manage to secure compliance with over 80 percent of their judgments, even in contexts where the states strongly object to their decisions.

The theory developed in this book can also be extended to explain a variety of other features of courts' behavior that have long puzzled students of judicial behavior. For example, what explains the decisions of some international courts to issue increasingly demanding judgments against particular states? What (apart from bias) might explain why some states are subject to harsher remedial measures than others? Why do national courts encourage dissenting opinions in some cases and in some contexts while discouraging them in others? What determines the type of reasoning used by courts and the types of authority they rely on in particular cases?

A. Courts as long-term strategic actors that seek to maximize their reputations

This book, like most of the literature on courts and judicial behavior, starts from the assumption that courts seek to implement their policy preferences. It proposes a theory of the accumulation and spending of reputational capital to explain how courts that lack the power to directly enforce their judgments are nonetheless able to induce states to comply with their decisions and thereby effectuate their policy preferences.

The core of the theory is simple: Courts build reputational capital by carefully calibrating their judgments to manipulate the probability that a state will choose to comply. Each time a state complies with a judgment, it strengthens the norm of compliance. Other states, viewing the act of voluntary compliance, reason that they will look worse if they fail to comply with future judgments rendered against them, thus making them more likely to comply with future judgments. As the court secures compliance in additional cases, the perceived reputational penalty for failing to comply with its judgments also grows, making it possible for the court to issue judgments that are gradually more demanding and costly for states to implement. As the book explains, the process by which this is done and the ways that courts calibrate their judgments differ from case to case, and the tactics used by courts to build their reputational capital are quite ingenious and complex. The bulk of the analysis is devoted to identifying these tactics, presenting case studies that demonstrate their power and identifying their limitations – limitations rooted in culture, politics, and the constraints of legal rules and court processes.

The book is organized as follows. After this Introduction, Chapter 2 presents the basic theory of judicial reputation, while situating it in the literature on judicial behavior more generally and exploring carefully the conditions and context in which it most powerfully applies. Reputation is attractive to courts, but states also have reputations. It is the interaction of states and courts that produces their respective reputations. For analytic reasons, the book distinguishes between high-reputation and low-reputation courts, although of course reputation is in fact a continuous variable. Similarly, states can be high-reputation or low-reputation states.

Building on the basic theory, Chapter 3 presents the constraints that courts face as they shape their strategy within the limits of doctrine and the rules of the legal system that circumscribe their discretion. It goes on to describe the possible counter measures that the executive can use against a national court and that states can use against international courts. Parties can use the threat of noncompliance, criticism, or exit of the court's jurisdiction, as well as other harmful responses, to exert their influence on courts and to constrain them to behave according to the parties' interests.

Chapter 4 carefully explores the wide variety of tactics national and international courts can use in order to improve their reputation. Such tactics include the practice of issuing increasingly demanding judgments when the court's reputation is improving and shifting to less demanding judgments when the court's reputation is declining, the shift toward methods of reasoning that expose judicial discretion when the court's reputation is high and hiding judicial discretion when the court's reputation is low, the attempt to support especially demanding judgments with reasoning that hides the judges' discretion, the practice of issuing more demanding judgments against states that are known not to comply with many judgments compared to states whose compliance practices are better, and several other more nuanced judicial practices.

Chapter 5 presents a case study of a national court, the Israeli Supreme Court, that demonstrates the use of judicial tactics by the court. The chapter also presents the responses of the executive against the court's strategy and the ways the court adapts to those responses by changing its behavior.

Chapter 6 presents a case study of an international court, the European Court of Human Rights, that also uses the tactics described in the book. The strategic analysis of the court's behavior explains two patterns in its judgments: a trend toward constantly increasing its demands from states and issuing more demanding judgments against states that often fail to comply with its judgments, compared to states that usually comply.

Chapter 7 investigates the behavior of courts and the different tactics they use in situations where they are not interested in increasing their reputation. Considering these situations helps identify and clarify more precisely the way that the desire to build reputation affects courts' actions. It also helps identify the conditions and contexts in which the theory outlined here will and will not be a powerful predictor of courts' actions.

Chapter 8 concludes and suggests preliminary normative implications of the book.

2 A theory of the reputation of courts

This chapter presents the basic concept of courts' reputation and the reason courts try to improve their reputations. It studies the reputation of parties facing the court, a concept that is necessary to study the court's behavior, and then presents the basic theory of how courts can increase their reputations by taking calculated risks. The chapter explains the concept of public support and the connection between public support and reputation and presents different methods for measuring courts' reputations. Finally, the chapter situates the theory in the literature on judicial behavior and explains when the theory is and is not applicable.

A. What is courts' reputation?

Before explaining the type of court reputation discussed in this book, it is useful to begin with a short explanation about the concept of reputation. When two actors interact in a repeated game, they observe each other's behavior and try to predict the future behavior of the actor faced. The belief each actor forms about the future behavior of the other actor can be referred to as that actor's reputation.[1] When more than two actors are interacting, information about their beliefs passes from one actor to another. A community of actors can form a prevailing belief about the future behavior of a single actor – this belief is that actor's reputation. Reputation can describe not only the predicted behavior of a specific actor, but also the predictions of the relevant community about the behavior of certain actors toward that actor.

The reputation of courts described in this book refers to the belief of the relevant community about the prospects of compliance with future judgments of the court. Therefore, the reputation of the court is determined by predictions about the behavior of parties that are subject to the court's judgments and not the predicted behavior of the court itself.

[1] Miller defines reputation as: "... a judgment about an actor's past behavior that is used to predict future behavior." *See* Gregory D. Miller, Hypotheses on Reputation: Alliance Choices and the Shadow of the Past, 12 *Security Studies* 40, 42 (2003).

A court with a high reputation is expected by the relevant community to be complied with more often than a court with a low reputation. As the next section shows, this expectation of the relevant community can be self-fulfilling by creating a greater reputational incentive to comply with high-reputation courts.

B. Why courts want to increase their reputation

Why would a court want be viewed as having a high reputation? A court's reputation is only a means to an end, and courts may pursue many different kinds of goals. The theory developed here is not concerned with the purpose courts should serve, only with the description of how courts act. Nevertheless, the theory has important normative implications, because the power courts possess as a result of their reputations can be used to achieve certain policy goals, whether good or bad.

Let us start with the idea that parties to judicial proceedings have their own reputations for compliance with courts and that these can be affected by court decisions. Party reputations are affected differently depending on the reputation of the court. When a party fails to comply with a judgment by a high-reputation court, it suffers a greater reputational sanction than it would if it failed to comply with a judgment by a low-reputation court, because noncompliance with a high-reputation court is more unexpected than noncompliance with a low-reputation court. When a party complies with a high-reputation court, it gains less reputation than it would gain for compliance with a low-reputation court because compliance with a high-reputation court is more expected than compliance with a low-reputation court. Because, for the courts examined in this book, compliance is usually much more expected than noncompliance, the reputational sanction from noncompliance is substantially larger than the reputational benefit from compliance. A high-reputation court therefore generates a larger reputational payoff – the sum of the reputational sanction for noncompliance and the reputational benefit for compliance – than a low-reputation court. The reputational payoff describes the incentive of parties to comply: If they comply, they will both avoid the reputational sanction for noncompliance and gain the reputational benefit associated with compliance.

A party facing a court will comply with it only if the material cost of compliance is lower than the reputational payoff. Therefore, the higher the reputational payoff, the more likely the party is to comply. Because high-reputation courts generate a higher reputational payoff than low-reputation courts, they are more likely to be complied with than low-reputation courts when they issue similar judgments. Costs of compliance can include not only monetary payments but also the costs of taking actions that lead to internal political resistance or that jeopardize long-term interests such as security or maneuverability. Although the court cannot observe the exact cost of compliance with its judgments, it can assess the approximate cost. This allows the court to assess the probability that its judgment will involve a higher reputational payoff than its material cost and will therefore lead to compliance.

In some situations the court's sincere preference is that the party subject to its judgment will undertake demanding actions and change its behavior. The court may compromise on its sincere preference and issue a less demanding judgment, however, in order to ensure compliance. Because a high-reputation court is more likely to be complied with than a low-reputation court, the high-reputation court can issue a more demanding judgment that is closer to its sincere preferences.

Parties are expected to comply with the judgments of high-reputation courts. Therefore, a high-reputation court gains a smaller reputational benefit than a low-reputation court in the case of compliance with a similar judgment. Conversely, a low-reputation court loses a smaller reputational benefit in case of noncompliance with a judgment than would a high-reputation court in the case of compliance with a judgment.

While high-reputation courts can lose more from noncompliance and earn less from compliance than do low-reputation courts, this does not create an incentive for courts to eschew efforts to enhance their reputation. Courts do not care about the ability to gain more reputation for its own sake. They care about their ability to promote their preferences by ensuring compliance with their judgments. Courts seek to increase their reputation because the higher the court's reputation, the greater its ability to ensure compliance with its judgments.

C. The reputation of parties facing the court

Because many of the courts discussed in this book do not have an effective enforcement mechanism that can use tangible material sanctions against noncomplying parties, it is necessary to investigate the reputational considerations of the parties facing the courts in order to understand the reasons for their compliance or noncompliance. This book deals with two types of parties: states facing international courts and the executive branches facing their own national courts. The reputational considerations of these two types of parties are similar in some respects but different in others.

States have many different kinds of reputations, including a reputation for compliance with international law[2] as well as reputation for other qualities such as aggressiveness and trustworthiness. This book focuses on what we might call *judgment-compliance reputation*, which is distinct from other kinds of reputation. Judgment-compliance reputation measures the expectation, in the relevant community of states, about the future compliance of a state with

[2] This concept is investigated in Andrew Guzman, *How International Law Works: A Rational Choice Theory* (New York: Oxford University Press), 2008.

judgments issued against it. High-reputation states are expected to comply more often than low-reputation states and will be expected to comply even with more demanding judgments.

Because a high-reputation state is expected to comply with judgments, when it does comply, it will gain a lower reputational benefit than a low-reputation state would gain for similar compliance. On the other hand, if a high-reputation state fails to comply with a judgment, it acts unexpectedly and will therefore suffer a greater reputational sanction than would a low-reputation state. Because most states are expected to comply most of the time with the courts considered in this book, the reputational sanction from each case of noncompliance is substantially higher than the reputational benefit for compliance. High-reputation states will therefore face a higher reputational payoff – the sum of the reputational benefit for compliance and the reputational sanction for noncompliance – for every decision whether to comply or not to comply. This means that the expectation that high-reputation states will comply more often will fulfill itself because the expectations from high-reputation states give them a higher incentive to comply than low-reputation states.

If a state persistently ignores judgments against it, however, noncompliance may become expected from it. In that case, the reputational benefit such a state can gain from each case of compliance may be greater than the reputational sanction for noncompliance. As the reputation of such a rogue state descends even further, its reputational incentive to comply will increase instead of decrease. Such a state can gain substantial reputational capital from the unexpected act of compliance. This book, however, deals only with states that are normally expected to comply and therefore cannot explain the behavior of such rogue states.

States' reputation would not deteriorate to the level where the state is never expected to comply, because at some point the gains of compliance increase and give the state a stronger incentive to comply with courts' judgments. Nor are high-reputation states able to acquire a perfect reputation that identifies them as expected to comply with every judgment regardless of its cost. The higher the state's current reputation, the lower the reputational benefit it can gain from each act of compliance. It therefore gets harder and harder to increase the state's reputation as it improves. Because the true cost of compliance is always unknown, the state's actions are not completely foreseeable in advance and therefore every individual act of compliance increases the state's reputation.[3] The decreasing pace of the growth in the state's reputation, however, prevents its reputation from growing infinitely.

[3] The effect of each act of compliance or noncompliance on the state's reputation described here differs from Guzman's model. Guzman claims that when a state acts according to existing perceptions about its reputation, its reputation will not be increased or decreased, although this action might make the beliefs of other states more stable, see *Ibid.* at 83–84

States can signal their low discount rate by behaving in a way that increases their reputation. A low discount rate means that a state is willing to incur costs in the present in order to facilitate gains in the future – it doesn't heavily discount the importance of future gains. A high discount rate, in contrast, means that a party doesn't care much about the future and is focused on gaining as much as possible in the present. A state's willingness to incur the immediate cost of compliance, even when high, serves as a signal that it cares about the future and doesn't discount the future benefits it can gain from acquiring reputation. If a state behaves in a way that shows it cares about the future, its treaty partners will view it as credible – they would expect the state not to break its promises in pursuit of easy short-term gains, but instead to try to maintain a good relationship with its treaty partners in the hope of maximizing its future benefits from this relationship.

My argument builds on and extends the important work of Andrew Guzman. Guzman investigated the reputation of states for compliance with international law, which will be termed here *compliance reputation* to distinguish it from *judgment-compliance reputation*.[4] He concludes that complying with international law is costly: A state that is willing to sustain this cost in order to improve its reputation

[4] Guzman's compliance-reputation is discussed at *Ibid.* at 33–36. Like the judgment-compliance reputation discussed here, it signals the state's discount rate.

will be a credible treaty partner. By similar reasoning, a state that is willing to comply with a demanding judgment values its future credibility and will be willing to comply with the costly dictates of international law in general. Therefore, states can gain compliance reputation by complying with judgments and building their judgment-compliance reputation.

The state's reputation also allows it to exert influence on other actors in order to suit its interests. If a high-reputation state fails to comply with a court, that court suffers a greater reputational damage than if a low-reputation state fails to comply with it, because such conduct is unexpected by the community of states. At the same time, noncompliance will cause the high-reputation state itself greater reputational damage than it would to a low-reputation state. If the court has a repeated interaction with a high-reputation state, that state can behave strategically: It can threaten the court with noncompliance even if such noncompliance will cost the state a greater reputational payoff than the material cost of the judgment. In the case of a high-reputation state, this threat is credible: The state is calculating that it can sustain the reputational cost of noncompliance better than the court can. This book argues that in some such situations in which high-reputation states credibly threaten not to comply with the court, the court exercises restraint in issuing a judgment. Therefore, having a high reputation can help a state face less demanding judgments from international courts.

Criticism is another threat that high-reputation states can use to constrain courts to act according to their interests. A high reputation lends legitimacy to a state's actions. When a high-reputation state criticizes a court, the court's public support is damaged to a greater degree than if a low-reputation state voiced the same criticism. If the court's public support is damaged, other states will view its judgments as incorrect or biased and will be less likely to comply. Criticism can be used not only against a court but against other states as well. Criticism by a high-reputation state is viewed as justified and can make the criticized state's actions appear less legitimate. Consequently, a high reputation can aid a state in extracting concessions from other states.

Judgment-compliance reputation focuses only on the effect of a state's acts of compliance or noncompliance with judgments on its reputation. This captures only some of the ways courts can affect the broader compliance-reputation of states. A full account of the reputational benefits states draw from courts can help explain why states create international courts in the first place. The broader compliance reputation of states is affected by courts in five different stages. The last stage, compliance or noncompliance with the judgment, also affects the state's judgment-compliance reputation.

The first stage is that of joining a treaty regime and thus submitting to the jurisdiction of an international court. Joining a treaty signals the state's willingness to comply with international law and therefore presumptively increases its compliance-reputation. If the court is an effective one that can inflict severe reputational sanctions on noncomplying states, the value of the state's commitment when it joins the treaty regime is increased and so is the reputational benefit gained from joining the treaty.[5]

The second stage occurs when a state acts contrary to its international obligations. This conduct, if it becomes known in the community of states, leads to rumors about the state's misconduct and damages its compliance reputation.

The third stage occurs when a state or an individual applies to the court and asks that a state be found in violation of its international obligations. The application to the court helps to crystallize and expose the latter state's violation and therefore harms its compliance reputation. The state can partly rebuild its compliance reputation by the way it responds to these allegations. For example, if the state willingly cooperates with the court, this may lower the reputational damage caused to its reputation.

Note that one can have the third stage without the second. That is, a litigant can bring a claim even if a state did not violate international law. The job of courts is to screen good claims from bad ones and to determine if a genuine violation occurred. Thus, the fourth stage occurs

[5] See Oona A. Hathaway, Do Human Rights Treaties Make a Difference?, 111 *Yale Law Journal* 1935, 2002, 2024 (2002).

when the court issues its decision. The court can find that the state did not violate its obligations or that it did violate its obligations, in which case the violation is described and explained. If the court finds the state committed the violation, the state's compliance reputation is damaged. If the court finds the state did not commit the violation, the state gains a reputational benefit. One of the reasons states support courts is that the court can find the state did not violate its obligations, or, alternatively, that the violation was less severe than the rumors against the state indicate.

The fifth stage only occurs if the court finds a violation. In this stage, the state can either comply with the judgment of the court and thus increase its judgment-compliance reputation, or fail to comply and damage its judgment-compliance reputation. The act of compliance also helps the state rebuild its compliance reputation, because compliance with judgments indicates the propensity to comply with international law in the future. This ability to rebuild some of its compliance reputation by compliance with the court's judgments is another reason states need courts.

It is important to note that the fifth stage, which is the stage this book analyzes, covers only part of the effects of the court on a state's compliance reputation. For example, when the court issues a very demanding judgment against a state, it may be indicating that the state is responsible for severe violations of international law and must undertake substantial steps to correct them. In such a case, the state's compliance reputation is severely damaged. However, if the state complies with this demanding judgment, it gains a substantial judgment-compliance reputational benefit. The judgment-compliance reputational benefit may also improve the state's general compliance reputation. This book does not attempt to answer the question of whether the compliance reputation the state gains if it complies with the demanding judgment is enough to offset the compliance reputation the state lost because the court found this severe violation. This book is focused only on the stage when the court issues a judgment that demands compliance to remedy the violation.

The interaction in the domestic arena, between the national court of last resort and the executive, is similar to that between an international court and its participating states in the international arena. The particular reputation of the executive indicates whether the public expects it to comply with the judgments of the national court. Whenever the executive fails to comply, its reputation for compliance is damaged, which means the public will expect less compliance in the future. Every time the executive complies, its reputation is increased.

The executive has an interest in maintaining its reputation for compliance with the national court. Compliance, which shows respect for the rule of law and the independence of the judiciary, comes at an immediate cost and leads to future benefits – it therefore signals the executive's low discount rate.[6] The low discount rate of the executive increases its credibility in the eyes of domestic interest groups. This allows the executive to close better deals with those interest groups. The signal that the executive has a low discount rate can also be received by an international audience. This increases the credibility of the executive as a treaty partner and allows it to conclude better deals with other states, international firms, and organizations. If the court's judgments receive high public support, the executive can increase its own public support by complying with them and thus improve its chances of reelection.

The reputation of the executive is more volatile than that of states and is subject to changes from other factors besides the record of compliance with the national court. When the personnel comprising the executive changes following elections, the expectations of the public, and thus the executive's reputation, may also change. For this reason, this book does not try to differentiate between high-reputation executives and low-reputation executives or assess the different behavior of courts toward them. Another reason for this choice is that the national court faces just one executive, and because the court's reputation measures

[6] Farber claims that maintaining the rule of law and the independence of the judiciary can help states financially by assuring investors their investments are safe. Farber also claims that the willingness to maintain the rule of law despite its immediate costs signals the low discount rate of states, *see* Daniel A. Farber, Rights as Signals, 31 *Journal of Legal Studies* 83 (2002).

the chances of compliance by the executive, the reputation of the court and the executive are inextricably tied to each other.

Because the government in power expects that it might be replaced after a short period, it may discount the future and put less emphasis on maintaining the reputation of the executive. This may render the politicians that control the executive less sensitive to its reputation, although these politicians may still consider significant damage to the executive's reputation dangerous even in the short run. Furthermore, the possibility of elections makes these politicians concerned about losing public support due to noncompliance with the court and strengthens the need for reputation in the short run in order to close political deals.

The possibility of change of government also reduces the effect of the reputation of states on state's behavior for similar reasons.[7] However, states have many lasting attributes and institutions, such as their domestic courts, and in some cases, a stable bureaucracy that remains unchanged after elections. Furthermore, international law does not allow states to escape their obligations simply because of a change in government or policy. For these reasons, the community of states will view a particular state's reputation as stickier and less liable to change following elections. This makes

[7] See Rachel Brewster, Unpacking the State's Reputation, 50 *Harvard International Law Journal* 231, 249 (2009).

the distinction between high-reputation and low-reputation states worth investigating.

A national court interacts with other actors besides the executive. It may be overruled by the legislature, or its judgments may be either ignored or followed by lower courts within the state's judiciary. A national court is also affected by the behavior of nongovernmental organizations (NGOs) that can regularly appear before it and by the judgments of international courts. Chapter 5 shows how the Israeli Supreme Court uses its relationship with these actors to improve its position vis-à-vis the executive branch.

D. How courts improve their reputations

Parties comply with the court when the reputational payoff is higher than the material cost of compliance. High-reputation courts generate a higher reputational payoff than low-reputation courts. Parties will therefore comply with more demanding judgments of high-reputation courts than of low-reputation courts. Compliance proves that the reputational payoff is higher than the material cost of compliance and thus signals that the court has a high reputation. Because the exact material cost of the judgment is never observed by the community that creates the court's reputation, each additional act of compliance signals that the complying party views the court's reputation as high and leads the relevant community to update its assessment of the court's reputation upwards. The more demanding the judgment complied with, the greater the benefit to the court's reputation.

In the domestic arena, the executive has greater information about the court's reputation than does any member of the general public observing the court's behavior. While the expectations about future compliance, which forms the court's reputation, are held by the public, the executive has a better assessment of the prevailing expectations in the public than any member of the public. Therefore, in the domestic arena, the court cannot trick the executive into believing that it has a high reputation simply by issuing demanding judgments. If a low-reputation court issues a demanding judgment, the executive will simply fail to comply, which would cause reputational damage to the court. For that reason, in the domestic arena, issuing demanding judgments can serve as a credible signal – high-reputation courts will gain from this conduct, and low-reputation courts will lose from it.[8] Thus, in the domestic arena, the practice of issuing demanding judgments can, by itself, increase the

[8] For a comprehensive theory of credible signals *see* Michael Spence, Job Market Signaling, 87 *The Quarterly Journal of Economics* 355 (1973), and Michael Spence, *Market Signaling: Informational Transfer in Hiring and Related Screening Processes*, 16–20 (Cambridge, MA: Harvard University Press), 1974. A similar theory that I found especially inspiring when thinking about courts was developed to explain phenomena in the animal kingdom: see Amotz and Avishag Zahavi, *The Handicap Principle: A Missing Piece of Darwin's Puzzle*, XIV (New York: Oxford University Press), 1997.

court's reputation. When compliance or noncompliance occurs, it serves as a separate signal that will also affect the court's reputation. Compliance will lead to an additional benefit to the court's reputation, and noncompliance will lead to a greater reputational damage than the reputation gained by the act of issuing the demanding judgment itself.

If the party against which the judgment is directed has the same information as the relevant community about the court's reputation, issuing demanding judgments does not serve as a credible signal. In the international arena, a state deciding whether to comply with a court ordinarily does not have superior information about the court's reputation compared with other states in the international community. For that reason, the court's issuing a demanding judgment does not by itself increase its reputation. However, a state's compliance with this judgment indicates that state's own high assessment of the court's reputation. The individual assessment of the complying state is not necessarily more accurate than that of any other state. Nevertheless, the reputation of the court is affected by the assessments of each state in the relevant community. Every state has an imperfect assessment of the prevailing expectation of the court and draws on the behavior of other states to update it. When a state indicates a high assessment of the court's current reputation by compliance, it leads all other states to update their assessments upward, which increases the court's reputation.

One way a court can try to increase the chances of compliance is by trying to support its judgment with a very constrained reasoning – a reasoning that hides its judicial discretion. After all, a party failing to comply with a judgment that uses constrained reasoning is showing lack of deference to the rule of law. Respect for the rule of law, just like compliance with the court, leads to benefits in the long run and therefore can indicate a low discount rate. Not following the rule of law can therefore damage the party's reputation by indicating that it does not value the future and can be expected not to comply with future judgments of the court if those judgments will not suit its immediate interests. This will lead to a greater reputational sanction on a party that fails to comply with a constrained judgment compared with a discretionary judgment. If a party complies with a discretionary judgment, it will gain more reputation than if it complies with a constrained judgment. Because the losses for noncompliance are always greater than the gains for compliance, the total reputational payoff is higher for constrained judgments.

If a party complies with a discretionary judgment, it therefore signals that the court has a high reputation and generates a sufficiently high reputational payoff despite the discretionary reasoning used. For that reason, compliance with a discretionary judgment increases the court's reputation more than compliance with a constrained judgment. If a national court issues a judgment with discretionary reasoning, this can directly increase its reputation because the executive will conduct an independent assessment of the court's reputation before it decides whether to comply.

To make the theory presented in this section more concrete, I will apply it to a judgment of the Israeli Supreme Court: *Eduardo v. Minister of Defense*.[9] This judgment concerned a petition to protect schools in the vicinity of the Gaza Strip from short-range rockets (Kassam rockets) fired by militants from the Gaza Strip on civilian centers in Israel. The minister of defense, arguing for the state, only agreed to protect some of the classrooms in the schools in the area. This method of protection would force other schoolchildren to move rapidly toward the protected classrooms in case of a rocket fire alarm. The time between the sounding of the alarm and the impact of the rocket is only about 15 seconds, but the alarm system does not detect every rocket. The state declared that while partial protection was not the best solution in terms of the children's security, it was sufficiently good, and protecting all the classrooms would be too costly. The full cost of protecting all the main classrooms and the relevant auxiliary classrooms was assessed by the state as 192 million NIS.[10] The state had already allocated 330 million NIS to the protection of schools near Gaza and feared that accepting the petition would set

[9] HCJ 8397/06 *Eduardo* v. *Minister of Defense* [2007] IsrSC 62(2) 198.

[10] At the time of the judgment 1 NIS = approximately 0.25 U.S. dollars.

a new standard of protection, costing it hundreds of millions NIS in the short run and maybe billions in the future.

In this case, the court could relatively easily ratchet up the demands of its judgment. The more classrooms that the court ordered the state to protect, the higher the standard of protection, and the shorter the timetables set for this protection, the more demanding the judgment. By issuing a very demanding judgment, the court would signal to the public its high reputation. This signal is credible because it is costly: If the executive were to fail to comply with the court, this would do more damage to the court's reputation than the reputational benefit the court gained from issuing the demanding judgment. Therefore, the court should be expected to issue a demanding judgment only if its reputation is high enough that it is likely to motivate the executive to comply. If the executive complies, the court will gain an additional reputational benefit, because the executive's compliance demonstrates the court's high reputation.

The court in this case in fact issued a very demanding judgment. It ordered that all the main classrooms be protected by the beginning of the next school year and that auxiliary classrooms be protected by a few months after the beginning of the school year. While it may have been prudent to attempt to increase the likelihood of compliance by accompanying such a demanding judgment with a very constrained reasoning, the court did not do so. Instead of indicating in its ruling that it was bound by the law rather than ruling according to its own discretion, the court in this case took a double risk and issued a reasoning clearly based on judicial discretion. The court ruled that the state had to balance between the significance of the military threat, the risk to human life, the material cost of protections, and other considerations. The court ruled that the state had not reasonably balanced those many conflicting considerations. This form of reasoning indicates the result derived solely from the judges' discretion. Under such a discretion-based ruling, noncompliance by the executive does less damage to the executive's reputation.

In this particular case, this greater risk of noncompliance materialized. This indicates that the court had overreached in issuing too demanding a decision accompanied by reasoning that was not constrained enough for its current reputation. Two weeks before the protection of all the classrooms should have been completed, the state submitted a request for a delay. In its request, the state claimed that protecting all twenty-four relevant schools was impossible, that it was possible to fully protect only seven of these schools while seventeen would have had to be rebuilt completely. Furthermore, the state complied with the timetables set by the court in only three of those seven schools. Asking for a substantial delay only two weeks before the date set by the court for compliance is only a little short of open noncompliance.

While the court might have gained some reputation by the fact that it felt secure enough to issue such a demanding judgment, it lost much more reputation when the executive did not comply with the judgment. Admitting defeat and attempting to cut its losses, the court granted the delay requested by the state. Moreover, the court even refused in its decision to grant the remedy requested by the petitioners of driving the schoolchildren to other schools, out of the reach of the short-range rockets.[11]

The next sections analyze more thoroughly the different components that affect the chances of compliance and the reputational effects of judgments.

1. Demanding judgments

In order to comply with a demanding judgment, the party against which the judgment was issued must undertake certain costly actions. The costs of compliance may be diverse and difficult to calculate, and the court and the community observing the judgment can only estimate these costs.

Sometimes the party against which the judgment was issued will need to pay a fine or damages in order to comply with the judgment. The overall cost of compliance with this requirement may still diverge from the sum the party needs to pay. For example, a state that needs to pay reparations according to the just satisfaction mechanism in the European Court of Human Rights (ECHR) may consider several additional factors that affect the costs of compliance. The state may view the payment of reparations

[11] HCJ 8397/06 *Eduardo* v. *Minister of Defense* (decision from November 13, 2007)

as an acknowledgment of guilt that will damage its reputation for compliance with international law or lead to domestic resistance. In other cases, a state may view the payment of reparations as a price, the paying of which absolves it from responsibility for the initial violation. Payment in these latter cases frames the state's action not as a violation but as a legitimate course of action.[12] In such cases, the state may consider that the payment enhances its reputation for compliance with international law and this benefit must be balanced against the sum it needs to pay. Finally, the state may be afraid that compliance will set a precedent and encourage other individuals to petition against its actions leading to future costs. This is also true in the domestic arena. For example, in the *Eduardo* case discussed above, the Israeli government was afraid that compliance with the court's judgment would set a new standard for its obligations to protect classrooms that would end up costing the state much more in the future.

Judgments may require other specific measures that are costly to comply with. For instance, judgments may demand repeating proceedings that were undertaken unfairly or the release of people who are unlawfully detained. The monetary cost of compliance with such a judgment may be minimal

[12] Similarly, behavioral science shows that sometimes setting a fine on the violation can be perceived as exonerating offenders from blame for the violation and therefore increases the chances that people will commit this violation. See Uri Gneezy and Aldo Rustichini, A Fine Is a Price, 29 *Journal of Legal Studies* 1, 13–14 (2000).

or nonexistent, but compliance can still be very demanding. Compliance with such a judgment can lead to public opposition against the government or damage the attainment of policy goals the government views as important. The judgment in the case of *Ilascu v. Moldova and Russia*[13] provides an illustration. This case concerned the detention and ill treatment of four persons in the Transdniestrian region of Moldova. This region is ruled by separatists from Moldova with the active support of Russia under the name "The Moldavian Republic of Transdniestria" (MRT). The applicants in this case were arrested in June 1992 and accused of fighting against the MRT and committing various crimes. They were mistreated, tortured, and sentenced by the "Supreme Court of the MRT." One applicant was sentenced to death and the others to many years of imprisonment. The ECHR found that Russia was responsible for the mistreatment of the applicants because of its support of the separatists. Moldova was also held responsible for not taking suitable diplomatic steps to assist three of the applicants. The court found several violations: Some of the applicants were subjected to torture and others to inhuman and degrading treatment in violation of article 3 of the Convention for the Protection of Human Rights and Fundamental Freedoms (the convention); the applicants were unlawfully deprived of their liberty contrary

[13] *Ilascu and others* v. *Moldova and Russia*, judgment of July 8, 2004, 2004-VII EUR. Ct. H.R. 179.

to article 5(1) of the convention because they were not tried by a competent court; and Russia and Moldova failed to discharge their obligations to allow individual application to the court in violation of article 34. The ECHR emphasized that any continuation of the unlawful detention would result in prolonging the violation of article 5 and a breach of article 46(1) of the convention that requires compliance with the ECHR's judgments.

In order to comply with the ECHR's judgment, Russia needed to secure the release of two applicants who were still detained (the others had been released before the judgment) and to pay a sum of approximately 600,000 Euros as just satisfaction. While this sum of just satisfaction was high relative to most ECHR judgments, it did not pose a serious financial burden for Russia, and the state paid this sum. However, the obligation to secure the release of the two applicants was more demanding on Russia. In order to secure the release of the applicants, Russia had to put pressure on the quasi-independent MRT to release high-profile political prisoners, which would have damaged Russia's relationship with an important ally. It would be especially difficult for Russia to apply this pressure on the MRT because Russia denied any responsibility for the actions of the MRT. Russia tried to present the payment of just satisfaction as full compliance with the judgment and was criticized for this several times by the Committee of Ministers of the Council of Europe, the body tasked with monitoring the enforcement of ECHR judgments. The last two applicants were released from detainment only three years after the judgment was issued by the ECHR, about the time their original sentence under the sham trial held in the MRT was served. This judgment demonstrates that undertaking specific actions can be politically demanding on states even if it is difficult to assess these costs in monetary terms. It also shows that states can try to comply with certain parts of the judgment in order to reduce the reputational sanction for noncompliance, even when they fail to comply with other more demanding and more important parts of the judgment.

Another element of compliance with some judgments includes the undertaking of general measures to prevent recurring violations of a similar kind. Many of the violations of the convention found by the ECHR result from continuing practices that affect not only the applicants but other individuals that are harmed as a result of the violation. The ECHR made it clear in the judgment of *Scozzari and Giunta* v. *Italy*[14] that compliance includes the obligation to choose the necessary means to end the violation found by the court and to redress its effects. However, in many cases states do not implement the necessary changes to prevent future violations, and other individuals harmed by the violation keep raising the issue before the ECHR. The increasing number of recurring cases inflates the ECHR's caseload and also exposes its inability to ensure full compliance with

[14] *Scozzari and Giunta* v. *Italy*, 2000-VIII EUR. Ct. H.R. 471 at 528.

its judgments. This led the ECHR in recent years to demand in several cases (the so-called "pilot cases") specific actions needed to amend structural problems. The phenomenon of pilot cases will be addressed in Chapter 6.

The court that applies judicial strategy will try to assess in advance the costs of the judgment that include all the factors discussed above. While the court may not be able to find the exact cost for the state, it can form an assessment of the cost and perceive that some cases are more demanding than others. As the court acquires greater experience and expertise, it can improve its ability to assess the magnitude of its judgments' demands. The greater the accuracy of the court's assessment, the lower the margin of error it needs to take when it issues its judgments. This allows it to issue more demanding judgments while still foreseeing compliance.

2. *Discretionary reasoning*

This book is focused more on the discretion that judges profess to employ in their decisions than on the actual breadth of their discretion. Judges can often reach the same conclusion in the same case in several ways. Some of those ways suggest that the decision is constrained by the law and derived from it, and some of those ways suggest the decision is reached by the application of judicial discretion. In those cases, the form of reasoning used is merely a matter of judicial rhetoric used to ratchet the reputational sanction on a noncomplying party and consequently the chances of compliance. However, in other cases, the forms of reasoning that indicate the use of judicial discretion can actually lead to a greater spectrum of judicial decisions. This greater freedom to shape the final result may actually be part of the reason that courts favor the use of discretionary reasoning in some cases. In those cases, reasoning is used to reach a certain result and it therefore cannot be traced to a deliberate attempt to improve the court's reputation in the way discussed in this book.

Different forms of reasoning profess more judicial discretion than others. The use of standards instead of rules, for instance, indicates that the court is using its discretion instead of adhering to strict manifestations of the law. Legal tools that balance many conflicting values whose boundaries are not accurately defined show greater discretion than tools that make more clear-cut decisions. For that reason, constitutional tests of proportionality are more discretionary than finding an act unconstitutional merely because it is not legislated in an adequate procedural manner or does not serve any legitimate purpose. Legal tools that admit there is a certain zone of legal options and that the court must circumscribe the boundaries of this zone are more discretionary than tools that define certain actions as being clearly illegal. Therefore, in administrative law, the court appears more constrained if it decides that an administrative act is flawed because the relevant agency acted without legal authority than if it decides the agency acted unreasonably.

One way for the court to indicate that its judgment is constrained by the law is to indicate that it reached a similar result in the past in similar cases. Issuing similar results in similar cases can suggest that there is one correct legal answer, and the court merely applies it without the use of judicial discretion. Courts frequently refer to their past judgments even if they are not bound by them to indicate they are not basing their decision on judicial discretion. By contrast, when the court stresses that it is digressing from its previous decisions, it indicates it is employing judicial discretion. Some forms of reasoning, such as evolutionary interpretation, stress explicitly that the court is changing the law instead of maintaining the same interpretation and can therefore indicate the use of judicial discretion.

Different methods of treaty interpretation exhibit different levels of judicial discretion. Textual interpretation and interpretation that follows the subjective views of the treaty partners are grounded in factual factors that form a greater constraint on the judges. However, teleological (purposive) interpretation allows the court to use its discretion in shaping the object and purpose of the treaty. Many times, teleological interpretation is applied in conjunction with evolutionary interpretation because the object and purpose of the treaty can be dynamic and change over time. Teleological interpretation can also be combined with interpreting treaties according to the Principle of Effectiveness, which allows the rights enshrined in the treaty to be interpreted expansively and the limitations on those rights to be interpreted narrowly.

It is frequently difficult to assess accurately and empirically what type of legal reasoning a court used and how much judicial discretion it professed. But there are certain proxies that indicate a greater or lesser likelihood of the application of judicial discretion by the court. As an example, if the court uses lengthy judgments, it is able to use a looser and less formalistic style and therefore to show greater discretion. This explains the findings of comparative empirical research that shows that powerless courts use shorter judgments. These judgments can hide the courts' discretion and help them secure compliance despite their weakness.[15]

Another useful proxy is the sources that judges cite in their judgments. If the judges cite mainly statutes, they show their fidelity to the elected legislature and to its pronouncement of the law. If, on the other hand, the judges cite mainly academic literature, they indicate that they are using their discretion to pick the sources that suit their own preferences instead of following legal constraints. Citation to former precedent may indicate the court decides its cases consistently, and as suggested above, this can reflect a lack of judicial discretion. On the other hand, citation

[15] See Jean Louis Goutal, Characteristics of Judicial Style in France, Britain and the U.S.A., 24 *American Journal of Comparative Law* 43, 60–61 (1976).

to decisions of other courts is susceptible to the claim that judges are using their discretion to pick the legal systems that happen to suit their preferences instead of being subject to any legal constraints.[16]

3. Dissent

Another way for the court to indicate that it is employing judicial discretion in a ruling is by showing disagreement among the judges. If the law were clear and the judges merely declaring it, members of the court would not adopt different visions of the law. The issuing of dissenting opinions by judges increases the appearance of judicial discretion. Unlike the forms of reasoning discussed in the previous chapter, which each judge can manipulate in her own judgment, adjusting the level of dissent must involve a collective action by the judges and therefore merits a separate discussion.

When a court issues a particularly controversial or demanding judgment or ruling, it can either lead to noncompliance or to severe criticism. In such cases, the court has an interest in projecting unity by avoiding dissent. Minimizing dissents helps present the judgment as derived from the law and not from individual preferences of the judges.[17] Noncompliance with a unanimous judgment will cause a greater reputational damage to the noncompliant party

[16] See Scalia's dissent at *Lawrence* v. *Texas*, 539 U.S. 558, 598 (2003).

[17] See Walter F. Murphy, *Elements of Judicial Strategy*, 66 (Chicago: The University of Chicago Press), 1964.

than noncompliance with a contested judgment. Suppressing dissent can therefore promote compliance. Suppressing dissent can also preempt criticism of the judges that adopt politically controversial decisions. In order to prevent dissent, judges who disagree with the decision of the majority may be pressured to submit and to join the majority decision. Judges are often susceptible to pressure from other judges that can either try to convince them to conform to their opinion or bargain and offer future support in return for a desired vote by another judge.

A typical example of an attempt to suppress dissent within the court in a very controversial decision is the judgment of *Brown* v. *Board of Education*[18] issued by the U.S. Supreme Court. The court's ruling that segregation in public schools was illegal would require difficult and costly changes to the public education system in the face of opposition and criticism from powerful social groups. Research shows that initially some justices opposed this judgment and were pressured not to dissent in order to project unity.[19] The opinion of the court was issued by Chief Justice Warren. It was very short, and no concurring or dissenting opinions were issued. Similarly, the demanding judgment of *United States* v. *Nixon*[20] was given

[18] *Brown* v. *Board of Education*, 347 U.S. 483 (1954).

[19] See Michael J. Klarman, *Brown* v. *Board of Education: Law or Politics?* at 18 (research paper No. 02–11 December 2002) available at http://ssrn.com/abstract_id=353361

[20] *United States* v. *Nixon*, 418 U.S. 683 (1974).

unanimously. This judgment required President Nixon to turn over tapes containing criminalizing material relating to the Watergate affair. The release of the tapes led to the resignation of Nixon under threat of impeachment.

Another way to project unity is to issue the judgment *per curiam* – by the court – rather than identifying authorship by individual judges. This practice also depends on the prevalent norm in the court at the time. For example, the Israeli Supreme Court issued many of its judgments in the 1950s per curiam, but stopped using this practice almost completely in later years.[21] Nevertheless, even in the 1990s, the court used per curiam judgments when it was issuing very controversial decisions, such as the decision to acquit an alleged Nazi war criminal because of doubts regarding his identity in the *Demjanjuk* case[22] (judgment issued in 1993) or the decision to deny a petition against the temporary deportation of 415 members of hostile organizations in the *Association for Civil Rights in Israel* case[23] (judgment issued in 1992). The latter judgment was issued per curiam, although several judges resisted it vehemently and intended to write strong dissents. Meir Shamgar, the powerful

[21] See Yoram Shachar, Miron Gross, and Ron Harris, Anatomy of Discourse and Dissent in the Supreme Court: Quantitative Analyses, 20 *Tel Aviv University Law Review* 749, 754 (1997) (Hebrew).

[22] CrimA 347/88 *Demjanjuk* v. *The State of Israel* [1993] IsrSC 47(4) 221.

[23] HCJ 5973/92 *Association for Civil Rights in Israel* v. *Minister of Defense* [1993] IsrSC 47(1) 267.

president of the court, suppressed these dissents, which led to the unanimous per curiam judgment.[24]

Unfortunately, while suppressing dissent may reduce the appearance of judicial discretion and is therefore beneficial when the court issues particularly controversial judgment, such judgments may provoke controversy and disagreement among the judges themselves and may therefore be exactly the kind of judgments where dissent is likely.[25] When judges decide whether to dissent, they consider not only the effect of their decision on the future reputation of the court, but also how this decision promotes their own preferences. If a judge disagrees with the views of other judges, she may dissent and proclaim her sincere views, putting her own preferences before the long-term interests of the court. A judge may also dissent in order to reduce the chances of compliance with the judgment, to appeal to the legislature or to future judges to change the decision, or to improve the credibility of his threats to dissent in the future.[26]

[24] See Nomi Levitsky, *Your Honor*, 183–188 (Jerusalem: Keter), 2001 (Hebrew).

[25] See P. S. Atiyah and Roberts Summers, *Form and Substance in Anglo-American Law: A Comparative Study of Legal Reasoning, Legal Theory and Legal Institutions*, 288 (Oxford: Clarendon), 1987.

[26] For a discussion of some of these possibilities, see Robert Post, The Supreme Court Opinion as Institutional Practice: Dissent, Legal Scholarship, and Decisionmaking in the Taft Court, 85 *Minnesota Law Review* 1267, 1353–1354 (2001); Stanley H. Fuld, The Voices of

In some cases, judges may dissent even though they view the decision reached by the majority as either correct or unavoidable. A dissent in such a case will not change the final result and can be used to improve the dissenting judge's image in the eyes of a particular segment of the public or other audience. A possible example is the *Yardor* case[27] decided by the Israeli Supreme Court. This case concerned a petition by a party that did not recognize the legitimacy of Israel against the decision of the election committee preventing it from participating in the Israeli parliamentary elections. Justice Haim Cohen wrote the first judgment in the case, writing that the party should be allowed to participate in the elections. Cohen was so resolved to position himself as the protector of the rule of law that he came to the first meeting of the justices with his judgment completely written, breaking with the tradition of the Israeli court, under which no justice writes his judgment before the conversations between the justices are over and the head of the panel has assigned the majority judgment. Cohen's unorthodox move forced the other two justices on the panel, Simon Agranat and Yoel Zussman, to rule that the party could not join the elections in order to avoid a result that all three justices, including Cohen himself,

Dissent, 62 *Columbia Law Review* 923, 927 (1962); Murphy, *op. cit.*, *supra* note 17 at 90.

[27] EA 1/65 *Yardor* v. *The Chair of the Electoral Committee of the 6th Knesset* [1965] IsrSC 19(3) 365.

probably viewed as unacceptable (in the *Kardosh* case, Cohen had joined the majority in preventing the same party from registering as a company).[28] At the same time, Cohen's minority opinion allowed him to present himself as the protector of human rights and the rule of law.[29]

The judgment of the Israeli Supreme Court in *Regional Council, Coast of Gaza*[30] provides an illustrative example of the difficulty of suppressing dissents in controversial cases even when it is in the court's interest to do so. In this judgment, ten justices out of eleven joined a per curiam decision, ruling that the implementation of the disengagement statute that authorized the evacuation of Israelis from the Gaza Strip was constitutional. The use of the rare per curiam judgment and the size of the panel indicate that the court was striving for unity in order to support its controversial judgment. However, Justice Edmond Levy issued a dissent, writing that the statute was unconstitutional because it contradicted the Israeli Declaration of Independence (which enjoys constitutional status), unreasonably changed policies advocated before the elections, and violated constitutional rights. Levy acted against the court's effort of

[28] See HCJ 241/60 *Kardosh* v. *Registrar of Companies* [1961] IsrSC 15(2) 1151, 1170–1173.

[29] See Pnina Lahav, *Judgment in Jerusalem: Chief Justice Simon Agranat and the Zionist Century*, 258–259 (Tel Aviv: Am Oved Publishers Ltd.), 1999 (Hebrew).

[30] HCJ 1661/05 *Regional Council, Coast of Gaza* v. *Knesset of Israel* [2005] IsrSC 59(2) 481.

projecting unity because he was opposed to the policy the court advocated. He may have inadvertently helped the court by showing the court was pluralistic and represented a spectrum of views, but this was certainly not his immediate intention. Further examples of the problems raised by dissent will be discussed in the analysis of the Israeli Supreme Court in Chapter 5.

In some cases, even though it may be in the interest of the court to indicate it applies judicial discretion, individual judges refuse to cooperate with the court's interest by dissenting. They may be unwilling to dissent for their own individual reasons, for example, in order to avoid attracting attention to the majority's decision.[31] In specific cases, judges may put their own preferences before the need of the court to either project unity or to indicate disagreement; thus it is difficult to learn about the strategy of the court from individual cases. However, patterns of dissent ranging over many years are less susceptible to the idiosyncratic behavior of judges. If the court shows much less dissent in a certain period, it may indicate an attempt to show less judicial discretion in this period by pressuring judges to conform with the majority opinion. If the court shows much more dissent, this indicates that judges are given more freedom to express their opinions and by this to show they exercise judicial discretion.

[31] See Richard A. Posner, *How Judges Think*, 10 (Cambridge, MA: Harvard University Press), 2008.

E. Reputation and public support

The court's reputation represents the beliefs of the relevant community about the prospects of future compliance with the court. The reputation of a national court is a measure of the extent to which the public believes that the executive will comply with future judgments of the court. The reputation of an international court is a measure of the extent to which the relevant community of states believes states will comply with the court in the future. Reputation measures only whether the relevant community thinks compliance with the court is likely or unlikely, not whether the judgment is good or bad. If the public thinks that a judgment is legally wrong or biased, they may decide not to criticize the executive for failing to comply with it. The executive may still have an interest in complying with the judgment in order to preserve its reputation for compliance.

If the relevant community generally considers a court's judgments to be legally correct, fair, and impartial, the court will have high public support. A party failing to comply with such a court's judgments will be subject to a greater criticism than a party failing to comply with a court that has low public support. Even if the public perceives a certain judgment as incorrect, but is generally supportive of the court, the public will criticize a party for failing to comply with it.[32]

[32] The general public support for the court is often termed *diffuse support* to distinguish it from the public satisfaction with a certain

Parties are more likely to comply with courts with high public support in order to avoid this greater level of criticism. If a court loses public support, noncompliance becomes easier, and therefore more likely, in the future.

If a national court issues demanding judgments that go against public opinion, compliance with these judgments may increase the court's reputation in the short run. However, such judgments may erode public support for the court and make it easier for the executive to avoid complying with future judgments without being subject to public criticism. When the executive perceives that this is the case and reduces its level of compliance, the court's reputation will also be damaged. Chapter 5 of this book suggests that this is what happened with the Israeli Supreme Court under the leadership of Aharon Barak around the year 2000.

F. Methods for measuring judicial reputation

Reputation measures the expectations of the relevant community about the chances of future compliance with the court. These expectations are hard to observe and to quantify directly. While it might be possible to ask the public about its beliefs in the probability of future compliance with

judgment, termed *specific support*. See James L. Gibson, Gregory A. Caldeira, and Lester Kenyatta Spence, Why Do People Accept Public Policies They Oppose? Testing Legitimacy Theory with a Survey-Based Experiment, 58 *Political Research Quarterly* 187, 188–189 (2005).

the court, the questions must be phrased very precisely to distinguish views about likelihood from the question of whether the public thinks compliance is good. In addition, a survey of the general public does not take into account that the views of certain members of the public have a far greater effect on the court's reputation than other less informed, less well-financed, or less sophisticated individuals. And the expectations of powerful interest groups who have formed their own beliefs about the court's and the executive's reputations may also count more than the expectations of the general public in shaping the behavior or actions of the court and the executive.

In the international arena the views of a few individuals in the governments, the civil societies, or the industries of the relevant states shape to a great degree the court's reputation. The views of these powerful actors are the ones that will shape the future behavior of the court and of the states under the court's jurisdiction. The general public within the states may have a much weaker impact. Surveys attempting to measure the public expectations about the court's future compliance must identify the relevant influential individuals.

A court's reputation can also be measured by assessing how much a party is willing to pay in order to avoid the reputational sanction for noncompliance and gain the reputational benefit for compliance, because the higher the reputation of the court, the higher the reputational payoff to a complying party. One way to make this assessment is to find out what is the most demanding judgment the party complied with in the past. Unfortunately, it is difficult to accurately quantify the most demanding judgment a party has complied with, as discussed in section D1.

It is also possible to use the intuition that if the court has a high reputation, parties will comply with its judgments more frequently. However, if courts act strategically and try to avoid noncompliance, they may deliberately lower their demands in most or all of their judgments. In that case, rates of compliance are not a perfect measure of judicial reputation, because these rates may reflect a tendency of the court to demand very little, rather than parties' willingness to comply.[33] Selection effects are also a problem: If individuals with a complaint against the executive or the state are more likely to bring the case (against the executive or the state) to the court if it is a high-reputation court, it is because they expect greater compliance with such a court. Paradoxically, this may cause high-reputation courts to have lower compliance rates, because high-reputation courts may have to deal with cases necessitating more demanding judgments.[34]

Another obstacle to accurately measuring a court's reputation is that it is often difficult to find accurate data about

[33] See Heiner Schulz, The Political Foundations of Decision Making by the European Court of Justice, 99 *ASIL Proceedings* 132, 134 (2005).

[34] See Eric A. Posner and John C. Yoo, Judicial Independence in International Tribunals, 93 *California Law Review* 1, 28 (2005).

compliance. It is also difficult to decide how to treat instances of delayed compliance.[35] If a party complies only after the amount of time set in the judgment passed or after an unreasonable time, this certainly does not indicate the same willingness to comply as immediate compliance. On the other hand, if compliance is still difficult and conditions have not changed completely, such compliance shows a willingness to suffer costs in order to comply with the court and cannot be dismissed as regular noncompliance. Compliance can also be partial. Parties can change their practices following the court's judgment but not in the way that fully follows the requirements set in the judgment. Many judgments consist of multiple demands including reparations, specific required actions, and general required measures. Parties can comply with one type of requirements and not with the others, and it would be difficult to determine if this constitutes compliance or not. Despite all these difficulties, compliance rates remain the most useful tool to assess the court's reputation because they attempt to measure the actual response of parties to the court's judgments.

Some other tools may assist in determining the court's reputation and complement the use of compliance rates. One of these indicators is usage rates.[36] The claim is that

[35] *Ibid.*

[36] *Ibid.* Posner and Yoo offer another measure for the effectiveness of courts: the overall success of the treaty regime, but it is very difficult to isolate the effect of the court on the treaty regime from other possible factors, *see Ibid.* at 29.

if parties regularly comply with the court, then petitioners will use it more often because they know that judgments in their favor will be enforced. There are several problems with this measure as well. The first problem is that different courts may be faced with a different number of conflicts, leading to a different number of potential cases. However, if there has been no significant change in the relevant arena that leads to more conflicts, a growth in usage rates can signal parties believe compliance is likely. But this raises other problems. A growth in usage can indicate that parties continue committing violations because they do not fear the future judgments of the court, which can therefore indicate the court has a low reputation. Sometimes an increasing number of cases may even show that states are not complying fully with the original judgment thus leading to more violations from the same unchanged conduct and consequently to more cases. The ECHR, for instance, is faced with a high number of repetitive cases, states that continue to act in a way that was deemed as a violation of the convention by the court. This indicates that these states are not complying with what is usually the most significant part of the judgment: undertaking general measures to prevent future violations.

In conclusion, it seems that all measures of the court's reputation are inaccurate and hard to quantify. Nevertheless, even an intuitive use of some of these measures can help to find big differences between the reputation of different courts or of the same court at different periods.

G. What this theory can and cannot explain

Previous theories explain judicial behavior in different ways. Legal models explain judgments as simply following the dictates of doctrine. Attitudinal models claim that judges pursue their preferences sincerely. Strategic models claim that courts or judges act strategically in pursuing their preferences as they consider the behavior of other actors.[37] The theory presented in this book looks at courts as long-term strategic players, suggesting that courts try to acquire the potential to further promote their preferences in the future as opposed to trying to shape the result in particular cases. Unlike other attempts at studying courts as long-term strategic players, this theory looks at the way courts can improve their future abilities by their judgments alone.[38]

The judgments of many courts raise a puzzle that legal, attitudinal, and short-term strategic models fail to explain. Sometimes courts employ reasoning that seems unconvincing and less authoritative than allowed by the law. Instead

[37] For this ordering of the literature, see Jeffrey A. Segal and Harold J. Spaeth, *The Supreme Court and the Attitudinal Model Revisited*, 44–114 (Cambridge, UK: Cambridge University Press), 2002.

[38] For another long-term strategic model of the Israeli Supreme Court, see Omri Yadlin, Judicial Activism and Judicial Discretion as a Strategic Game, 19 *Bar Ilan University Law Review* 665 (2003) (Hebrew). Yadlin shows how the institutional arena can affect the prospect of legislative override of the court's judgment.

of indicating that they are constrained by the law, judges profess to employ judicial discretion. Unless judges have a certain hidden preference for using this type of reasoning, this behavior does not seem to make sense – it would only appear to damage the chances of compliance and does not seem to bring any immediate benefit to the court. John Hart Ely addressed this puzzle in his book *Democracy and Distrust*, where he stated that judicial activism can lead to expectations of future judicial activism and increase judicial power.[39] More recently, David Law attempted to resolve this puzzle by presenting a new theory of judicial review. Law claims that by supplying less obvious focal points for coordination (which means issuing judgments that are less persuasive), courts enhance their future ability to coordinate behavior around their judgments.[40]

In this book I provide a different explanation for courts' use of discretionary reasoning: If a court's discretion-based judgment is complied with, the court's reputation is increased to a greater extent than in the case of a judgment that appears more constrained. Courts are not concerned with coordinating behavior of multiple actors around the focal points they supply. Rather, a specific party complies with the court to avoid a reputational sanction for

[39] John Hart Ely, *Democracy and Distrust: A Theory of Judicial Review*, 48 (Cambridge, MA: Harvard University Press), 1980.

[40] David S. Law, A Theory of Judicial Power and Judicial Review, 97 *Georgetown Law Journal* 723, 780–781 (2009).

noncompliance. The higher the court's reputation, the higher this reputational sanction will be, which explains the court's incentive to use discretionary reasoning in order to rapidly increase its reputation.

The theory of courts as long-term strategic actors that seek to increase their reputation explains several observed patterns in judicial behavior. The patterns are explained as judicial tactics: different behavior that suits the court's interests under different conditions. The theory, however, can explain only the judgments of certain courts in certain situations; the explanatory power of the theory will be diminished under different conditions.

This book claims that courts try to promote their future ability to obtain compliance, because compliance allows courts to fulfill their preferences. When parties comply with the court for reasons that are not related to the court's reputation – for instance, because the court has a strong enforcement mechanism – the theory will have less explanatory power. The theory is therefore more applicable to international courts, which usually have weak enforcement mechanisms. The actions of national courts can be explained by the theory in cases involving issues of public law, such as constitutional cases, in which they issue judgments against the executive. In these types of cases, national courts are unable to use the executive itself to enforce their judgments and must therefore rely on the force of their reputational sanctions.

The theory assumes that states gain from compliance with international courts, because compliance indicates their willingness to sustain costs in order to comply with their international commitments. If an international court is viewed as heavily biased regarding certain states, or as promoting an agenda that is resisted by the community of states, compliance with its judgments may not increase the reputation of the complying state. The results in those cases will therefore not be explained by the theory. If a state is averse to the basic values of the community of states of which it is part, it may willingly develop a reputation as a rebel state. Such states may be more concerned with maintaining relationships with other states that rebel against the general community of states and therefore may even earn rebel-reputation in this sub-community of rebels through noncompliance with the court.[41] Because the incentives of those states are different than those of most states, the court may also behave differently toward them and therefore those cases are not explained by the theory.

There are other possible situations in which compliance does not serve as a signal in the way depicted in this book. If the court's judgments are usually met with noncompliance, like the Inter-American Court of Human Rights, then every act of compliance will lead to a greater benefit than the reputational cost of an act of noncompliance. This may lead the court to forsake the careful strategy of trying to ensure

[41] For a discussion of the sub-communities of rebel states, see Alex Geisinger and Michael Ashley Stein, A Theory of Expressive International Law, 60 *Vanderbilt Law Review* 77, 126 (2007).

compliance with its judgments and instead take wild risks in the hope of generating a few cases of compliance that would produce big reputational payoffs. Another possibility is that an ineffective court may focus on other aspects of judicial decision making instead of trying to promote compliance, which is highly unlikely regardless of the court's methods. Even an international court that usually obtains compliance from a certain group of states may behave differently regarding generally noncompliant states or when, for some specific reason, noncompliance is expected in a certain case. Compliance is also less relevant to the court's behavior if it issues a judgment that, for some external reason, is certain to be complied with, or requires no tangible act of compliance. In those situations, courts may behave differently than the theory predicts, as is discussed in Chapter 7.

This book shows how courts and the judges within them are subject to many constraints and suggests tactics that can be used only within the realm of discretion left by these constraints. Therefore, the greater the constraints on the court or the ability of interested parties to influence the judges, the less likely the court is to employ long-term judicial strategy.[42] National courts of last resort are more

[42] The use of the word *strategy* to denote a basic plan for judicial behavior and the word *tactic* to denote specific maneuvers under this strategy follows the terminology used at Murphy, *op. cit., supra* note 17 at 9–10. Murphy studies behaviors judges can use besides writing judgments to increase their power, see *Ibid.* at 199. This book, however, deals only with strategic use of judgments.

likely to practice the tactics listed here than lower courts, because they do not fear the prospect of appeal and their judges are usually better insulated from political influence. Courts of last resort usually deal with cases where the law is less clear, and therefore doctrine allows the court a greater discretion. Because the tactics employed here necessitate a good understanding of the law and of policy issues, courts of last resort with professional and experienced judges will usually exhibit better strategic behavior.

The behavior of ad-hoc tribunals and arbitrators is not explained by this theory, because such organizations do not have a long time horizon. Because arbitrators are not concerned with maintaining the reputation of an organization, they may try to increase their own prestige and their ability to draw future clients instead.[43] Even a permanent court will heavily discount the future when faced with some extremely important cases, either in terms of the law or in terms of material implications. Those cases can therefore lead to unique and different behavior. The court is more likely to behave strategically when it has a large caseload, because this allows it to sacrifice the results of some cases in the hope of increasing its reputation for the future. Because this theory is based on signals, the parties must be able and

[43] As an example, Cooter claims that private judges will be particularly inclined to give decisions that are beneficial for the litigants and to ignore their effects on third parties in order to promote more litigation, see Robert D. Cooter, The Objectives of Private and Public Judges, 41 *Public Choice* 107, 130 (1983).

likely to observe the court's behavior and the behavior of the parties that it faces. When judgments are published and commented upon, and when academics and the media scrutinize compliance with judgments, chances that the court will employ a long-term strategy increase.

In many cases, international courts deal with two states that contest each other, and this makes it difficult to adjust the costs of the judgments strategically: A judgment that is demanding for one state may be favorable to the other. Therefore, it is supranational courts – courts hearing cases that pit individuals of minimal political significance against states – that serve as the best examples of the theory. This book deals with the possibility of counter-strategies used by states against supranational courts in case of repeated interaction. The court must adjust to the possibility of such responses by employing more nuanced tactics. A court that faces many states and is therefore less concerned with repeated interactions with each individual state can therefore more easily practice the basic strategy described in this book.

The two case studies presented in Chapters 5 and 6 exhibit optimal conditions for the theory. The Israeli Supreme Court, when seated as the High Court of Justice, deals with complex cases directed mainly against the executive. It is a court of last resort, with a substantial caseload and judgments that are closely scrutinized in Israel. Insights learned from the analysis of the Israeli Supreme Court can be applicable to many other courts of last resort that enjoy judicial independence and share the other qualities discussed above. The European Court of Human Rights is a supranational court that faces many different states, has a large and constantly growing caseload, and is usually complied with despite the lack of an effective enforcement mechanism. The analysis of this court can throw light on other supranational courts with similar attributes such as the European Court of Justice.

The theory explains, with a few necessary changes detailed in the following chapters, the behavior of national courts of last resort and the behavior of supranational courts. The theory can therefore highlight the structural similarities between these two types of courts that lead to similar behavioral patterns. Both types of courts act as long-term strategic players that care about the promotion of their preferences in future cases and will often behave in similar fashions. As an example, the European Court of Human Rights, although a supranational court, is considered as starting to act as a constitutional court. It not only administers individual justice, but also tries to improve the protection of human rights across Europe.[44]

The theory presented in this book is a theory of the behavior of courts. Judges within the court may not

[44] See Joshua L. Jackson, *Broniowski* v. *Poland*: A Recipe for Increased Legitimacy of the European Court of Human Rights as a Supranational Constitutional Court, 39 *Connecticut Law Review* 759, 777–781 (2006).

necessarily use the tactics discussed here deliberately, or even be aware of them; it is the institutional structure of the court that makes the court act as if it rationally pursues the strategy discussed here. Judges and other individuals working within the court may sometimes exhibit different behavior and interests. The institutional structure of the court can minimize the individual biases of judges and lead the court on a path that is motivated by a long-term strategy. However, this does not mean that this theory can never explain the behavior of individual judges. Some judges may value their future ability to promote their preferences. Those judges may gain this ability either by improving their bargaining power relative to other judges within the court or by improving the court's reputation. Sometimes judges will opt for behaviors that are detrimental to the court's reputation in order to improve their own bargaining power by, for example, dissenting when it is in the court's interest to project unity. In other cases, however, judges will behave in a manner intended to increase the court's reputation and consequently their own power to affect society. In these cases, their individual behaviors could be explained by the theory.

H. Conclusion

This chapter suggests that courts in some situations shape their judgments in order to increase their reputations. The reputation of courts is increased if parties comply with their judgments, especially if those judgments are demanding or use discretionary reasoning. National courts can also credibly signal their high reputation directly by issuing demanding judgments or judgments with discretionary reasoning. The higher the court's reputation, the harder it is to increase it. When the court's reputation is high, it will gain less reputation for every act of compliance and will lose more reputation for every act of noncompliance, compared with a low-reputation court. This factor prevents courts from infinitely increasing their reputations. Another factor that can resist the attempts of courts to increase their reputations is that the public may resist the court's attempts to overreach and lower its support for the court. The court is also subject to many types of constraints, some of which are legal constraints that limit the ability of the court to operate within the law and others that are external constraints that include possible responses parties can use to restrain the court. These constraints are the subject of the next chapter.

3 Constraints on courts

This book presents a theory of courts as strategic actors that try to maximize their reputation. In order to maximize their reputation, courts shape the remedies and the reasoning of their judgments in different ways. The ability of courts to shape their judgments, however, is limited by the constraints imposed by legal doctrine and the procedural rules that regulate the behavior of courts, limitations that this chapter refers to as *legal-internal constraints*. Courts are trying to increase their reputation so they can secure compliance with their future judgments, but the parties that face the court can respond to this judgment by noncompliance. Noncompliance will lower the court's reputation and also prevent it from shaping policy in the current case. The prospect of noncompliance is therefore an external constraint on the court's discretion. Besides the option of noncompliance, a party that is dissatisfied with the court's judgments can damage the court's interests in many other ways. Courts seek to avoid this damage and must therefore consider the possibility of such responses as external constraints on their behavior. This chapter will discuss the different responses that the executive can exercise against a national court as well as the responses that states can exercise against an international court and will try to compare the constraints imposed on national and international courts. Third parties may affect the interaction between the court and the party subject to its judgments and either increase or decrease the constraints imposed on the court. The influence of third parties will be briefly discussed in this chapter. Finally, the chapter investigates the tradeoff that exists between the internal and external constraints on the court. A court that is bound by doctrine, or appears to be bound by it, may be better able to resist political pressures because parties subject to its jurisdiction may find it more difficult to retaliate against it.

A. Legal-internal constraints

Judges can apply strategy only insofar as they have discretion to shape their judgments. Although the claim that judges enjoy judicial discretion is considered a truism, this discretion is still bounded by the constraints of legal doctrine and the rules of the judicial system.

Judges are supposed to uphold the law, and therefore when the law suggests only one possible decision clearly and unequivocally, judges seem to have no room for discretion. Legal Realism suggests three main reasons why judicial decision making nevertheless involves judicial discretion. The first reason is the inherent indeterminacy of legal rules, which results from the vagueness of human language and the impossibility of foreseeing the future.[1] The second reason is the prevalence of conflicting rules that apply to the same issue. The third reason is the need to classify the facts into a relevant legal category, a process that involves the choice between different categories.[2] The reasons put forward by the legal realists suggest that judges may be able to choose between several possible results and several forms of reasoning as they decide cases. These reasons do not prove that judicial discretion exists in every case. Some cases may be clear cut and involve no judicial discretion – those cases are termed "easy cases." The existence of easy cases and their prevalence can be debated. It must be clear, however, that the theory of judicial strategy presented in this book has nothing to say about such easy cases. Strategy can be applied only where there is judicial discretion; in other words, strategy can be applied only in hard cases that

[1] See H. L. A. Hart, *The Concept of Law*, 124–126 (London: Oxford, Clarendon Press), 1961.

[2] See Hanoch Dagan, The Realist Conception of Law, 57 *University of Toronto Law Journal* 607, 613–616 (2007).

involve choices made by the judges.[3] The resolution of easy cases therefore involves no judicial strategy.

Judges usually try to present their decisions as determined by the law even if they have judicial discretion, thus making it difficult to distinguish between easy cases and hard cases. There are good reasons, however, to believe that the judgments analyzed in this book and some other judgments of similar courts are hard cases and involve judicial discretion. Most cases where the law is clear and obvious do not reach the courts at all. Individuals coordinate and settle their differences in the shadow of the law all the time; otherwise, society would soon collapse. Easy cases that reach the judicial system will usually be settled before a judgment is written, because both parties will anticipate the same result. Supreme Courts and supranational courts have many mechanisms that ensure only cases where the law is unclear will be litigated. For example, when the Israeli Supreme Court sits as the High Court of Justice, it requires that petitioners exhaust all alternative remedies.[4] A similar requirement for the exhaustion of domestic remedies exists in the European Court of Human Rights.[5]

[3] *See* Aharon Barak, *Judicial Discretion*, 58–66 (Tel Aviv: Papyrus), 1987 (Hebrew).

[4] For a discussion of the duty to exhaust remedies by the petitioner and its limits, see HCJ 1661/05 Regional Council, *Coast of Gaza* v. *Knesset of Israel* [2005] IsrSC 59(2) 481, 581.

[5] See Convention for the Protection of Human Rights and Fundamental Freedoms, Art. 35.

In either of these cases, if the state or the executive realize there is a clear violation of the law, each will probably settle the issue before a negative judgment is handed out. Moreover, in the U.S. Supreme Court, the judges can also choose their cases by the certiorari process and increase the chances of judging only cases where the law is controversial.[6]

There are also ways to verify that judicial discretion was exercised in a particular case, which suggests judicial strategy is possible. If several judges disagree about the result or the reasoning, this can indicate that the case involves judicial discretion. If different results or different forms of reasoning are used in cases that are factually similar, either in the same court or in different courts in the same system, this can help prove the existence of judicial discretion. This book analyzes these kinds of judgments to demonstrate the existence of judicial discretion and therefore the possibility of judicial strategy.

Significant shifts in the way judgments are decided over a period can also indicate that judicial discretion is being exercised, at least in some of the cases, and that judges use this discretion to further policy goals. Trends in judgments, however, can usually also be explained by selection effects,

[6] For the claim that the U.S. Supreme Court is more likely to grant review in the certiorari stage if there is conflict between different courts or precedents, see Thomas G. Walker and Lee Epstein, *The Supreme Court of the United States: An Introduction*, 87–89 (New York: St. Martin's Press), 1993.

that is, a decision of parties to litigate only certain cases based on the expected decision of the court.[7]

Even if a case is a hard case and the judges can exercise judicial discretion when they decide it, their discretion may not be absolute. In fact, discretion has been compared to the hole in the doughnut, which exists only within a belt of restriction.[8] Aharon Barak identifies three objects of judicial discretion: discretion regarding the construal of the relevant facts, discretion regarding the application of the norms to the facts, and discretion regarding the construal of the relevant norms.[9] While a measure of discretion may exist in each of these activities, this discretion is always bounded by the norms and the facts that actually pertain to the case. As a result, while judges can make choices when they decide cases, there are only certain choices they can make, and there are certain decisions they cannot reach and certain forms of reasoning they cannot use.

[7] For instance, individuals may bring cases when compliance is unlikely to high-reputation courts because only such courts can secure compliance. See Eric A. Posner and John C. Yoo, Judicial Independence in International Tribunals, 93 *California Law Review* 1, 28 (2005). (See Chapter 2 *supra* note 34). Parties can also choose to settle cases when one of the parties has a higher chance of victory, leading to a 50 percent chance of victory for plaintiffs, unless they have different litigation costs than the defendants. See George L. Priest and Benjamin Klein, The Selection of Disputes for Litigation, 13 *Journal of Legal Studies* 1 (1984).

[8] See Ronald Dworkin, *Taking Rights Seriously*, 31 (Cambridge, MA: Harvard University Press), 1978.

[9] Barak, *supra* note 3 at 35–41.

Judges are not only limited by doctrine, but also by two other sets of constraints imposed by any legal system: procedural constraints and substantial constraints. Procedural constraints limit the form of what can be considered legitimate, both in the sense of the judicial process and the actual judgment. For instance, a legitimate judgment must be reasoned. Although there are different possible forms of reasoning, the judgment must disclose some form of logical reasoning. Substantial constraints, on the other hand, limit the choices judges can make even further and demand that a judgment be reasonable. Several choices that can be presented as concurring with doctrine can therefore be excluded as unreasonable.[10]

There is a key difference between the amount of discretion judges actually exercise in the case and the amount of discretion their reasoning admits. In a case where doctrine and the rules of the legal system leave a measure of discretion, the judges can choose between several forms of reasoning. Some hide judicial discretion and present the case as mandated by the existing law, and some admit judicial discretion was exercised in reaching the result. The choice between forms of reasoning that expose or hide judicial discretion can be strategic. This book argues that judges may profess judicial discretion as a way to increase their reputation or may hide their judicial

[10] Barak, *supra* note 3 at 46–51.

discretion as a way to preempt noncompliance or other actions that can damage the interest of the court.

The judgments issued by the court are authored by individual judges, who may serve individual goals or follow their own individual interests. The decisions of judges can be shaped by certain background conditions that can help predict their choices. The individual behaviors of the judges may contradict the court's long-term strategy. However, the behaviors of judges should not be viewed as a constraint on the court. Instead, they limit the explanatory power of the theory of the court acting as a unit. Within the boundaries of judicial discretion, the behavior of the court can be explained according to the theory presented here. But this theory cannot explain every judgment, for many reasons: One of them is the conflicting behaviors of individual judges.

B. External constraints on national courts

The executive may respond to the judgments of a national court in a variety of ways that can damage the court's reputation or its other interests. Some of the executive's responses may reflect its immediate interests and have no intention of harming the court. As an example, if the executive finds that compliance with a judgment will jeopardize its interests, it may choose not to comply. This will damage the court's reputation, although this was not the intention of the executive. The executive can also intentionally diminish the court's ability to affect the executive's interests in the future. For instance, if the executive restricts the court's jurisdiction, it can prevent the court from issuing certain judgments that contradict its interests. The executive can also harm the court in order to deter the court from attempting future actions that do not suit the executive interests. For instance, the executive can lower the court's budget in order to make the court understand that it will respond by doing further damage to the court, if the court continues to issue demanding judgments. A national court must strive to avoid the damaging responses that the executive may use against it. These possible responses, therefore, constrain its behavior.

This book focuses on the way the executive and the national court interact. While in some legal systems based on coalition governments the legislature is partly controlled by the executive, the legislature is a different institution with different interests; it will therefore not be addressed fully here. Some of the actions described in this chapter demand legislative actions even if they are initiated by an executive decision. For the sake of simplicity, those actions will be described as undertaken by the executive.

1. Noncompliance

Most judgments issued by national courts against the executive require the executive to undertake certain actions. For example, the executive can be required to pay certain sums to certain people, to release prisoners, to disclose information, to cease certain practices, or to undertake certain works of construction or demolition. The executive can fail to comply with such judgments by not following the instructions of the court. When the executive fails to comply, its policy contradicts the directions of the court and therefore the court's policy preferences are frustrated. Furthermore, noncompliance signals the executive's belief that the court's reputation is low and will therefore damage the court's reputation.

When making the decision whether to comply or not to comply, the executive considers whether the material cost of compliance is greater than the sum of the reputational benefit it will gain if it complies and the reputational sanction for noncompliance ("the reputational payoff"). If the material cost of compliance is higher than the reputational payoff, the executive has every reason not to comply, even if it does not intend to harm the court. Unless the executive has some other interest to help the court or to change its behavior in accordance with the court's judgments, it will fail to comply to suit its immediate interest. If the court can assess accurately the material cost of the judgment in advance and can also assess the reputational payoff, it will avoid issuing judgments that cost more than the reputational payoff in order not to give the executive reason not to comply. The court may err in its assessment and issue judgments that are too demanding. This will sometimes lead to noncompliance.

Other cases of noncompliance can be explained as a strategic response of the executive. If the executive continually complies with the court's judgments to suit its immediate interest, the court's reputation will continue to grow, and the court may try to issue more and more demanding judgments. The executive can deliberately fail to comply with a judgment even if compliance costs less than the reputation it would lose by noncompliance, in order to signal to the court it will not comply with future demanding judgments. That the executive has an iterated relationship with the court can lend credibility to its threat not to comply with future judgments. The executive considers the future implications of facing a high-reputation court and may find it profitable to lose reputation in the short term in order to prevent the court from increasing the court's own reputation or from shifting to demanding judgments.[11] The signal sent by strategic noncompliance is credible if the executive can fail to comply with judgments for longer than the court can withstand this noncompliance. Unlike supranational courts that face many different states and can rebuild the reputation they lose by noncompliance from one state when other states comply with their judgments, national courts

[11] The executive's commitment is conditional; for the threat to be effective, the court must expect the executive not to comply with judgments only over a certain level of demands and otherwise to comply. Schelling investigated similar cases of commitment to a conditional choice. See Thomas C. Schelling, *The Strategy of Conflict*, 48 (Cambridge, MA: Harvard University Press), 1960. Schelling also suggests that in a repeated interaction, a party can demonstrate its commitment in the first few rounds. See *Ibid.* at 41.

face only one executive and are therefore more vulnerable to strategic noncompliance.

Strategic noncompliance can be used to signal to the court that it should lower its demands, but strategic noncompliance can also be used simply to lower the court's reputation. If the executive fails to comply repeatedly, the court's reputation may be damaged to such an extent that it will not be able to create a reputational sanction strong enough to lead to compliance in the future.

But noncompliance is hard to detect because the executive almost never declares openly that it will fail to comply with the court's judgments. Such a declaration will cause a very substantial damage to the executive's reputation. Instead, the executive may try to hide its noncompliance and present its actions as fulfilling the court's judgments. If the judgment is vague or imprecise, the executive may change its practices to create an appearance of compliance, without actually conforming to the dictates of the court. In that case, it may be hard to verify that the new policy is also illegal, and the court will have to undertake a new trial to make such a decision. The executive can fail to comply with the court's judgments and ask for repetitive extensions of time to comply with the judgment. The executive can also fail to comply with parts of the judgment and comply only with some of its dictates.

The court loses reputation when noncompliance is exposed to the public. For that reason, the court may also have an interest to help the executive hide its noncompliance. The Israeli Supreme Court, for example, has been faced with many instances of noncompliance in recent years and yet never used an injunction of contempt of court against the executive. Part of the reason for this behavior of the court was an attempt not to admit openly that the executive failed to comply with the court's judgments. This strategy may work well for a while, but eventually the practice of noncompliance will usually be exposed. This is what happened in Israel in the beginning of the 21st century as will be discussed in Chapter 5.

If the court fears noncompliance, it may try to leave itself a way to retreat from the judgment. The *Eduardo* example discussed in the last chapter shows that the Israeli Court retreated from its judgment after noncompliance became imminent and granted the requested delays to the executive. Another example of this behavior comes from *Worcester* v. *Georgia*,[12] a case handed down by the U.S. Supreme Court in 1832. In this case, the plaintiff, Worcester, was convicted by a lower court in Georgia for violating a Georgia law against residing within the Cherokee nation without a license. Chief Justice Marshall delivered the judgment of the Supreme Court, stating that the act under which the plaintiff was convicted was void since it was "repugnant to the constitution, laws, and treaties of the United States."[13] Accordingly, Worcester's conviction

[12] *Worcester* v. *Georgia*, 31 U.S. 515 (1832).
[13] See *Ibid.* at 561.

was declared null, and Georgia was ordered to release him from prison. But Georgia ignored the judgment and did not release Worcester, and President Andrew Jackson did not intervene. The popular myth is that Jackson remarked after the decision "John Marshall has made his decision, now let him enforce it." What Jackson probably said in fact is perhaps less catchy but does not indicate any greater intention to enforce the judgment – "The decision of the Supreme Court has fell still born, and they find that they cannot coerce Georgia to yield to its mandate."[14] Formally, President Jackson could not send U.S. marshals to enforce the Supreme Court's decision until the Georgia state court formally refused to comply. But the Georgia authorities simply ignored the decision – they did not denounce it. And the Supreme Court adjourned before it could report Georgia's disobedience.[15] There is reason to believe that the Supreme Court could have issued a new mandate that the federal marshals would be required to enforce, but deliberately did not do so.[16] Apparently the Supreme Court understood that

[14] See Paul F. Boller, Jr. and John George, *They Never Said It: A Book of Fake Quotes, Misquotes and Misleading Attributions*, 53 (New York: Oxford University Press), 1989; Ronald A. Berutti, The Cherokee Cases: The Fight to Save the Supreme Court and the Cherokee Indians, 17 *American Indian Law Review* 291, 292 (1992).

[15] See Prucha Francis Paul, *The Great Father: The United States Government and the American Indians*, 212 (Lincoln: University of Nebraska Press), 1984.

[16] See William F. Swindler, Politics as Law: The Cherokee Cases, 3 *American Indian Law Review* 7, 16 (1975).

its judgment would not be met with compliance and chose to minimize the friction with the president by allowing him not to enforce the decision without formally denouncing it.

2. Criticism

If the executive finds that a judgment damages its interests, it may choose to criticize the court for issuing the judgment. If the criticism against the court is issued by an official agent of the executive, such as a minister in a press conference, it can damage the court's reputation. Criticism is an open confrontation with the court and can therefore damage the executive's reputation by indicating that the executive may fail to comply with future judgments. Criticism will usually not damage the executive's reputation as much as noncompliance, because if the executive complies despite its criticism, it indicates a willingness to comply in the future as well. A lot depends, however, on the severity of the criticism. If a criticism is harsh enough and salient enough, it may cause the executive's reputation the same damage as would an act of noncompliance. The reputational damage to the executive that criticizes the court depends on the court's reputation. The higher the court's reputation, the greater the executive's reputational damage will be. When the executive criticizes the court, it therefore signals that the court has a low reputation; this signal damages the court's reputation. In order to prevent this reputational damage, the court may try to avoid issuing judgments that will lead to severe criticism by the executive.

When the executive criticizes the court repeatedly, it can damage the court's public support. The public supports the court if the members of the public think that the court's judgments are correct, just, and unbiased. The executive can criticize the court in order to change public opinion about the content of the court's judgments and lower the public support for the court. The public can change their views about the content of the court's judgments whether the executive or its agents, or someone else the public trusts such as a prominent journalist, voice the criticism. The effect criticism has on public opinion does not result from a signal of the weakness of the court, but rather from the force of the arguments raised against the court's judgments.

Criticism can help to signal to the court that the executive is dissatisfied with the court's judgments and can be used to communicate a threat that in the future more severe responses, such as noncompliance, will be used against the court. Criticism can also make the threat of such future responses credible by eroding the public support for the court. Once the erosion of the support for the court begins, there is a chance that the public will become so enraged with the court's behavior that it will force the executive not to comply. Alternatively, the executive may have no interest to avoid noncompliance because the court's reputation and public support will be low. The court that realizes there is a possibility that the executive may be forced not to comply in the future if the executive continues to criticize the court, may restrain itself to please the executive.[17]

3. Curbing the court's jurisdiction

Courts cannot make policy independently – they must hear a case brought to them by a litigant. For a national court to affect policy, it must hear cases that involve policy issues. Furthermore, courts need a variety of cases so that they can choose the cases that are best suited to issue strategic judgments that can help increase their reputation. Courts can only decide cases that are under their jurisdiction. Courts may be able to shape the boundaries of their jurisdiction by their judgments to a certain extent, but the boundaries of jurisdiction are usually not under the complete control of the court. If the court's jurisdiction is restricted, it therefore loses the ability to decide cases that can help it shape policy and increase its reputation. The executive and the legislature can initiate changes that curb the jurisdiction of the court as a way to retaliate against the court and damage its interests. Curbing the court's jurisdiction is a severe measure of retaliation against the court, which will usually lead to a severe reputational sanction against the executive

[17] A similar tactic in the realm of international power politics was termed *brinkmanship* by Schelling: If a nation cannot threaten a total nuclear war, it can advance ground troops to a spot that creates such friction with the enemy that it may be impossible to prevent the war in the nearby future. This may force the enemy to retreat. See Schelling, *supra* note 11 at 199–201.

because it demonstrates a lack of commitment to the rule of law. For that reason, the executive will not use this measure unless it has a substantial interest to damage the court. However, because the potential damage this action will cause to the court is great, the court will avoid pushing the executive to this desperate measure.

To complete the picture, it must be stated that sometimes courts have jurisdiction over cases they would rather not decide. The Israeli Supreme Court must decide all cases that come to it and is therefore often forced to delay cases strategically or to dismiss cases on technical grounds in order to avoid decisions that can harm it.[18] The Judiciary Act of 1925 improved the strategic position of the U.S. Supreme Court because the act decreased the court's mandatory jurisdiction and increased its discretionary jurisdiction; this allowed the court to choose its battles according to its strategic interests.[19] Usually courts gain from having a wide jurisdiction from which they can choose the cases they wish to decide; a threat to this jurisdiction is a constraint on their decision making.

[18] See Yoav Dotan, Pre-petitions and Constitutional Dilemmas Regarding the Role of Government Lawyers, 7 *Mishpat Umimshal* 159, 193–194 (2004) (Hebrew).

[19] See Robert Post, The Supreme Court Opinion as Institutional Practice: Dissent, Legal Scholarship, and Decisionmaking in the Taft Court, 85 *Minnesota Law Review* 1267, 1272–1273 (2001); Walker and Epstein, *supra* note 6 at 77–78.

4. Changing the law

The legislature can overrule some of the court's judgments by changing statutes after they were interpreted by the court. In the Israeli legal system, the government is supported by a coalition that enjoys a majority of votes in parliament; therefore, the executive can exercise significant control over the legislature and overrule judgments that contradict the executive's interests. Statutes can also be changed in order to either change the legal situation in a way that contradicts judicial preferences or limits the powers of the judiciary. Nevertheless, because these actions are primarily the province of the legislature, they will not be addressed further here.[20]

5. Establishing new courts

One way to damage the jurisdiction of a national court is to transfer some of its powers to another court. The executive may be wary of damaging the jurisdiction of a national court because doing so will damage the legitimacy of the executive's actions. If a new court that can legitimize

[20] Others have looked at the way courts strategically respond to the possibility of legislative override; see William N. Eskridge, Jr., Reneging on History? Playing the Court/Congress/President Civil Rights Game, 79 *California Law Review* 613 (1991); William N. Eskridge Jr., Overriding Supreme Court Statutory Interpretation Decisions, 101 *Yale Law Journal* 331 (1991); Omri Yadlin, Judicial Activism and Judicial Discretion as a Strategic Game, 19 *Bar Ilan University Law Review* 665 (2003) (Hebrew).

the executive's actions is constructed, however, the executive can more easily damage the jurisdiction of the older court and transfer some issues to the jurisdiction of the new court. One of the threats that was posed by the executive against the Israeli Supreme Court was to construct a new Constitutional Court and transfer to it the power of deciding constitutional cases. The plan was eventually forsaken, but the judges may have taken the threat to heart and changed their behavior to avert it.

Even if the executive and the legislature do not impair the jurisdiction of the old court, the existence of another court with concurrent jurisdiction is detrimental to the powers of the old court. If the executive can rebuild its reputation by complying with the new court, it may be more willing not to comply with the old court. When another court exists, the executive may also be more willing to damage the old court in other ways, such as cutting its budget or criticizing it. If the executive can forum shop between the two courts, this also damages the position of the old court, which may be forced to change its judgments to suit the interests of the executive in order to make it transfer cases to it and not to the new court.

A court can be threatened even by the construction of lower courts over which it has appellate jurisdiction. While the court may be able to overrule the judgments of lower courts on appeal, its ability to decide appeals may be limited by its finite resources. McNollgast show that the more lower courts are in existence and the more cases they decide, the more likely the higher court is to compromise on its preferences to give fewer lower courts a reason to digress from its judgments.[21] Furthermore, if the higher court wishes to maintain a coherent policy, but is willing to compromise on its content, the existence of many lower courts will increase the higher court willingness to defer to the executive. The executive may not set policy according to the higher court's preferences, but its policy will be coherent, something that will not be true if the decision is left to many separate lower courts. Peter Strauss claims that the concern that lower courts will set an incoherent policy was the reason for the decision of the U.S. Supreme Court in the *Chevron* case.[22] The court decided in this case that if a statute is unclear, the Federal Courts of Appeals should not impose their own interpretation, but rather defer to the administrative agency. This judgment demonstrates how the existence of many lower courts increases the tendency of the court to defer to the executive in order to avoid an inconsistent policy.[23]

[21] McNollgast, Politics and the Courts: A Positive Theory of Judicial Doctrine and the Rule of Law, 68 *Southern California Law Review* 1631, 1647 (1995).

[22] *Chevron U.S.A. INC* v. *Natural Resources Defense Council Inc et al.* 467 U.S. 837 (1984).

[23] Peter L. Strauss, One Hundred Fifty Cases Per Year: Some Implications of the Supreme Court's Limited Resources for Judicial Review of Agency Action, 87 *Columbia Law Review* 1093, 1120–1121 (1987).

6. Influencing judicial selection and sanctions against judges

This book focuses on the strategic behavior of the court and not of the judges sitting within the court. The judgments of the court, however, are written by judges and the behavior of these judges therefore shapes the behavior of the court. In different legal systems, the executive has different degrees of influence on the selection of judges. If the executive can control the selection of judges, this allows it to select judges that suit the interests of the executive, and not necessarily the interest of the court. If judicial selection is effective in the sense that the executive knows the line the judges will advance on the bench, then the executive can control the court's decision making.

If judges are insulated from political pressures once they are on the bench, they may choose to change their views. Judges, however, may already be entrenched in their views, either because they sincerely continue to hold them or because they feel committed to the previous views they expressed. If judges are not insulated from political influence once they are on the court – because, for example, the executive can control the salaries of judges or the type of work assigned to them or take other actions that either improve or damage their condition – the executive has further leverage to shape the behavior of the court. Similarly, if judges expect other positions or benefits controlled by the executive after they leave the bench, the executive has an additional way to affect judges' decisions.

Another method that can be used to change the court's behavior is to increase the number of judges on the court and appoint new judges – to pack the court. U.S. President Franklin Roosevelt threatened to increase the number of justices on the Supreme Court when they resisted his social and economic reforms during the New Deal. Some scholars claim that even though this initiative was never implemented, the mere threat was enough to make the justices change their policies.[24]

If the executive can control the judges, it can control the decisions of the court and lead to decisions that are favorable to the executive's interests even if they damage the court's interest in increasing the court's reputation. The executive has an interest, however, in preserving an image of the court's independence. If the public believe that the court is independent, they are likely to view the court's decisions as more demanding than they actually are. This allows the executive to increase its reputation by complying with judgments that are not as demanding as they seem. If the court has an image of dependence on the executive, this can help the court to issue demanding judgments that the public will perceive as less demanding than they actually are and will therefore require the executive to comply with them. For that reason, if the executive

[24] See J. Mark Ramseyer, The Puzzling (In)Dependence of Courts: A Comparative Approach, 23 *Journal of Legal Studies* 721, 728–729 (1994).

appoints a judge that seems dependent on it to a position it cannot control, this judge can change her skin and issue extremely demanding judgments.

For example, when the U.S. President Dwight Eisenhower appointed Chief Justice Earl Warren to the U.S. Supreme Court, he viewed Warren initially as dependent, as did many in the public. Eisenhower later regretted his choice when Warren became the most activist Chief Justice in the court's history, referring to Warren's appointment as "The biggest damned-fool mistake I ever made."[25] Decision makers in Israel made a similar mistake when they appointed Zvi Berenson to the Supreme Court. Berenson's nomination was initially opposed by the opposition party because he previously served as the legal adviser to the highly influential workers' union in Israel (the Histadrut) and before his nomination served as the chief manager of the Labor Office. Nevertheless, shortly after his nomination, Berenson became an activist critic of the actions of the government.[26]

Yet while the court can gain from an image of dependence, especially when its reputation is low and it needs to present its judgments as less demanding to ensure compliance, the judges themselves may want to appear independent. Judges can care about their prestige in legal and

[25] See http://pbs.org/wnet/supremecourt/democracy/robes_warren.html.

[26] See Itzhak Zamir, On Justice Zvi Berenson, 2 *Mishpat Umimshal* 325, 327 (1994) (Hebrew).

academic circles and for that reason foster an image of independence even at the expense of the court's long-term interests.

7. Manipulating the court's budget

Courts depend on adequate funding for their existence. To increase the court's reputation, the court must be able to issue many well-reasoned decisions in a timely fashion. This requires attracting talented and committed judges, which in turn requires paying them well. Budgets are also needed to pay the salaries of many other officials, such as clerks, legal advisers, secretaries, and supporting staff and to maintain buildings, libraries, and computer services. If the executive controls the court's budget, the executive can offer to increase this budget in return for judgments that suit its interests and to damage the budget as a penalty for decisions it disapproves. Affecting the court's budget or the salaries of judges is a powerful countermeasure that can be used against the court. In democracies that stress judicial independence, mechanisms are usually put in place to prevent the executive from changing the budget of the court. Those mechanisms, however, are often imperfect.[27]

[27] Cross and Nelson show that in the United States, despite the protection of judicial salaries, Congress can have a significant influence on judicial resources. Congress can withhold salary increases, change the budgets allocated to the court, refuse to authorize new judgeships, or even threaten to reduce judgeships. See Frank B. Cross and Blake J. Nelson, Strategic Institutional

C. External constraints on international courts

This book is focused mainly on the type of international courts termed supranational courts – that is, courts that allow individuals to submit applications against states. A prominent example of a supranational court is the European Court of Human Rights discussed in Chapter 6. In contrast, in international courts such as the International Court of Justice (ICJ), the dispute of two states is brought before the court. In these cases, the court must take into account the possible retaliation of both states in case its judgment contradicts their interests. Many times a decision that suits the interests of one state will damage the interests of the other state. In order to minimize the damages of retaliation by both states, the court must adopt sophisticated methods to satisfy the interests of both states at least in part.[28] Supranational courts have to take into account the possible retaliation of only one state that stands to lose from a finding of violation against it. Individuals and NGOs that bring the case against such a state may also respond negatively to a judgment that does not accept their application, but their ability to retaliate is limited compared to that of a state.

Effects on Supreme Court Decisionmaking, 95 *Northwestern University Law Review* 1437, 1465–1469 (2001).

[28] See Yuval Shany, Bosnia, Serbia and the Politics of International Adjudication, 45 *Justice* 21, 23–24 (2008).

Because supranational courts face one state at a time, their position is similar to a national court facing an executive. This section is therefore structured in a way that resembles the last section, which dealt with responses against national courts. In the interest of brevity, it does not repeat insights that are evidently applicable to both situations. Although supranational courts face one state at a time, they have jurisdiction over several states. This means that a supranational court can face different states in different cases, and those different states can all try to respond against the court. This gives supranational courts an advantage over national courts; the executive can respond strategically against a national court without having to coordinate its behavior with other parties. In contrast, in order to strategically damage the interests of a supranational court, several states have to collude and act collectively. Otherwise, if only some states retaliate against the court, it may use the support of other states to rebuild its reputation and improve its position.

Different states have different power to constrain international courts. If a state has a high reputation for compliance with the court, it can cause the court more damage if it fails to comply with its judgments. A high-reputation state can also cause more damage to the public support of the court if it criticizes its judgments. Chapter 4G will argue that courts take into account the reputation of the state that faces them and show greater deference to high-reputation states.

1. Noncompliance

When a supranational court finds that a state violated its obligations, the state has a duty to end this violation by taking the necessary measures, such as changing legislation or administrative practices. Even if the judgment is phrased in a way that only declares the violation, it creates a binding obligation to remedy it as Chapter 2D1 above demonstrates. If the state decides not to comply with this obligation, it will suffer a reputational damage; the higher the reputation of the court, the higher will be this reputational damage. If the state fails to comply, it therefore signals that it assesses the court's reputation as low and because of that it expects a low reputational sanction for noncompliance. This signal will cause all other states to lower their assessment of the court's reputation and will therefore damage the court's reputation. A high-reputation state will suffer a greater reputational damage for noncompliance because noncompliance goes against the expectations of other states. Therefore when a high-reputation state chooses not to comply with the court, this will cause an especially great reputational damage to the court.

Judgments of supranational courts often include an order to undertake certain immediate actions, such as paying reparations. The state may comply with this part of the judgment and use this partial compliance to hide the fact that it failed to comply with the main part of the judgment. A state may also comply after a substantial delay or comply in bad faith, for instance, by prosecuting certain officers according to the court's judgments but doing so in sham trials. Noncompliance may be hard to detect and to verify because of the problems of delayed, partial, and insincere compliance, but when cases of noncompliance multiply, states will eventually detect them and the reputation of the court will be damaged.

2. Criticism

A state may respond against an international court by criticizing its judgments. Criticism can affect the way other states view the content and quality of the court's judgments. If the state that criticizes the court can convince other states that the court's judgments are legally flawed, unjust, or biased, then the other states will reduce their support for the court. If the court has lower support, this means states can fail to comply with its judgments in the future without incurring severe criticism from other states. This increases the chances that the court will suffer future noncompliance.

States can also target their criticism to the ears of their own public. If the public does not support the court, the public will not pressure their executive to comply; in some cases they may even demand noncompliance. Once criticism is unleashed against the court, it is impossible to restrict its repercussions: The public may shift its views dramatically against the court and demand serious means from the executive, perhaps even a withdrawal from the court's jurisdiction. International courts must take the possible harmful results of criticism into account and do their best not to give states a reason to criticize them.

Criticism can damage the court's support even if it is not voiced by an agent of a state. The degree of damage caused to the court's public support depends on the quality of the arguments raised against the court and on the credibility of the party that criticizes it. Criticism that is voiced by a state representative in a formal setting, however, will also damage directly the court's reputation because it indicates the state is willing to incur the reputational damage that results from confronting the court. When a state criticizes the court, it indicates its willingness not to comply in the future and loses reputation as a result. The higher the court's reputation, the greater will be this reputational damage. For that reason, a willingness to criticize the court indicates the state views the court's reputation as low and will therefore damage the court's reputation in the eyes of all other states. Criticism will usually damage the court's reputation less than noncompliance, because criticism does not prove the state is willing to disregard the court's judgments. The effect on the court's reputation, however, depends on the severity of the criticism. The reputational damage also depends on the reputation of the state. High-reputation states stand to lose more reputation from criticizing the court because such criticism is unexpected. If a high-reputation state criticizes the court – indicating its willingness to suffer high reputational damage – it signals that it views the court's reputation as low and will therefore cause greater damage to the court's reputation than a low-reputation state. High-reputation states will also be viewed as more credible and therefore their criticism will cause more damage to the court's public support.

3. *Exiting the court's jurisdiction*

The most severe method of retaliation states can use against international courts is to exit the treaty regime altogether. If a state leaves the treaty regime, the court loses the ability to affect this state's policy in the future and thus the ultimate goal of the court is undercut. If a state exits the treaty regime, it will also cause a substantial damage to the court's reputation. The state indicates it is willing to suffer the reputational damage of leaving the court's jurisdiction completely, and by this signals to the other states that the court has a low reputation.

When a state exits a treaty regime, it risks damaging its relationship with other states that joined the same treaty. This makes states unlikely to exit treaties unless they have a substantial interest to do so. States may find ways to curb the court's jurisdiction or to avoid being subject to its judgments even without using the ultimate method of exit. One form of partial exit is to withdraw consent to the court's compulsory jurisdiction even without leaving the treaty. For example, after the ICJ rejected the preliminary objections of the United States in the *Nicaragua* case,[29]

[29] Case Concerning Military and Paramilitary Activities in and Against Nicaragua (jurisdiction of the court and admissibility of the application) [1984] ICJ Rep. 392 (Judgment of 26 Nov 1984).

the United States withdrew its agreement to the courts' compulsory jurisdiction.[30]

The more flexibility a state has to tailor intermediate forms of exit, the greater its ability to damage the court without jeopardizing its interests, and hence the greater its ability to constrain the court. The evolution of the rules that set the jurisdiction of the ECHR illustrates this phenomenon. Before Protocol 11 to the European Convention on Human Rights came into force in November 1, 1998, states could join the ECHR without agreeing to compulsory jurisdiction. This meant that states held both a carrot and a stick that could be used to constrain the court. If states viewed the court's judgments as beneficial, they could consent to the court's jurisdiction in future cases and even agree to accept compulsory jurisdiction. If states disagreed with the court's judgments, they could withhold their agreement to the court's jurisdiction. States could even issue a declaration agreeing to compulsory jurisdiction for a limited amount of time, which would allow them to threaten not to renew this declaration if the court digressed from their preferences. Similarly, before Protocol 11, states could agree to the court's jurisdiction without allowing private individuals to petition the court and claim a violation.

[30] See Tom Ginsburg, Bounded Discretion in International Judicial Lawmaking, 45 *Virginia Journal of International Law* 631, 658 (2005).

This allowed states to use the promise of accepting individual petition as leverage against the court.

The ability of states to constrain the court by the use of partial exit depends not only on the doctrinal rules that allow or forbid this measure, but also on the reputational costs of using such measures against the court. When it became the norm in the European Council to agree to compulsory jurisdiction and individual petition for the ECHR, states could not withhold these powers from the court without incurring a substantial reputational damage. This change in the expectation of states lowered the ability of states to constrain the court. Nevertheless, the acceptance of Protocol 11 – which made compulsory jurisdiction and individual petition mandatory – and of interim resolution DH(2001)(80) – which required new members to the council to accept the convention as amended by Protocol 11 – improved the position of the ECHR vis-à-vis the states.

Many treaties contain provisions that limit the ability of states to legitimately exit them. For example, article 58 of the European Convention allows states to denounce the convention only five years after they joined it and only after six months notice. Denunciation will not release the state from obligations incurred before the denunciation took effect. States may, however, exit the treaty informally by simply declaring their unwillingness to comply with the convention and the organs set to enforce it. This form of exit, which is performed in contradiction of the rules of the convention, may cause the state a greater reputational damage than an exit that conforms to the rules of the convention. Strict rules that prevent formal exit may therefore make states less likely to leave the treaty regime. Strict rules may also express a general perception that exiting the treaty regime will be viewed unfavorably by the other states, making exit even more damaging to the state reputation. Nevertheless, even if formal exit is foreclosed completely, the possibility of informal and illegitimate exit is always a threat that states hold against the court.

States may damage the interest of an international court such as the ICJ even without exiting it, simply by avoiding the court. If states do not ask the court to settle their disputes, the court will not be able to discuss new cases and increase its reputation. International courts are therefore constrained by their need to convince states to submit disputes to their decision.

4. Changing the treaty

If states are dissatisfied with the court's judgments, they may initiate a treaty amendment that overrides the court's interpretation of the treaty and creates a new legal regime. States can also change the treaty not in order to avoid incurring a specific obligation but rather to retaliate against the court by damaging its interests. The court's interests can be damaged if the amendment limits its jurisdiction or changes provisions that suit the court's preferences.

If several states are dissatisfied with the court, they may decide to suspend the court completely. This is the most extreme measure that states can use because it can completely incapacitate the court. There is at least one precedent for such an extreme act: States of the Southern African Development Community (SADC) decided to amend the rules pertaining to the SADC tribunal in response to a judgment in favor of disposed Zimbabwean farmers that antagonized many of its members. Until the amendment process is completed, the SADC court is effectively suspended. The states prevented the reappointment of judges and the replacement of retired judges. The states also prevented the court from hearing any cases or from receiving any new ones.[31]

Treaty amendment is usually an extremely difficult process that demands collective action by many different states. This renders international courts more immune to an override of their decisions than national courts, which can be overridden by a statute amendment in the national legislature. At the same time, because international courts are not as essential to the well-being of member states as a national court is to its own state, it seems that if the court upsets enough powerful states in the treaty regime, the states may react with extreme measures such as suspending the court.

[31] See Communiqué: Extraordinary Summit Heads of State and Government of the Southern Africa Development Community, Windhoek, Republic of Namibia, May 20, 2011.

5. *Establishing new courts*

States can threaten to exit the treaty regime or to avoid the court in order to constrain it to decide according to their wishes. The threat to exit the treaty regime will only be effective, however, if it is credible. If states gain from the services provided by the court and have no alternative venue to provide these services, they will not be able to leave the court, and their threats of exit will therefore not be credible. If states are under the jurisdiction of another court that provides similar services, their ability to exit or to avoid the court will be improved and so will their ability to constrain the court by threats of exit. Therefore, states can improve their bargaining power vis-à-vis the court by joining the jurisdiction of other courts or by creating new treaty regimes that provide similar services. Once a competing court is joined, states can forum shop between the two different courts. A court that wants to continue and affect the policy within the states will have to compromise and cater to their interests. Joining the jurisdiction of competing courts is one example of the tendency of powerful states to create multiple treaty regimes and increase their power as a result, a tendency described by Benvenisti and Downs.[32]

As an example, consider the recent threat to create a competing international court in order to limit the power of

[32] See Eyal Benvenisti and George W. Downs, The Empire's New Clothes: Political Economy and the Fragmentation of International Law, 60 *Stanford Law Review* 595, 627 (2007).

the ECHR. Alexander Torshin, the Russian Federation Council First Deputy Chairman, suggested that the Commonwealth of Independent States (CIS), an organization that includes several formerly Soviet republics, will change its existing human rights commission into a human rights court that will serve as an alternative to the ECHR. According to Torshin's proposal, citizens of the CIS will have a choice between the two human rights courts.[33] This proposal, if accepted, will threaten the ability of the ECHR to affect the policy of CIS states because it will allow any state that the ECHR finds in violation of the Convention to get a stamp of approval and rebuild its reputation by receiving a lenient judgment from the new alternative court. CIS states may find it easier not to comply with ECHR judgments, to criticize them, or even to leave the jurisdiction of the ECHR if they know that an alternative international court can provide them with the benefits provided by the ECHR with much lower costs to their interests. If such a proposal is accepted, the ECHR may realize that it has to serve the interests of CIS states in order to defend itself from their retaliation.

6. *Influencing judicial selection and sanctions against judges*

The behavior of the court is to a large extent determined by the behavior of the judges who author its judgments.

[33] See www.kyivpost.com/content/russia-and-former-soviet-union/russian-council-member-proposes-establishment-of-c-114160.html

Therefore, states can try to constrain the behavior of international courts by constraining their judges. If states can affect the selection of judges, they can choose judges who are either loyal to the state's interest or who have preferences that suit those of the state. If states can control the reelection of judges to the court or if judges can expect other benefits from the state once they retire, the state gains another leverage to affect the judges.[34]

International courts need to maintain an image of impartiality in order to keep the support of the public for their actions. If an international court is considered dependent on certain states, rival states may view the court as hostile to their interests and be less likely to comply with the court. The public in those states will not demand compliance because they view the court's judgments as biased and damaging to their state's interests. For that reason, judicial selection for international courts is usually calculated to ensure that each state will have only little control over the selection process. In the ECHR, for instance, each state under the court's jurisdiction offers a list of three candidates, and a judge is selected from this list by a majority at the Parliamentary Assembly.[35] Erik Voeten shows that the different judges that collectively decide

[34] See Eric A. Posner and Miguel F. P. de Figueiredo, Is the International Court of Justice Biased?, 34 *Journal of Legal Studies* 599, 608 (2005).

[35] Convention for the Protection of Human Rights and Fundamental Freedoms, articles 20, 22.

cases on the chamber balance each other and ensure that even if a judge is biased toward her own country, she will rarely determine the result that favors her country.[36] In an attempt to further decrease the control of states over the judges, Protocol 14 to the European Convention determined that judges will be elected for a period of nine years and cannot be reelected. Previously, judges were elected for six years and could be reelected, which gave the states an ability to reward judges that suit their interests by nominating them for reelection.

The behavior of an international court is not determined solely by the behavior of the judges. Sometimes legal advisers and other professional staff can impact the nature of the court's judgments. In the ECHR, the legal staff is directed by the registrar and not subordinated to individual judges. Judges have a particularly great need for the staff because they may not be perfectly comfortable writing in English or French, the two official languages of the court. Paul McKaskle cites these two facts as reasons for the great effect of the legal staff on the behavior of the ECHR.[37] If states can influence the legal staff or the registrar, they therefore gain leverage to affect the court.

[36] See Erik Voeten, The Impartiality of International Judges: Evidence from the European Court of Human Rights, 102 *American Political Science Review* 417, 426 (2008).

[37] Paul L. McKaskle, The European Court of Human Rights: What It Is, How It Works, and Its Future, 40 University of San Francisco *Law Review* 1, 26–31 (2005).

7. Manipulating the court's budget

International courts depend on states to finance their budget. To process cases and issue well-written judgments, they need to have money to pay for the work of judges and legal and administrative staff. A substantial budget is also needed to publicize the court's decisions and make them more accessible to the public. The ECHR, for instance, does not limit itself to publishing judgments; it issues press releases and detailed factsheets that summarize its case law, it collects and edits statistical data, and it holds public hearings. Public hearings and intensive fact finding are becoming increasingly important for international courts; they are especially important for courts such as the IACHR that have low rates of direct compliance with their judgments.[38]

Tom Ginsburg draws attention to the significant differences in the budgets of different international courts and suggests that courts that are better financed serve the interests of powerful states that control their budget.[39] If states can control the budget of an international court and change it to punish or reward the court, they hold a powerful tool to manipulate the court's actions. Mechanisms can be put in place to prevent individual states from denying money

[38] See James L. Cavallaro and Stephanie Erin Brewer, Reevaluating Regional Human Rights Litigation in the Twenty-First Century: The Case of the Inter-American Court, 102 *American Journal of International Law* 768, 792–795 (2008).

[39] Ginsburg, *supra* note 30 at 666–668.

from the court. For instance, the ECHR does not have a separate budget. Instead, its budget is part of the general budget of the European Council, which is subject to the approval of the Committee of Ministers.[40] This arrangement means that individual states cannot deny payments to the court directly. The budget of the European Council, however, is paid by the member states according to scales that take into account population and gross national product. States that pay a substantial part of the European Council's budget, or that hold political capital for other reasons, may therefore try to exercise their influence to change the court's budget in the Committee of Ministers.

D. Comparing the constraints on national and international courts

This chapter is structured in a way that highlights the similarities between the responses that can be imposed on national and international courts by the parties subject to the jurisdiction of these courts. The vulnerability of national courts to some responses is greater than the vulnerability of international courts. For example, the executive can mobilize the legislature to overrule a judgment by a national court. In contrast, overruling a judgment by an international court is much more difficult and requires a coordinated

[40] See www.echr.coe.int/ECHR/EN/Header/The±Court/How±the±Court±works/Budget

action by several states. The executive may also be able to control the budget of a national court, to curb its jurisdiction, or to influence judicial selection. But even very powerful states may be less able to use similar responses against an international court. On the other hand, states can exit the jurisdiction of an international court, something that the executive cannot do with regard to the jurisdiction of the national court. Moreover, states can also avoid the jurisdiction of an international court more easily than the executive can avoid the jurisdiction of the national court.

The ability of parties to respond strategically against the court depends on more than just the formal steps needed to complete these responses. In fact, it depends primarily on the reputational damage the party will suffer if it attempts such a response. Noncompliance with a high-reputation court will cause the noncompliant party a greater reputational damage than noncompliance with a low-reputation court. Other hostile responses, such as criticizing the court, will also cause parties more damage if used against a high-reputation court rather than a low-reputation court. Therefore, high-reputation courts can require parties to comply with more demanding judgments and still expect compliance. In this sense, a high-reputation court is less constrained than a low-reputation court.

A high-reputation court will suffer a greater reputational damage from each case of noncompliance than a low-reputation court, because noncompliance with the high-reputation court is unexpected. If a party does not try to deliberately damage the court or credibly signal to it that it will fail to comply in the future, however, the party will be ready to comply with more demanding judgments by high-reputation courts compared to low-reputation courts to avoid the reputational sanction. If the party does attempt to signal to the court that it will not comply with future demanding judgments, this signal will only be credible if the party can withstand the reputational sanction for noncompliance longer than the court can withstand the reputational damage caused to it by noncompliance. If the court has a high reputation, it will be able to sustain a greater damage to it than a low-reputation court can before this will jeopardize its ability to influence parties and fulfill its long-term goals. At the same time, the party that strategically fails to comply with a high-reputation court will suffer a greater reputational damage and will be less able to withstand it than a party that faces a low-reputation court. Parties therefore have less leverage against high-reputation courts than against low-reputation courts. They will be less able to credibly commit not to comply with high-reputation courts than they would be able to credibly commit not to comply with low-reputation courts.

National and international courts may have different levels of reputation. An international court with a high reputation may therefore be less vulnerable to responses from states than a national court with a low reputation. The opposite can also be true: A national court may have a higher reputation than an international court and therefore be less constrained.

While much depends on the reputation of each individual court, it seems that usually national courts have higher levels of domestic support.[41] This may result from the rule of law culture they are part of, from the fact that they are usually more veteran courts, or from the fact that they deal with a more homogenous society.[42] Consequently, an executive that fails to comply with a national court can expect more substantial public criticism than a state that fails to comply with an international court. On the other hand, international courts have several different states under their jurisdiction. Therefore, if some states fail to comply, the court can rebuild its reputation by convincing other states to comply with its judgments.

It is hard to determine whether in general the strong points of international courts outweigh those of national courts. Only specific information about individual courts can lead to such an assessment.

E. The influence of third parties on judicial constraints

The focus of this chapter has been on the responses that the executive can use against a national court and that states

[41] See Eyal Benvenisti, Reclaiming Democracy: The Strategic Uses of Foreign and International Law by National Courts, 102 *American Journal of International Law* 241, 271 (2008).

[42] See Yonatan Lupu, International Judicial Legitimacy: Lessons from National Courts, 14 *Theoretical Inquiries in Law* 437, 451–453 (2013).

can use against an international court. A national court is exposed to powerful responses from other parties, however, that may have different interests than the executive. For the sake of simplicity, this chapter discusses the ability of the legislature to overrule judgments of the court as part of the possible responses of the executive. In some legal systems the executive indeed has a substantial influence on the behavior of the legislature. Even in such systems, however, the legislature is a different institution that might have different interests. The executive and the legislature may compete for power, and this contest may be used by the court to increase its own influence. Eyal Benvenisti showed that the Israeli Supreme Court tried to strengthen the inherently weaker legislature to increase the friction between the legislature and the naturally stronger executive. This friction between the two government branches increases the need for the court as a mediator between them, improving the court's position in the power relations between the branches.[43]

The political arena that a national court faces can be further fragmented into small interest groups. Each of these groups promotes its own interest through the use of economic power or through the funding and control of political parties, associations, NGOs, public petitioners, and other organizations. Interest groups can marshal public

[43] Eyal Benvenisti, Judicially Sponsored Checks and Balances, 31 *Hebrew University Law Review* 797, 813–818 (2001) (Hebrew).

opinion for or against the court and by this affect the public support for the court. One way the court can gain the assistance of interest groups is by letting them have a voice in the proceedings, either as direct petitioners or as friends of the court (*amicus curiae*). The Israeli Supreme Court example discussed in Chapter 5 demonstrates how the court can use public petitioners strategically to improve its position, especially in a time when its public support is low.

When the national court and the executive interact, they cannot ignore the influence of parties beyond the state's borders. For example, international courts can demand certain standards from the national court and threaten to criticize it if it does not conform to these standards, forming another constraint on the decisions of national courts. This constraint, however, may actually improve the ability of the national court to face the political pressures of the executive. In this case, the national court may use the constraint imposed on it by the international court as a way to credibly commit not to compromise on its position in the face of pressure from the executive.[44] International courts and the international community can also criticize

[44] The idea that being bound to a certain position can actually improve your bargaining power was investigated by Schelling as part of the concept of commitment; see Schelling, *supra* note 11 at 28. Putnam further investigates this condition where an agent is bound by a principal and gains bargaining power as a result; see Robert D. Putnam, Diplomacy and Domestic Politics: The Logic of Two-Level Games, 42 *International Organization* 427, 440 (1988).

the actions of the executive that will need the national court to legitimize its actions. This too can improve the bargaining power of the national court in its interaction with the executive.

International courts can also improve the position of national courts vis-à-vis the executive in a different way, as noted by Benvenisti. Benvenisti claims that national courts serve the need of the executive to appear bound by its own legal system in the face of external political pressure.[45] If the court helps the executive resist foreign pressures, it may be able to gain important concessions from the executive as a result. The influence that international courts have on national courts is also demonstrated in Chapter 5.

Foreign countries can also exert their influence on the relationship between the national court and the executive. An example is the case of *Martin* v. *Hunter's Lessee*.[46] This case established the supremacy of the U.S. Supreme Court in matters of federal law over lower courts. This judgment reversed a decision of the Supreme Court of Virginia to allow confiscation of land from a British subject, a confiscation that was previously overruled by another judgment of the Supreme Court – *Fairfax's Devisee* v. *Hunter's Lessee*.[47] It appears that this decision in favor

[45] Benvenisti, *supra* note 41 at 248.
[46] *Martin* v. *Hunter's Lessee*, 14 U.S. 304 (1816).
[47] *Fairfax's Devisee* v. *Hunter's Lessee*, 11 U.S. 603 (1813).

of a British subject was possible because the United States at this point was striving to maintain friendly relations with Great Britain. In this way, the interest of a foreign power assured the court its decision will be complied with and paved the way for a decision that increased the power of the U.S. Supreme Court inside the United States.[48]

This chapter has depicted the way international courts are constrained by states that can respond strategically to their judgments. The international arena, however, contains many other important parties that can shape the constraints imposed on international courts. NGOs are important parties that the international court must take into account when it makes its decisions. NGOs can bring cases and supply information to the court, either as direct petitioners or indirectly by funding legal assistance to petitioners or by providing detailed amicus curiae briefs. NGOs can help to provide the court with favorable publicity or take part in important negotiations where states change the structure and the founding documents of the court. NGOs also help to monitor the enforcement of the court's judgments.[49]

International courts must realize that the behavior of states under their jurisdiction is constrained by the preferences of their public and important interest groups within it.

[48] I owe this idea to William Eskridge Jr. More information about this period can be found at Jean Edward Smith, *John Marshall: Definer of a Nation*, 430 (New York: Henry Holt and Company), 1996.

[49] See Shai Dothan, Luring NGOs to International Courts (unpublished draft).

The international court can try to mobilize segments of the domestic public and use their influence on the state for the court's advantage. As an example, the ICJ's decision in the case of *Avena*[50] ruled that based on violations of the Vienna Convention on Consular Relations, the U.S. state courts' convictions and death sentences of several Mexican nationals must be reviewed and reconsidered. The ICJ may have believed that the United States would not comply with its judgment, but that the judgment would win some internal support and shape the policies of the United States for the long run. Indeed, the ICJ judgment won the support of none other than President George W. Bush, who issued a memorandum to the Attorney General stating that the United States would comply with the *Avena* decision and state courts would give effect to it. Finally, the U.S. Supreme Court in the case of *Medellin*[51] decided not to give effect to the ICJ judgment and declared it is not binding domestic law, and even the president cannot give effect to it because it is the authority of Congress to give domestic effect to international obligations. Although at the end, the United States failed to comply, the ICJ doubtlessly won important support within the United States for its position.[52]

[50] Case Concerning Avena and Other Mexican Nationals (*Mexico* v. *U.S.*), [2004] ICJ Rep. 12.

[51] *Medellin* v. *Texas*, 552 U.S. 491 (2008).

[52] I thank W. Michael Reisman for this idea.

A key player that can shape the behavior of the state toward the international court is this state's own national court. National courts can help monitor the enforcement of international courts' judgments in their own state. They can also increase the support within the state for the judgments of an international court by issuing similar judgments. International courts can therefore expect compliance even with demanding judgments when they have the support of the national court. An illustrative example is the case of *A* v. *United Kingdom*.[53] The ECHR discussed in this case the detainment of foreign nationals who were suspected of terrorist activities and could not be deported because they might be subject to mistreatment in their home countries. The ECHR's judgment ruled that an emergency existed at the time but that the detainment constituted a disproportionate and therefore an impermissible derogation even under an emergency and was therefore a violation of the right to liberty of the detained. The ECHR could issue such a demanding judgment without fearing noncompliance or severe criticism because it simply followed the track of the House of Lords, which issued a very similar decision in the same case.[54] The ECHR notes that it is extremely rare for the government to contest before the ECHR a judgment

[53] *Case of A and others* v. *the United Kingdom*, judgment of February 19, 2009, *Reports of Judgments and Decisions* 2009.

[54] *A* v. *Secretary of state for the home department* [2004] UKHL 56, 16 December 2004.

of its own highest court.[55] While these cases may indeed be rare, a supranational court can try to ground its judgments in the decisions, the attitudes, or the reasoning of national courts as a way to gain support and to secure compliance with its judgments.[56]

F. Conclusion and the tradeoff between external and internal constraints

This chapter described two forms of constraints on national and international courts: legal-internal constraints and external constraints. The constraints on courts limit their ability to manipulate their judgments to suit their interests, including the interest discussed in this book of increasing the court's reputation. Courts can try to minimize the constraints they will face in the future by increasing their reputation and by shaping the doctrine they use. The next

[55] See *A* v. *United Kingdom*, *supra* note 53, at par. 157.

[56] Similarly, Sadurski described the cooperation between the ECHR and the Polish Constitutional Court that led to *Hutten-Czapska* v. *Poland*, judgment of June 19, 2006, 2006-VIII EUR. Ct. H.R. 57. See Wojciech Sadurski, Partnering with Strasburg: Constitutionalisation of the European Court of Human Rights, The Accession of Central and East European States to the Council of Europe and the Idea of Pilot Judgments, 9 *Human Rights Law Review* 397, 414–420 (2009). Regarding the ways international courts can gain support for their judgments while interacting with states and their national courts, see Shai Dothan, How International Courts Enhance Their Legitimacy, 14 *Theoretical Inquiries in Law* 455 (2013).

chapter discusses different tactics that courts can use to achieve this goal.

As courts strive to reduce the constraints on their judgments, they must keep in mind that a possible tradeoff exists between external and internal constraints. If a court is bound by strong legal constraints because doctrine unequivocally mandates a certain result, this may reduce the ability of the parties under its jurisdiction to respond against its judgments. The executive or the state may lose much more reputation if it fails to comply with a judgment that is constrained by doctrine than if it fails to comply with a judgment that is a result of judicial discretion. This book argues that courts can use their reasoning to make judgments appear more constrained or more discretionary according to their strategic interest. Even though courts can shape the appearance of judicial discretion to a certain extent, their ability to shape this appearance and to affect the public perceptions of the constraints of doctrine is limited. Therefore, if the doctrine on certain issues is clear, this does form a constraint on courts. This doctrinal constraint, however, can aid the court to resist external pressures of parties.

4 Tactics to increase courts' reputation

The preceding chapters presented a theory of courts that views them as strategic actors who try to increase their reputation. According to this theory, courts wish to increase their reputation in order to improve the chances that parties will comply with their future judgments. The higher the court's reputation, the higher the reputational sanction for noncompliance, and therefore the higher the incentive of parties to comply with the court. When parties comply with the court's judgments, the court's reputation is increased because the complying party has signaled that it expects a high reputational sanction for noncompliance, which indicates the court has a high reputation. Compliance with a demanding judgment signals that the court's reputation is especially high by indicating that the reputational incentive to comply is greater than the costs of compliance with this judgment. Therefore, compliance with a demanding judgment will increase the court's reputation more than compliance with a less demanding judgment. When the court uses discretionary reasoning, this reduces the reputational sanction for noncompliance. Therefore, compliance with a judgment that uses discretionary reasoning will increase the court's reputation more than compliance with a judgment that uses constrained reasoning. If a court issues a demanding judgment or a judgment that uses discretionary reasoning and its reputation is not high enough to give the state an incentive to comply, however, this judgment will not be complied with. Noncompliance will damage the court's reputation by signaling that its reputation is too low to induce states to comply. Courts therefore need to practice a strategy that will signal they have a high reputation without leading to noncompliance.

This chapter describes a strategy that allows courts to increase their reputation. In some cases, courts should issue demanding judgments or judgments that use discretionary reasoning that they nevertheless expect states to comply with. If a lower-reputation court were to issue such a judgment, parties would fail to comply with it, but if the court that issues this judgment has a high enough reputation, it can induce parties to comply. A court that uses this strategy is "walking on the brink of noncompliance"; it issues judgments that will be complied with due to its high reputation, but would have led to noncompliance if issued by a lower-reputation court.

The chapter breaks this basic strategy into specific tactics courts can use to implement it. Courts can shift to issuing demanding judgments and judgments using discretionary reasoning when their reputation is high and retreat to issuing less demanding judgments and to using constrained reasoning when their reputation is low. As long as the court's reputation remains the same, it should support demanding judgments with more constrained reasoning and less demanding judgments with more discretionary reasoning. The court should develop doctrine incrementally, shifting to more demanding judgments slowly and relying on its past judgments to legitimate this move. If the court introduces a new doctrine that increases its power, or is not supported by past judgments, it can decide not to implement it in the same case and not to require specific actions to comply with the judgment.

An international court interacts with different states that have different levels of reputation; high-reputation states can cause greater damage to the court's reputation by failing to comply or by criticizing it. International courts should address this threat by issuing less demanding judgments against high-reputation states. At the same time, international courts must try not to appear biased in favor of certain states. This is especially difficult when the court adjudicates a dispute between two states, in which case the court should try to please both parties to the conflict.

Finally, in some cases courts will need to take actions that damage their reputation in order to promote one of their preferences. They will need to "spend" their reputation and gain something in return.

A. Walking on the brink of noncompliance

As elaborated in Chapter 2, in order to increase their reputation, courts must signal that their audience views them as having a high reputation. Courts create this signal by issuing demanding judgments or judgments that use discretionary reasoning. If parties comply with these judgments, this signals that they view the court as having a high reputation, and this will further increase the court's reputation.

Even though a state that complies with an international court does not necessarily have more information about the court's reputation than any other state in the international arena, it still possesses some information about the common belief that constitutes the court's reputation and takes part in forming that reputation and updating it as conditions change. Therefore, when a state complies with an international court, it increases the court's reputation.

Because an executive that faces a national court has more information about the court's reputation than any member of the public, the court cannot fool the executive into thinking it has a high reputation simply by issuing a demanding judgment or by using discretionary reasoning. If the executive does not think the court's reputation is high enough to generate a reputational sanction that can force it to comply with the judgment, it will fail to comply and thus cause the court a reputational loss. For that reason, national courts that issue demanding judgments or use discretionary reasoning are creating a costly signal, and therefore a credible one, that can increase their reputation. If the executive complies with this judgment, this will indicate to the public that the court's reputation is indeed high and will therefore further increase the court's reputation.

Issuing demanding judgments and using discretionary reasoning can therefore potentially increase the reputation of international courts if states comply with them. This practice itself increases the reputation of national courts and would increase the court's reputation even further if the executive were to comply.

Yet courts can also lose reputation by issuing these kinds of judgments. If a judgment requires a party to undertake actions that are more costly to it than the costs of suffering the reputational sanction for noncompliance and losing the reputational benefit it would gain had it complied, then that party would fail to comply. Noncompliance will damage the court's reputation because it signals to the public that the court's reputation is not high enough to induce compliance.

Similarly, when the court uses discretionary reasoning, the reputational sanction a party will suffer in case of noncompliance is lower than if the judgment employed constrained reasoning. This makes parties more likely not to comply with judgments that use discretionary reasoning – noncompliance that would damage the court's reputation.

When the court issues judgments, it faces risk as it assesses its own reputation, the reputation of the party subject to the judgments, the costs of compliance, and the discretion professed by the reasoning. In order to maximize the benefit to its reputation, the court must issue the most demanding judgments and use the most discretionary reasoning that will still induce parties to comply. This practice is risky because the assessments of the court about the various factors mentioned above may be inaccurate. The court may think that it has a higher reputation than it actually has according to the public belief. It may think the party it faces has a higher reputation than it has and is therefore more reluctant not to comply. The court may not assess the costs of fulfilling the requirements in the judgment correctly, inaccurately thinking they can be accomplished cheaply when in fact these requirements would lead to significant costs for the complying party. As Chapter 2D1 argues, the costs of compliance to parties are manifold and complex, and the court may often fail to assess them correctly. The court may also believe that the reasoning used will appear constrained by the law, when in fact the public perceives it as reflecting judicial discretion. When such mistakes are made, judgments may not be complied with and the court's reputation will suffer as a result.

When the court issues a demanding judgment, it increases the chances that this judgment will require the state to make changes that it is either unable or unwilling to comply with, which will lead to noncompliance. When the court uses discretionary reasoning, it increases the risk that reputational sanctions will not be substantial enough to lead states to comply. Courts that try to increase their reputation must therefore take risks. They must *walk close to the brink*, taking a certain chance that they will fall down the slope because their actions lead to noncompliance.

In order to prosper, courts must take *calculated* risks. They must use certain tactics to improve their chances of increasing their reputation as much as possible. Some of these tactics are described throughout this chapter. As courts apply them, however, they always draw on imperfect sources of information and therefore are always taking a risk that their judgments will not be complied with. Because courts operate under uncertainty, they can only maximize their *expected* reputational gains from different actions.

Courts can improve the accuracy of their information as they invest resources in studying the beliefs of the public or the costs of compliance with their judgments. Better information means that the court can more accurately assess when states will fail to comply and can therefore create smaller margins of error by issuing more demanding judgments and using more discretionary reasoning, while maintaining a high likelihood of compliance.

Courts can also improve the quality of their tactics and utilize their ability to manipulate their judgments in an increasingly skillful manner even while operating under imperfect information. More experienced courts that have a long history to learn from and courts that have more professional and talented judges or legal assistants may have better information and better tactics than younger courts and courts that employ lower-quality judges.

Courts do not and should not walk on the brink of noncompliance in every case. Some cases are manifestly unfounded or need to be rejected on technical grounds. Many cases are easy cases where the doctrine is clear and judges do not have a judicial discretion that they can use to employ strategy. In other cases, the requested remedy is not demanding, and compliance is therefore easy to secure. The court can choose the opportunities to walk on the brink of noncompliance only from the cases that can reasonably be used to issue demanding remedies or utilize discretionary reasoning. Even from this pool of cases only a few should be strategically manipulated. Even courts that issue hundreds of judgments every year and are under close scrutiny by the media and academia can get sufficient public attention to significantly increase their reputation in a handful of cases every year. Courts need to pick carefully the cases that they want to render salient and in these cases apply strategy wisely. The success of the court's strategy depends to a large extent on the wise choice of the case where it is used.

If the court does not issue demanding judgments at all, the public will infer that its reputation is low, because otherwise the court would have tried to issue demanding judgments to further increase its reputation. Therefore, timidity by the court can serve as a signal that damages its reputation. However, if the court issues demanding judgments too often, even if they are complied with, it risks losing public support by indicating that it contradicts the preferences of the general public. Courts that overreach and lose their public support may later face noncompliance because the parties that fail to comply will not suffer severe public criticism. This can eventually damage these courts' reputation.

B. Matching the remedy to the court's reputation

In some cases, the court can ratchet the demands of the judgment and determine the costs of compliance. The court can never assess fully the costs of compliance, however, which means there is always a risk that reputational sanctions will not be high enough to motivate the party facing the court to comply. Nevertheless, the court has some assessment of the costs that allows it to identify a threshold over which it expects the state not to comply because the costs of compliance are higher than the reputational sanctions. As the court requires that party to undertake actions that pass this threshold, the expected likelihood of noncompliance rises significantly. Courts will not pass this threshold knowingly. They will try to issue judgments that parties have a reputational interest to comply with, unless they are motivated by some reason besides promoting their reputation. Sometimes courts erroneously assess the costs of the judgment, however, and suffer noncompliance as a result.

Courts can only increase their reputation if they come near the threshold from time to time. Only judgments that are demanding enough that compliance with them indicates the court has a high reputation can further increase the court's reputation. When a court has a high reputation, it can issue more demanding judgments while staying clear of the threshold over which noncompliance is expected. Therefore, the clearest application of the court's strategy of walking on the brink is the tactic of matching the remedies the court issues to the current level of its reputation. When the court's reputation is high, it will issue more demanding judgments than when its reputation is low.

Because courts do not come near the threshold in every case, the comparison of two judgments issued at different times will not necessarily reveal whether the court increased or decreased its reputation. If many judgments are surveyed, however, and they show that the court increases its demands over time, this can demonstrate that the court has increased its reputation over that period. Chapter 6 surveys judgments of the ECHR in an attempt to demonstrate that it issued increasingly demanding judgments, a behavior that correlated with its increasing reputation. Further examples will not be provided here because the theory can be best demonstrated when the nature of the court's judgments across a long period is analyzed. It is much easier to correctly identify a trend in the judgments of a single court than to find unique examples of courts with low reputation and compare their judgments to the judgments of courts with higher reputations. Courts differ from each other in the nature of the doctrine they apply and in the political constraints they operate under, often rendering such a comparison useless.

As long as the court increases its reputation, the theory recommends that it should issue increasingly demanding judgments. If the court's reputation declines, however, for instance because of persistent noncompliance, it needs to shift to less demanding judgments. This strategic restraint is a dangerous exercise because it exposes the court's weakness and may do further damage to its reputation. It may be the court's only option, however, if it wants to avoid noncompliance, which can do even greater damage to its reputation. Chapter 5 surveys recent judgments of the Israeli Supreme Court that demonstrate it shifted to less demanding judgments as its reputation declined.

C. Matching the reasoning to the court's reputation

Another way for courts to walk on the brink of noncompliance is to issue judgments with discretionary reasoning in some cases. Parties will comply with judgments that use discretionary reasoning only if they are issued by a high-reputation court, therefore courts should issue such judgments only when their reputation is high enough to secure compliance. The court must avoid using a reasoning that is too discretionary to lead to compliance, taking into account the demands of the judgment and the reputation of the court and the party facing it. At the same time, the court should, in some cases, use a reasoning that will only lead to compliance with a court at its current level of reputation, in order to further increase its reputation. As long as courts apply this tactic, they will use more discretionary reasoning when their reputation is higher.

When courts use a certain form of reasoning consistently, they signal to the public that their decisions are not discretionary, but rather follow certain doctrines and legal conventions. Courts can therefore increase the chances of compliance if they stick to certain forms of reasoning. Even when courts change their reasoning in an attempt to show their discretion, they will usually do so slowly because judges and legal assistants grow accustomed to certain styles of writing and interpretation. For these reasons, unlike a shift to more demanding judgments that can affect only a few landmark cases, a change in the court's reasoning can encompass a significant part of its caselaw. It is therefore possible to use quantitative empirical data to identify differences between the forms of reasoning used by different courts or by the same court in different time periods.

Comparative research highlights the differences between the style of judgments in Britain, the United States, and France. It finds that in the 18th century British judgments started to lengthen and were substantially longer than the judgments of the French and American systems. The British tradition of writing long judgments evolved at a time when the British courts had much more power and legitimacy than the American or the French courts. Longer judgments usually reveal greater judicial discretion than shorter judgments.[1] Therefore, there seems to be a correlation between the reputation of the court and the practice of revealing less judicial discretion. In later years, the French judicial system, which started out with extremely short judgments, gathered reputation and slowly lengthened its judgments. It never reached the length of British judgments, however.[2] This does not necessarily indicate that even in recent years the French courts have a lower reputation than the British ones. Judges may follow the tradition established within the court even decades after the original conditions that gave rise to this tradition changed. This demonstrates the danger of comparing the practices of different courts. Courts' practices may differ for a host of reasons, including conditions that shaped their behavior early in their history. Chapter 5 focuses instead on one court, the Israeli Supreme Court, and tries to analyze trends in its reasoning over the last sixty years. It suggests that the court shifted to discretionary reasoning as its reputation increased, a change that can be explained by the tactic described here. The focus on a single court allows better isolation of the changes that led to this shift in the court's reasoning.

[1] Jean Louis Goutal, Characteristics of Judicial Style in France, Britain and the U.S.A, 24 *American Journal of Comparative Law* 43, 58, 61–62 (1976).

[2] *Ibid*. at 60–61.

Besides the reasoning used in the judgment, another factor that can expose the court's discretion is the practice of dissent. When judges dissent, they expose the fact that other legal results can be reached in the same case and therefore judges applied their discretion to reach the judgment. When the court has a low reputation, it is thus more important that judges present a united front and not dissent than when it has a high reputation. Judges who seek to serve the court's interest will therefore be more willing to hide their personal views in order to project unity and to pressure other judges to do the same in periods when the court's reputation is low. There is some evidence for a correlation between a low reputation and fewer dissents in the Israeli Supreme Court, which is described in Chapter 5. Similar correlations have also been discovered in the U.S. Supreme Court. Scholars found that Chief Justice Marshall led his court toward greater use of unanimous decisions in periods when the status of the judiciary was low.[3] Under Chief Justice Taft the same court suppressed dissents in the first half of the 1920s when the court was under attack. When these attacks subsided, the court shifted back to allowing more dissents.[4]

[3] Nuno Garoupa and Tom Ginsburg, Reputation, Information and the Organization of the Judiciary, 4 *Journal of Comparative Law* 228, 243 (2009).

[4] Robert Post, The Supreme Court Opinion as Institutional Practice: Dissent, Legal Scholarship, and Decisionmaking in the Taft Court, 85 *Minnesota Law Review* 1267, 1314–1319 (2001). (But at

D. Matching the remedy to the reasoning

In order to walk on the brink of noncompliance, the court must issue judgments that would be complied with only if issued by courts with its current level of reputation or higher. In some cases, the court can manipulate both the remedy, which determines the costs of compliance, and the reasoning, which determines the reputational payoff that motivates parties to comply. As long as the court has the same level of reputation, it should use more constrained reasoning in judgments that include a demanding remedy and more discretionary reasoning in judgments that include a less demanding remedy. This tactic allows the court to walk near the brink of noncompliance without passing it. It ensures that the court's judgments will be complied with and would serve to increase its reputation by signaling its high reputation.

Many judgments are technical and clear in terms of the law, and the required remedy is either clear or obviously not demanding. In these judgments, the court cannot manipulate strategically either the remedy or the reasoning, and therefore cannot strategically use this judgment to increase its reputation.

In many other judgments, courts can manipulate the reasoning, but the final result and the remedy are clear.

1319–1328 the paper presents other possible reasons for these shifts, including personal changes within the court and changes in Taft's leadership.)

In these judgments, the judges should choose to use constrained reasoning if the remedy they are forced to issue is demanding. If the remedy is not demanding, the court can use discretionary reasoning in an effort to increase its reputation. However, the court does not have to manipulate the reasoning in every case. Only few cases are salient enough to really increase a court's reputation, and in some of these cases the court should try to strategically match the reasoning to the remedy.

Other judgments leave the judges no room for discretion regarding the reasoning. Usually this means the reasoning will appear constrained and will not reflect any discretion. In many cases, the law is clear and therefore the judges cannot exercise or profess to use judicial discretion. In such cases, the court can issue a demanding remedy and require parties to undertake costly actions to comply with its judgment. Demanding remedies will only be issued in a few cases, but cases that already employ constrained reasoning are usually a better place for the court to increase its demands.

Some authors argue that judges first determine the remedy they wish to issue and then determine the reasoning that can lead to this result;[5] others stress the importance

[5] Benjamin N. Cardozo, *The Nature of the Judicial Process*, 45–46 (New Haven, CT: Yale University Press), 1921. Pnina Lahav, *Judgment in Jerusalem: Chief Justice Simon Agranat and the Zionist Century*, 107 (Tel Aviv: Am Oved Publishers Ltd), 1999 (Hebrew).

of the reasoning process in shaping the judge's decision.[6] It is probably true that the need to use legally acceptable reasoning shapes the remedy the judge thinks is appropriate, and the intuition the judge has regarding the appropriate remedy shapes her use of reasoning. When judges decide collectively, they argue with each other and use legal arguments to convince each other.[7] This further intertwines their beliefs about the appropriate remedy and their reading of the law. The decisions about what reasoning to use and what remedy to issue are therefore often inseparable. Usually this decision is determined by the legal perceptions and the policy preferences of the judges. In some cases, however, judges can use strategic calculations to shape the reasoning and the remedy in a way that suits the court's long-term reputational interest and reflects the tactic described here.

One way to demonstrate the use of this tactic is to compare the reasoning used in demanding judgments with the reasoning used in less-demanding judgments. The hypothesis that courts will use a more constrained reasoning in the demanding judgments is difficult to support by quantitative methods, because courts will issue deliberately demanding judgments only in few cases. However, if the court deals with a highly salient issue and changes the remedy completely in

[6] Aharon Barak, *The Judge in a Democracy*, 37–38 (Jerusalem: Keter), 2004 (Hebrew).

[7] See Frank B. Cross and Emerson H. Tiller, Judicial Partisanship and Obedience to Legal Doctrine: Whistleblowing on the Federal Courts of Appeals, 107 *Yale Law Journal* 2155 (1998).

two separate judgments, issuing in one judgment a very demanding remedy supported by constrained reasoning and in the other judgment a remedy that is not demanding that is supported by discretionary reasoning, this would support the hypothesis. Chapter 5 analyzes such pairs of judgments issued by the Israeli Supreme Court.

If a special effort by the court to hide its discretion is identified in an especially demanding judgment, this lends further support to the hypothesis that courts use this tactic. Chapter 2D3 identifies unique instances where the U.S. Supreme Court and the Israeli Supreme Court suppressed dissent and tried to present a united front to support a very demanding judgment. The most famous example mentioned there is the American judgment *Brown* v. *Board Education*,[8] which was issued unanimously and used the appearance of constraint to support the incredibly demanding remedy of ending school segregation.

E. Incrementalism

Many authors have stressed that courts develop their doctrines incrementally.[9] Courts slowly shift to judgments that are more demanding. They do not immediately set

[8] *Brown* v. *Board of Education*, 347 U.S. 483 (1954).

[9] See J.H.H. Weiler, The Transformation of Europe, 100 Yale Law Journal 2403, 2447–2448 (1991) (describing this practice in the European Court of Justice (ECJ)); Laurence R. Helfer and Anne-Marie Slaughter, Toward a Theory of Effective Supranational

precedents that damage the interests of other parties, but rather shape these precedents step by step in a series of separate decisions. When courts introduce doctrines that increase their discretion, or simply change the law dramatically, they will try to support the doctrines in several judgments that rely on each other and cumulatively fortify this doctrinal shift. The reasons courts increase their demands and shape their doctrines incrementally can be highlighted by the theory of courts presented here.

Considering first the slow shift to more demanding judgments, several explanations that concur with the theory can be provided. If courts issue more demanding judgments as their reputation increases, and if courts increase their reputation gradually over time, then courts should slowly increase their demands as long as their reputation increases. The incremental shift toward more demanding judgments can therefore be simply explained by the incremental nature of growth of the court's reputation. This explanation may account for long-term trends toward issuing increasingly demanding judgments, but can only partially explain judgments issued in relatively quick succession that increase their demands from states.

It may be wise to progress judgments' demands incrementally even if the court's reputation does not change significantly in the interim. By this method, over time courts

Adjudication, 107 *Yale Law Journal* 273 (1997) (describing this practice in the ECJ and the ECHR).

may assemble and analyze more accurate and abundant information about their reputation, the reputation of the parties facing them, and the costs of their judgments for them. This will allow courts to take smaller margins of error as they gather experience and issue more demanding judgments while still foreseeing compliance.

If the court increases its demands in a series of judgments, it can study the responses of parties to each of these judgments. If the court realizes that its judgments lead to hostile responses, such as noncompliance or criticism, it can retreat to more restrained judgments.[10] It is significantly less harmful for the court to commit a small retreat and revert to more restrained judgments after facing some minor resistance than to leap forward in a single judgment and then abruptly restrain itself after facing a damaging response. Violent countermeasures directed against the court can be avoided if the court restrains itself in time. Furthermore, small retreats into restraint can be hidden from the public and do less damage to the court's reputation

[10] See Charles E. Lindblom, The Science of "Muddling Through," 19 *Public Administration Review* 79, 86 (1959) (suggesting that administrators can set new policy incrementally to test the results of their policy change); Martin Shapiro, *The Supreme Court and Administrative Agencies*, 73–91 (New York: Free Press), 1968 (studying the practice of incremental decision making in courts); Michal Tamir, Sunk Cost and Stare Decisis, 1 *Haifa Law Review* 211, 285–286 (2004) (Hebrew) (explaining incremental decision making in courts as resulting from cognitive biases of judges such as a preferences for the status quo).

than a visible about-face, which indicates the court's low reputation that cannot support demanding judgments.

Incrementally increasing the court's demands not only protects the court's reputation, it also decreases the chances of making bad policy. Incremental progress decreases the costs of acquiring information about the policy results of the judgment and decreases the chances of significant policy errors.[11]

If the court issues a series of judgments that slowly increase their demands, many of these judgments are likely to be complied with. This will not only increase the court's reputation, it can also ingrain a habit of compliance among bureaucrats, thereby determining the behavior of governments. If the individuals who determine the response of parties to the court's judgments grow accustomed to compliance, they are more likely to comply with future judgments of the court and allow it to continue to shape policy and increase its reputation.

Besides increasing their demands incrementally, courts also shape doctrine incrementally. When they wish to adopt a new doctrine, especially a doctrine that increases their discretion or gives them additional power, they will usually

[11] These benefits are similar to the benefits of the practice Sunstein dubbed *minimalism:* deciding cases narrowly by focusing on the specific case and shallowly by not explaining the theory behind the decision; see Cass R. Sunstein, *One Case at a Time: Judicial Minimalism on the Supreme Court*, 4 (Cambridge, MA: Harvard University Press), 1999.

shift toward this new doctrine in a series of small doctrinal changes undertaken in different judgments. Courts can increase the appearance of constraint in their judgments by showing they are consistent. Therefore, if courts avoid abrupt changes in their reasoning and seem to apply the same doctrines, this can increase the chances of compliance with their judgments by hiding the discretion they employ. Chapter 5 shows that the Israeli Supreme Court issued some important judgments in pairs issued at almost the same time. This allowed the court to refer to its recently released judgment and appear consistent. Chapter 6 demonstrates that the ECHR developed the doctrine that allowed it to require specific actions from states in so-called Pilot Cases in a series of judgments that slowly formed this essential judicial tool.

Courts can try to project consistency by citing their previous judgments, even if they are not binding precedents.[12] Many courts cite mainly new judgments and stop citing judgments several years after they were issued.[13]

[12] See Yonatan Lupu and Erik Voeten, Precedent in International Courts: A Network Analysis of Case Citations by the European Court of Human Rights, 42 *British Journal of Political Science* 413, 438 (2011)) showing that ECHR judgments cite previous ECHR judgments, although they are formally not binding precedents to increase the chances that national courts will support them).

[13] See Yoram Shachar, Ron Harris, and Miron Gross, Citation Practices of the Supreme Court, Quantitative Analyses, 27 *Hebrew University Law Review* 119 (1996) (finding that the Israeli Supreme

This practice may result from the fact that legal issues reappear in every generation and give the court an opportunity to cite new sources of law that reflect the application of established law to current conditions.[14] Another explanation is practical – judges find it easier to access and to master newer judgments. This phenomenon can also be explained, however, by the fact that courts constantly change doctrine incrementally, rendering older judgments obsolete. Judges may even have a personal incentive to change doctrine in order to increase the chances that their own judgments will be cited by the next generation of judges. These explanations apply in varying degrees depending on the type of case and the type of court being examined.

F. Distinguishing remedy and precedent

When international or national courts issue a judgment that increases their doctrinal powers or impinges on the interests of states or the executive, these parties can fail to comply with the judgment. By failing to comply, these parties not only damage the reputation of the court, they also indicate that they view the new doctrine as illegitimate and may fail to comply with other judgments that employ this doctrine in

Court cites mainly new judgments and referring to similar findings in the U.S. courts).

[14] See Oliver Wendell Holmes, The Path of the Law, 10 *Harvard Law Review* 457, 458 (1897).

the future. Many courts realized that the best way to disarm parties of the weapon of noncompliance is simply to require no actions in terms of compliance. In this way, the doctrine is added to the court's arsenal with no ability for the parties whose interests may be affected by this precedent in the future to resist.

This tactic was dubbed the *Marbury* v. *Madison tactic*, after the landmark judgment by U.S. Supreme Court Chief Justice Marshall.[15] The details of this renowned case are worth reciting. Marbury was a supporter of the Adams administration. This administration nominated him during its last days in office to become a justice of the peace in the county of Washington in the District of Columbia. Marbury petitioned the court to receive a writ of mandamus ordering the new secretary of state, Madison, to deliver his commission. Marshall ruled that the refusal to deliver the commission to Marbury violated his rights.[16] At the same time, however, Marshall denied the petition because the Supreme Court did not have original jurisdiction to issue a writ of mandamus. Marshall annulled the clause in the judiciary act of 1789, which gave the Supreme Court original jurisdiction to issue writs of mandamus, because it contradicted the Constitution, which, according to Marshall, gives the court only the authority to issue writs of mandamus under appellate jurisdiction.[17] Therefore, the judgment set a precedent

[15] *Marbury* v. *Madison*, 5 U.S. 137 (1803).

[16] *Ibid.*, at 167–168. [17] *Ibid.*, at 175–179.

of judicial review: It empowered the court to annul statutes that contradict its interpretation of the Constitution. This precedent was set in a case that upheld the interests of government and denied the petition against it, thus preventing it from noncomplying.[18] Furthermore, the court acquired the greatest doctrinal power in its possession by annulling a clause that actually increased the court's powers. This made it difficult for the executive to criticize the judgment as unwarranted judicial power grabbing.[19]

When the Israeli Supreme Court acquired the power of judicial review and slowly expanded it in a series of judgments, it followed this tactic as Chapter 5B4 demonstrates.

This tactic can also be exercised by international courts; in fact, some authors claim that the European Court of Justice (ECJ) mastered the use of this tactic.[20] An illustrative example is the ECJ *Charmasson* case.[21] In this case Charmasson argued that a quota for banana imports, which was imposed by the French government on October 28, 1969,

[18] Thomas G. Walker and Lee Epstein, *The Supreme Court of the United States: An Introduction*, 10 (New York: St. Martin's Press),1993.

[19] I thank Maxwell L. Stearns for this idea.

[20] Helfer and Slaughter, *supra* note 9 at 314–315.

[21] Case 48/74 *Mr. Charmasson* v. *Minister for Economic Affairs and Finance*, 1974 E.C.R II-1383. This analysis draws on Geoffrey Garrett, R. Daniel Kelemen, and Heiner Schulz, The European Court of Justice, National Governments, and Legal Integration in the European Union, 52 *International Organization* 149, 162–163 (1998).

did not conform to the timetables for eliminating restrictions on trade according to article 33 of the Rome Treaty.[22] The court ruled that the quota scheme was part of a national marketing organization, which could preclude the application of article 33 until the end of a transitional period on December 31, 1969. Because the quota was enacted before the end of the transitional period, the ruling favored the French government, thereby preempting any chance of noncompliance. However, the precedent damaged French interests by deciding that its banana marketing organization could not be used after the end of the transitional period. Because the judgment was issued on December 10, 1974, years after the transitional period ended, the negative effect on the French interest was immediate.

To a certain extent, an international court can make more effective use of this tactic than a national court, because the precedents set by the international court affect manifold states. If the court issues a precedent that damages the interests of a certain state and does not require any actions, it avoids the possibility of noncompliance, but it may incur criticism or face other hostile measures by this state. However, this precedent may actually suit the interests of other states under the court's jurisdiction. States that profit from this precedent will support the court and defend it against any attempts to harm it by the recalcitrant state.

[22] Treaty Establishing the European Community, March 25, 1957.

The tactic described here prevents parties from failing to comply by not requiring them to do anything. A slightly modified tactic can require only limited and easily performed actions from a party in a judgment that sets a precedent harmful to its interests. In this situation, a party may fail to comply with the judgment, possibly to protest against the precedent set by the court. However, the party is less likely not to comply because the remedy is not demanding and can be cheaply complied with. If the party chooses to comply, the new precedent will seem to receive its approval, and the court will be able to use it in the future with high probability of compliance.

G. Matching the demands to the party

International courts usually have many states under their jurisdiction, and these states may have varying levels of reputation and different interests. States that are expected to comply with most of the court's judgments are termed *high-reputation states*. Other states are expected to comply with fewer judgments and are termed *low-reputation states*. The past practice of a state is a good indicator of the other states' expectations of it. Therefore, states that usually complied with past judgments will be identified as high-reputation states, and states that failed to comply with more judgments will be identified as low-reputation states. The higher the state's reputation, the greater the reputational sanction it will suffer if it fails to comply with the court, because noncompliance contradicts the expectations of other states and will therefore make them radically change their assessment of this state's type and lower its reputation.

If the court faced every state only once, it could require the state to undertake actions that were only slightly less costly than the state's reputational incentive to comply. In that case, the state would comply with the judgment. States that face the court only once cannot deter the court's decision and shape its future behavior. Such states decide whether to comply based on the costs and benefits of compliance in only the case at hand. Because high-reputation states face a greater reputational sanction in case of noncompliance, the court would be able to issue more demanding judgments against high-reputation states in such a single-shot game. However, the court faces each state multiple times. In other words, most states are repeat players. States who are repeat players can threaten to not comply with the court's judgments, even if noncompliance contradicts their immediate reputational incentive: If the reputational damage caused to them by noncompliance is higher than the costs of compliance with the judgment. If a high-reputation state fails to comply with the court, it will substantially damage the court's reputation by indicating that its judgments are ignored even by states that used to comply with them in the past. This gives high-reputation states a potent threat against the court. They have the ability to do significant damage to the court's reputation if the court issues judgments that contradict their interests.

States that face the court repeatedly can threaten to not comply with judgments, even against their immediate interest, only if they can credibly commit to continue noncompliance if the court continues to issue demanding judgments against them. If the court can sustain noncompliance longer than the state can continue not to comply, the state will eventually have to surrender and comply with the court's judgments, exposing the court's strength in front of the other states.

While high-reputation states suffer a substantial damage in case of noncompliance, the damage caused to the court by their noncompliance is even greater. States have many different interests besides maintaining their reputation for compliance with a specific court. International courts, on the other hand, must rely on their reputation to have any effect on the state's behavior. The court cannot afford to suffer persistent noncompliance by a high-reputation state, but such a state may sustain the damages caused by noncompliance to protect its other interests. This means that high-reputation states can sustain the damage they suffer in case of noncompliance longer than the court can persevere in the face of noncompliance by a high-reputation state.

High-reputation states therefore have a credible threat not to comply with demanding judgments. Consequently, high-reputation states do not need to exercise their threat because the court restrains itself in advance and avoids issuing demanding judgments against high-reputation states. In a few cases the court may miscalculate and issue a demanding judgment against a high-reputation state. In that case, the state may criticize the court, fail to comply, or just signal its dissatisfaction with the judgment, and the court will usually reverse course and shift to more restrained judgments against this state in the future.

States can respond to demanding judgments against them by other means besides noncompliance, such as criticism, which further strengthens the position of high-reputation states vis-à-vis the court compared to the position of low-reputation states toward this court. States can criticize an international court when it issues judgments that damage their interests. Criticism by high-reputation states indicates that they may consider noncompliance as an option in the future. Because high-reputation states suffer greater reputational damage when they fail to comply than low-reputation states suffer when they fail to comply, the indication of willingness not to comply by high-reputation states that criticize the court would cause the court a greater reputational damage than criticism by low-reputation states. High-reputation states, which fear the damage to their reputation caused by noncompliance, can therefore threaten to criticize the court and this threat will influence the court to adhere to their interests rather than to the interests of low-reputation states whose criticism causes the court only minimal damage.

Criticism does not only damage the court's reputation, it can also change public perception of the quality of the court's judgments, thereby diminishing the court's public support. High-reputation states that criticize the court will be viewed as more credible because of their good practices than low-reputation states and can therefore cause greater damage to the court's public support. If a high-reputation state criticizes the court, other states may view its judgments as wrong and unjust and will in turn be more likely not to comply with future judgments against them.

States can also direct their criticism at a national audience in an attempt to sway domestic public opinion against the court. If the domestic public is convinced that the court's judgments are biased or incorrect, they are more likely to endorse future noncompliance by their government and may even demand that their state leave the court's jurisdiction by exiting its founding treaty. High-reputation states may face a particularly high damage to their reputation if they exit the court's jurisdiction, because this conduct cuts against the high expectations of the international community from them. But even high-reputation states may not be able to resist a public that is vehemently opposed to the court for a long time. A strategic high-reputation state can deliberately stir up resistance to the court to pose the threat that future exit is an option. The court that cannot accommodate an exit by a high-reputation state may have to surrender to this pressure and shift to restrained judgments against it.[23]

[23] This type of strategic behavior is described more fully in Chapter 3C2.

A low-reputation state holds no credible threat against the court, because the court can withstand its noncompliance without suffering a severe reputational damage. But theoretically, a group of low-reputation states can collude and decide that all would not comply with demanding judgments by the court, even if noncompliance causes more damage to their reputation than the costs of compliance. If many low-reputation states consistently fail to comply with the court's judgments, the court may not be able to withstand this damage to its reputation. A threat posed by a large group of low-reputation states that act collectively can therefore force the court to restrain itself. However, collusion between several states is very difficult to sustain. States must be able to prevent free riding within the group. That is, they must be able to detect states that comply with demanding judgments contrary to their agreement and punish them. States may find it very difficult to punish states for *complying* with the court, an action that usually increases their reputation in the eyes of other states. Furthermore, the threat of noncompliance by many states will only deter the court if it is aware of their agreement and their resolve not to comply. But when this agreement is made public, the states' reputation will suffer because they openly declare their decision not to comply with the court.

For the reasons mentioned above, international courts should issue more demanding judgments against low-reputation states than against high-reputation states. Yet, it is very difficult to prove that this is indeed the courts' practice. High-reputation states may have higher standards of human rights protection and will therefore have to face lower costs to comply with the same standard of behavior than would a low-reputation state. In that case, applying the same standards to all states will result in demanding judgments from low-reputation states and less demanding judgments against high-reputation states. In some situations, the court can therefore justify the difference in its demands from different types of states as an impartial application of the law.

Furthermore, courts must try to preserve their image of impartiality and try to prevent any accusation of bias. Therefore, even if the court does demand a higher standard of behavior from low-reputation states than it does from high-reputation states, the court will try to hide this fact by distinguishing between the facts of the judgments. Courts may even behave strategically to prevent accusations of bias. They may deliberately issue a few restrained judgments against low-reputation states or demanding judgments against high-reputation states just to appear impartial. Nevertheless, Chapter 6C1 tries to draw on specific examples from the judgments of the ECHR to demonstrate the tendency to demand more from low-reputation states compared to high-reputation states.

Some of the doctrines used by the court increase its ability to require the states to undertake costly actions. If such a doctrine is used against a high-reputation state, it may respond by noncompliance or by criticizing the court, causing the court significant damage. Courts can introduce such new doctrines in judgments issued against low-reputation states. After these doctrines are introduced and used several times against low-reputation states, they become accepted and consistent practice of the court. Consequently, the court can appear constrained and reveal less discretion when it uses the same doctrine in the future. This would allow the court to use the same doctrine against high-reputation states while facing a lower likelihood of noncompliance and while reducing the ability of these states to criticize its judgments. Chapter 6 demonstrates how the ECHR introduced the doctrine of Pilot Judgments that allowed it to demand specific actions from states in a series of judgments against low-reputation states before it applied the same doctrine to high-reputation states.

If the court issues a judgment against a high-reputation state and this state criticizes the judgment, the court may retreat and in future judgments shift back to doctrines that are more acceptable from the state's perspective or are less demanding toward it. Similar criticism by a low-reputation state may not lead the court to restrain itself, and the court may continue to issue demanding judgments against this state. The court may prove its persistence by refusing to retreat in the face of resistance by low-reputation states, forcing them to comply with its judgments. Chapter 6 gives examples of such different behavior by the ECHR when it faced resistance by low-reputation and by high-reputation states.

H. Pleasing both parties

The theory presented in this book applies mainly to supranational courts such as the ECHR, which receive applications of individuals against states. Some international courts, such as the International Court of Justice (ICJ) receive contentious cases in which one state raises claims against another. Courts that receive contentious cases may find it difficult to manipulate their judgments by walking on the brink of noncompliance, because usually if they issue a demanding judgment against one state, it will be favorable to the other state and vice versa. Courts that decide contentious cases will also find it harder to favor the interests of high-reputation states in their conflicts with low-reputation states than would supranational courts. When two states face each other in the same dispute, it is much easier to compare the court's treatment of them and to detect any sign of bias. The losing state would often have a special incentive to expose this bias and criticize the court.[24]

Although the theory cannot be neatly applied to international courts that decide contentious cases, these courts share many of the motivations of supranational courts. These courts both wish to secure compliance with their judgments in order to be able to promote their preferences.

[24] See Shai Dothan, How International Courts Enhance Their Legitimacy, 14 *Theoretical Inquiries in Law* 455, 461 (2013).

These courts both wish to preserve the support for their judgments by appearing impartial.

One method courts that decide contentious cases can use to increase the chances of compliance and to preserve their support is to reach some form of compromise between the interests of the two sides to the dispute. If both sides gain some of their objectives, they are both more likely to comply and less likely to criticize the court. Scholars claimed that the ICJ uses such a strategy in some of its judgments.[25]

Sometimes it is impossible to split the cake in the middle and grant concessions to both parties. In these types of situations, the court can still try to appease the losing party by using a rhetoric that accepts some of its arguments or looks favorably at its side of the debate. The *Oil Platforms* case[26] decided by the ICJ is a possible example. In this case, the ICJ decided that U.S. attacks on Iranian oil installations were not necessary and did not constitute self-defense under international law. These attacks therefore could not be justified under the treaty between Iran and the United States, which Iran claimed the United States breached by its attack.[27] However, the court decided that at the time there was no relevant commerce between Iran and the United States, and therefore the freedom of commerce

[25] Yuval Shany, Bosnia, Serbia and the Politics of International Adjudication, 45 *Justice* 21, 24 (2008).

[26] Case Concerning Oil Platforms (*Iran* v. *U.S.*) [2003] ICJ Rep. 161.

[27] The Treaty of Amity, Economic Relations and Consular Rights between the United States and Iran (August 15, 1955).

protected by the treaty was not breached and Iran's demand for reparations was denied.[28] The result of the judgment is favorable to the U.S. interests, but the reasoning that strongly criticizes the U.S. actions may have partly appeased Iran for losing the case.[29]

Even supranational courts and national courts may care about both sides of the dispute before them in some cases. Sometimes applicants and petitioners before these courts are organizations that can appear before the court repeatedly, and the court may wish to maintain their support. The court can maintain the support of these organizations and their willingness to appear before the court in the future by granting them at least part of the requested remedy or by using a rhetoric that is supportive of their arguments. Similarly, if the executive loses the case, the court can still try to appease it by looking favorably at some of its claims.[30]

I. Spending reputation

This book studies the attempts of courts to increase their reputation. Reputation, however, is only a means to an end. The court fulfills its ultimate goal of promoting its preferences by using its reputation to shape the behavior of parties

[28] *Oil Platforms* case, par. 98–99.

[29] See Dothan, *supra* note 24.

[30] See Alon Harel, The Courts and Homosexuality: Dignity or Tolerance? 4 *Mishpat Umimshal* 785, 789–790 (1998) (Hebrew) (finding this strategy in the behavior of the Israeli Supreme Court).

under its jurisdiction in future cases. Sometimes, the court may have to forfeit the goal of increasing its reputation in order to secure its immediate preferences. For instance, if compliance with a certain ruling is primary to the court, it may support this ruling with carefully constrained reasoning to prevent any chance of noncompliance, even if doing so will not increase its reputation as much as the use of discretionary reasoning, which poses minimal chance of noncompliance. In such cases, courts have to balance the potential generated by a high reputation for promoting their preferences in the future against their immediate preferences in the case at hand. Different courts may have a different *discount rate* for the future – they may show a greater or a lower willingness to jeopardize their immediate policy preferences in return for a higher reputation that will allow them to promote their preferences in the future.[31]

In some cases, the court may consider an issue so important that it may be willing to suffer noncompliance and the resulting damage to its reputation in order to change the behavior of the relevant party. If the court issues an extreme judgment, the party may not comply fully, but may still respond by changing its practices in a way that concurs with the court's preferences, or at least comes nearer to them than the party's current practices. The case of *Cooper* v. *Aaron*[32] decided by the U.S. Supreme Court may

[31] I thank Ian Ayres for this idea.

[32] *Cooper* v. *Aaron*, 358 U.S. 1 (1958).

serve as an example. Prior to this judgment, the Court decided to forbid segregation in public schools in *Brown* v. *Board of education.*[33] Later in *Brown II*[34] it directed district courts to take the necessary measures to end segregation "with all deliberate speed." Despite these decisions, segregation in public schools in southern states continued almost without a change.[35] The town of Little Rock, Arkansas, devised a gradual desegregation plan that was supposed to start with the admission of nine black children to high school. Members of the local government resisted the desegregation plan, which led to such civil unrest that the school could not function properly. The school board petitioned the district court to withdraw the admission of the black children and delay the desegregation plan for two and a half years. The district court accepted this request but was reversed by the court of appeals. The Supreme Court decided the case almost immediately – only a day after certiorari was given. In a short unanimous judgment, issued per curiam, the Supreme Court affirmed the judgment of the court of appeals. The full judgment issued later ruled that every type of state support for segregated schools contradicts the Fourteenth Amendment to the U.S. Constitution. *Cooper* v. *Aaron* demanded immediate

[33] *Brown* v. *Board of Education*, 347 U.S. 483 (1954).

[34] *Brown* v. *Board of Education* 349 U.S. 294 (1955).

[35] See Gerald N. Rosenberg, *The Hollow Hope: Can Courts Bring About Social Change?* 52 (Chicago: The University of Chicago Press), 2nd edn., 2008.

desegregation, even though it was evident that segregation would not end instantly. In fact, some of the judges themselves may not have wanted segregation to end without any delay. However, the Court's firm stance may have been calculated to speed up the process of desegregation and lead the practice of the states closer to the policy preferences of the Court. In this sense, the Court may have been willing to suffer noncompliance and damage to its reputation to help promote its preferences in a specific case.[36]

In these cases, the court *spends* its reputation – it suffers damage to its reputation in exchange for promoting its preferences in a specific case. The court's willingness to spend its reputation depends on the strength of its preferences regarding the issue at hand and on the importance it ascribes to the future – its discount rate. It may also depend on the current level of the court's reputation. If the court has a high reputation, it may feel confident that it can respond to future challenges, despite suffering a reputational sanction. This may make high-reputation courts more willing to spend their reputation than low-reputation courts, thereby further improving the ability of high-reputation courts to promote their preferences.

The preferences of the court can be presented as a sum of the preferences of the judges within it, often represented by the preferences of the median judge. Judges in the minority may not be able to determine the final result of the

[36] I thank William N. Eskridge for this idea.

judgment, but they can take actions that affect the court's reputation. For instance, a judge may choose to dissent to serve her own goals when it is the court's interests to project unanimity.[37] Other judges on the court may pressure judges not to dissent when doing so contradicts the court's reputational interest. The greater the court's need to increase its reputation, the greater these pressures may become. Some judges may withstand all efforts to convince them, however, and decide to jeopardize the court's reputation in order to serve their own goals.

The willingness of judges to damage the court's interest in order to serve another goal is demonstrated by the opinions of the U.S. Supreme Court justices in the case of *Bush* v. *Gore*.[38] In this case, the Court had to decide whether to allow a recount of votes for the presidential election in some counties in Florida in accordance with the judgment of the Florida Supreme Court. This case was a true hot potato; the Court's decision could have determined the result of the presidential elections, and therefore could be rejected by half of the country, damaging the Court's public support. With lower public support for the Court, the executive could more easily fail to comply with the Court in the future, which would damage the Court's reputation. Considering the Court's concern for its public support, it may

[37] The ways that dissent can serve the preferences of individual judges are discussed in Chapter 2D3.

[38] *Bush* v. *Gore*, 531 U.S. 98, 111 (2000).

have been wise not to accept the case at all or at least to defer to the Florida Supreme Court and allow the recount, as Justice Breyer urged the court to do in his dissent. Instead, the Court's majority opinion annulled the decision of the Florida Supreme Court to initiate the recount. Furthermore, several justices wrote scathing dissents against the majority's decision, exposing the political motivation behind the Court's decision. Authors debate the question of whether the Court's decision in *Bush* v. *Gore* damaged the support for the Court or if it proved a victorious use of judicial power.[39] However, even if the justices who wrote the majority and minority opinions considered that their opinions could hurt the Court's interests, they may have decided they preferred to fulfill their political ideology, so they followed their narrow political partisanship.[40]

J. Conclusion

This chapter presented the tactics courts use as they try to increase their reputation. The tactics presented here can serve both as recommendations for how courts should act if they wish to improve their reputation and as predictions of how courts usually act in situations in which they value

[39] See David S. Law, A Theory of Judicial Power and Judicial Review, 97 *Georgetown Law Journal* 723, 762–764 (2009).

[40] See Alan M. Dershowitz, *Supreme Injustice: How the High Court Hijacked Election 2000*, 174–175 (New York: Oxford University Press), 2001.

their reputation. The conditions under which courts will act as reputation maximizers are discussed in Chapter 2G.

The few examples mentioned in this chapter only serve to illustrate how courts act. These examples can give the reader tools to analyze judgments from a new perspective and to check whether they conform to the theory that courts seek to increase their reputation. To demonstrate the behavior of specific courts and show that their judgments conform to the theory, a more thorough analysis is necessary. This is the purpose of the next two chapters, which apply the theory to one national and one international court. Chapter 5 analyzes the behavior of the Israeli Supreme Court and presents the different tactics it uses. Chapter 6 studies the behavior of the European Court of Human Rights. These two courts can indicate how other national and international courts would act under the conditions that make courts act as reputation seekers.

When other conditions apply, courts may behave either similarly or differently according to their specific interests. Chapter 7 demonstrates how courts act under different conditions when the theory does not apply. This demonstration serves to illustrate that the claims made in this chapter are falsifiable. They do not cover every possible action of courts. Under different conditions, different behavior may be observed.

5 National court case study: Israeli Supreme Court

The Israeli Supreme Court serves as an ideal case study for the theory presented here for two reasons. First, it presents conditions under which courts are likely to behave as reputation maximizers: It issues many judgments that demand significant actions from the executive every year, and they are usually complied with despite the lack of an enforcement mechanism. The Court's judgments often involve ambiguous doctrine that allows the Court discretion that it can use strategically. Second, the Israeli Supreme Court shares many attributes with other important courts of last resort in democratic countries, such as the U.S. and the Indian Supreme Courts. This suggests that the theory can explain the way many significant judicial systems work.

This chapter begins with a short background on the Israeli Supreme Court that emphasizes attributes necessary to understanding the theory presented in this book. The chapter then goes on to describe the way the Court strategically decides cases in order to increase its reputation. The Court's practices are shown to conform to the tactics that can improve the Court's reputation, according to the last chapter. After presenting the Court's strategy, the chapter describes the way the executive retaliated against the Court and tried to shift the balance of power with the Court to its favor. Finally, the chapter shows how the Court responded to the executive response by adopting more sophisticated judicial tactics designed to maintain its reputation in the face of new conditions, such as a hostile executive and low public support.

A. Background

The Israeli Supreme Court is the highest appellate court in Israel; it hears appeals on judgments and other decisions of the District Courts.[1] The Court also sits as the High Court of Justice and hears cases in which it grants relief for the sake of justice, provided these cases are not under the jurisdiction of other courts.[2] It can order the release of unlawfully detained persons and can order state and

[1] Basic Law: The Judiciary, art. 15(b).

[2] *Ibid.*, at art. 15(c).

local authorities and any person carrying a public function to do, or refrain from doing, any act in the lawful exercise of their authority.[3]

The Court sits in Jerusalem[4] and currently consists of 15 justices, including a president and a deputy president. Justices are appointed by the president of Israel upon selection by the Judges' Selection Committee. The committee has nine members: the president of the Supreme Court and two other justices of the Supreme Court, the Minister of Justice and another minister designated by the government, two members of the Knesset (the Israeli parliament), and two representatives of the Israeli bar. The Minister of Justice serves as the chairperson of the committee.[5] Justices are eligible for nomination to the Supreme Court if they have served as District Court judges for five years, if they are members (or are eligible to be members) of the Israeli bar who served as lawyers, judges, or other legal officials or law professors for 10 years (at least five of them in Israel), or if they qualify as "eminent jurists."[6] Usually, only the most senior jurists in Israel are nominated to the Supreme Court. The justices' tenure ends when they reach the age of 70: After that, they have three months to complete any cases they started

[3] *Ibid.*, at art. 15(d). Orders to judicial authorities are discussed in more detail in articles 15(d)(3)-(4).

[4] *Ibid.*, at art. 15(a).

[5] *Ibid.*, at art. 4.

[6] Courts Law (Consolidated Version) 5744–1984, art. 2.

before they must retire.[7] Each justice has a senior and a junior legal adviser and two clerks who intern at his or her office for a period of a year; they are often assisted by a foreign volunteer.

The precedents of the Court bind all other courts in Israel.[8] The Court is not constrained by the Basic Law: The Judiciary to follow its own previous judgments, but many judgments of the Court stress the importance of following its precedents. The Court often refers to its own judgments and usually tries not to digress from them unless they are found to be clearly wrong, or if the judgments become incompatible due to changing conditions.[9]

The Court receives thousands of cases each year, including extremely salient cases that touch on the most sensitive issues in Israeli politics: the Arab-Israeli conflict, the occupied territories, religion and state relations, and budgetary

[7] *Ibid.*, at art. 13 and 15. After retiring from the court, some justices have gone on to fill other high public positions, such as the state comptroller.

[8] Basic Law: The Judiciary, art. 20(2).

[9] The degree to which the Court is constrained to follow its own previous decisions was debated within the Court, with some justices preferring consistency over allowing the justice to follow his or her own conscience and some adopting the opposite view. The differences of opinions within the Court about this issue are described at Yoram Shachar, Solidarity and Generational Sequencing in the Israeli Supreme Court, 16 *Bar Ilan University Law Review* 161 (2000).

issues. The Court decides all the cases that reach it and pass the hurdles of standing and admissibility.

Over the years, the Court increased the number of potential cases it can decide by lowering the barriers of standing. The Court allowed petitions from people who were not directly affected by the act in question and made it possible for members of Parliament, public lawyers, and NGOs to bring many salient cases to the Court.[10] It also adopted the doctrine that every issue is amenable to judicial decision and almost all issues are fit to be decided by the Court, including political issues that were avoided in the past.[11]

However, the Court has significant discretion regarding the reasoning it uses and the remedy it grants when it decides cases, which affects the salience of the final judgment. The Court can also delay the decision in certain cases for many years, partly diffusing the controversy around certain cases. The impact of a case is greatly influenced by the timing of the decision and also by previous judgments of the Court.[12] Many of the judgments the Court issues are

[10] See Menachem Mautner, *The Decline of Formalism and the Rise of Values in Israeli Law*, 104 (Tel Aviv: Ma'agalay Da'at Publishing House), 1993 (Hebrew); Ruth Gavison, Mordechai Kremnitzer, and Yoav Dotan, *Judicial Activism: For and Against – The Role of the High Court of Justice in Israeli Society*, 11–13 (Jerusalem: Magnes Press), 2000 (Hebrew).

[11] See Maunter, *supra* note 10 at 103–104; Gavison, Kremnitzer, and Dotan, *supra* note 10 at 13–15.

[12] For the claim that the Israeli Court uses postponing tactics to delay the decision in cases until it finds it beneficial to decide them,

technical, but every year many dozens of its judgments have substantial political influence and public exposure.

The Court usually sits in panels of three justices, although the president and the deputy president of the Court can decide before a case begins to refer it to a panel of an odd number of justices greater than three, and a panel in the middle of discussing a case can also decide to add more justices. Panels are usually enlarged in cases that are particularly controversial or difficult. Certain preliminary or intermediate decisions and requests can be decided by a panel of a single justice.[13] The president of the Court can choose the justices who sit on each panel.[14] A panel of three

see Yoav Dotan, Pre-petitions and Constitutional Dilemmas Regarding the Role of Government Lawyers, 7 *Mishpat Umimshal* 159, 193–194 (2004) (Hebrew).

[13] Courts Law (Consolidated Version) 5744–1984, art. 26. For data on the percentage of judgments issued by three-justice panels, *see infra* note 22.

[14] *Ibid.*, at art. 27. The president may delegate this power to the deputy president according to art. 29(3). Gross and Shachar found conclusive evidence that the panels are not randomly selected. However, their data cannot prove or disprove a manipulative use of the president's power to reach a certain result. The intuitive criteria they test, such as an attempt by the president to add to panels in which he sits less veteran justices or justices who usually sit in panels dealing with the same type of cases, can only partly explain how panels are chosen. This suggests that there are other hidden criteria that might influence this practice. See Miron Gross and Yoram Shachar, Searching for Methods in Bench Selection in the Israeli Supreme Court: Quantitative Analysis, 29 *Hebrew University Law Review* 567 (1998).

justices that issued a judgment can decide to refer it to a review by five or more justices. A party that is dissatisfied with the Court's judgment may ask for a review by an enlarged panel. In that case, the president, or a justice or justices he or she appointed, may grant a review if the judgment contradicted the Court's previous judgments or when the decision justifies a review because of its importance, difficulty, or novelty.[15]

B. The court's strategy

The Israeli Supreme Court acts strategically to increase its reputation over the long term. In order to increase its reputation, the Court, in some cases, walks on the brink of noncompliance. Some of the Court's judgments are demanding or use discretionary reasoning that would lead to noncompliance if the Court's reputation was lower. The Court expects compliance with those cases, however, because of the level of its reputation.

This section will demonstrate four tactics that are discussed in Chapter 4 used by the Court to practice this strategy: shifting to discretionary judgments as the Court's reputation increases, supporting demanding judgments with constrained reasoning and less demanding judgments with discretionary reasoning, changing doctrine

[15] Courts Law (Consolidated Version) 5744–1984, art. 30.

incrementally, and issuing less demanding judgments in cases that set precedents that increase the Court's power.

1. Shifting to discretionary reasoning as the court's reputation increases

The Israeli Supreme Court has been active for more than 60 years. Over this time, it issued many groundbreaking judgments, and most of them – at least until recently, as described in the next section and according to popular belief – were complied with.[16] The result was a significant growth in the reputation of the Court. The theory suggests that, as the Court's reputation increases, it should shift to judgments that use more discretionary reasoning. This chapter demonstrates that the Court's practice supports this hypothesis.

This chapter will not discuss the possibility that the Israeli Supreme Court shifted to more demanding

[16] See Aharon Barak, *The Judge in a Democracy*, 72 (Jerusalem: Keter), 2004 (Hebrew) (arguing that the sanction of contempt of court was never used against the state in Israel because the state always complies fully with judgments of the court). See also Daniel Friedmann, *The Purse and the Sword: The Trials of the Israeli Legal Revolution*, 30–31 (Tel Aviv: Miskal – Yedioth Ahronoth Books and Chemed Books), 2013 (Hebrew) (arguing that in Israel's early years the Court's judgments were usually complied with by the executive. There were only rare exceptions to this rule, such as the failure to comply with the court's order to allow the Arab-Israeli dwellers of the villages Ikrit and Biram to return to their lands from which they were evacuated).

judgments as its reputation increased. Although many have this impression,[17] this is a claim that is very hard to support. Israel has undergone many changes in the last 60 years, greatly increasing its economic and military power. Consequently, the executive has tremendously increased its ability to sustain costs. This renders a comparison of the demands of judgments across decades inaccurate.

While this chapter does not prove the claim that the Court shifted to more demanding judgments, the opposite claim, that from the 1950s to the 1990s the Court shifted to less demanding judgments, seems to contradict the prevailing view of the Court. The shift to more discretionary methods of reasoning is therefore not meant to balance a shift to less demanding judgments; instead, it results from a rise in the Court's reputation.

Menachem Mautner was the first to investigate the notion that the Israeli Supreme Court used formalistic reasoning during the 1950s, but toward the 1980s shifted to a values-based form of reasoning (hence showing greater judicial discretion). He provided several explanations for this phenomenon, including a suggestion that the Court was strengthened because its liberal values were increasingly accepted by important elites in Israeli society.[18] If important elites did accept the Court's ideology, this could have led to greater public support for its judgments,

[17] See Friedmann, *supra* note 16, at 8.
[18] Mautner, *supra* note 10, at 126–127.

because elites viewed them as just and correct, thereby increasing the criticism on a noncompliant executive, even when the Court used discretionary reasoning. Simultaneously, the Court shifted toward discretionary judgments, correlating with the increase in its reputation due to its high rates of compliance over the years. This correlation cannot prove that the increasing reputation of the Court caused these trends in behavior, because many other variables, including changes in the Israeli society as described by Mautner, might have affected the Court's behavior. This correlation, however, can be explained by the theory presented in this book.

Mautner's claims about the shift in the Court's reasoning can be checked empirically as long as there is an agreement about what constitutes more formal forms of reasoning. While types of reasoning may be difficult to code, it may be easier to identify other characteristics of the judgment that can serve as proxies for the type of reasoning used. One of those factors is the length of the judgment. Writing a lengthy judgment allows the justices to use looser forms of reasoning, which expose their individual discretion. For that reason, comparative research found that powerless courts try to increase the legitimacy of their judgments by writing shorter decisions.[19] Empirical research shows that

[19] See Jean Louis Goutal, Characteristics of Judicial Style in France, Britain and the U.S.A., 24 *American Journal of Comparative Law* 43, 60–61 (1976).

the judgments of the Israeli Court have steadily increased in length between the beginning of the 1960s and the year 2000: Only then did the trend toward longer judgments stop and even begin to reverse.[20] The stable trend of lengthening the Court's judgments is consistent with the claim that the Court issued increasingly more discretionary judgments over the years as its reputation increased.

Another method to assess the nature of the Court's reasoning is to study the sources that it refers to in its judgments. Yoram Shachar suggested that when the Court refers to its own previous judgments, it exposes its discretion. When it refers to academic writing, it partially hides its discretion behind external sources, and when it refers to legislation, it disguises its discretion perfectly and can claim that it is only fulfilling the will of parliament. In my view, the nature of citations to previous judgments could be debated: While they do not refer to external sources, they

[20] Yoram Shachar, The Citation Space of the Supreme Court 1950–2004, 50 *Hapraklit* 29, 32–33 (2008). At 36 Shachar shows how the data refute the possibility that these trends are explained by technological changes in data processing. The decline in the length of judgments after the year 2000 may be a sign of the Court's attempt to increase the legitimacy of its judgments in recent years, a trend analyzed at section D. However, this constitutes only weak evidence because the relevant data reaches only to the year 2004 and there are other, perhaps more plausible, possible explanations. Shachar suggests two such explanations: the retirement of a core of veteran justices or the approaching end of their terms and a general trend in legal culture toward shorter writing, see *Ibid.*, at 34–35.

show the Court is consistent, which suggests it is following the law and not issuing ad hoc decisions. Reference to legislation, however, clearly shows less discretion than reference to scholarship. Shachar found that over the last 50 years, the Court had decreased the proportion of citations to legislation and increased the proportion of citation to academic writing.[21] This shows that the Court became more willing to forsake the guise of fulfilling the will of the legislature and instead referred to sources that could easily support every decision it wished to reach.

Dissent among the justices increases the appearance of judicial discretion in the judgment. The preferences of individual justices can conflict with the interests of the Court and render practices of dissent in individual cases an inaccurate measure of the Court's strategy. Idiosyncratic dissents, however, cannot explain trends in the practices of dissent over many years. If trends in the rates of dissent appear despite the random noise of individually dissenting justices, the trend could suggest strategic behavior of the Court as a collective. Data that show the Israeli Court increased the proportion of dissents over the years can therefore support the claim that the Court is issuing more discretionary decisions as its reputation grows.

Shachar, Gross, and Harris measured the number of dissents in published judgments issued by three-justice panels, which comprise most of the important judgments

[21] See *Ibid.*, at 37–39.

issued by the Court.[22] Their data show several trends in the amount of dissent in those judgments: Between the years 1948–1955 the number of judgments with dissents increased to a peak of 11.5%, yet within two years this number plummeted to 2.2%. From the 1957 low, the percentage of judgments with dissents grew steadily for 20 years and reached 15.2% by 1978. In the following decade (1978–1987), the number declined, only to increase once more in the 1990s.[23] While there are several trends in these data, they seem to support the claim that from the 1950s to the 1980s, the Israeli Court could have increased the appearance of discretion in its judgments by increasing dissent.

In addition to issuing a judgment unanimously, the justices can hide judicial discretion by issuing a judgment

[22] Shachar et al. find that in their database covering published judgments in the years 1948–1994, 88.6% of the judgments were given from a panel of three justices; *see* Yoram Shachar, Miron Gross, and Ron Harris, Anatomy of Discourse and Dissent in the Supreme Court: Quantitative Analyses, 20 *Tel Aviv University Law Review* 749, 752 (1997) (Hebrew). Only about 12% of the cases opened in the Court during that period led to published judgments, but a substantial portion of the cases that reach the court end without a significant legal decision and without disagreement between the justices (see *Ibid*., at 751). The authors estimate that in the entire case law of the Court the percentage of judgments with disagreement is less than 1% (*Ibid*., at 756). This paragraph is focused on published judgments in the Shachar et al. primary database because those judgments are the main arena for the evolution of the law in the court.

[23] *Ibid*., at 768.

per curiam – signed collectively by the panel instead of by individual justices. In this way, the individual views of each justice are hidden and the judgment is presented as supported by the entire Court. The decline of the use of per curiam judgments over the years, to the point where they almost disappeared and served only for uniquely controversial cases, further supports the claim that the Court shifted to more discretionary reasoning over the years.[24]

2. Matching demanding judgments with constrained reasoning

If the Court issues two cases at approximately the same time and uses both of these cases to walk on the brink of noncompliance, then the judgment that issues a demanding remedy should be supported by relatively constrained reasoning, and the judgment that is not demanding can use more discretionary reasoning.

The main difficulty in demonstrating a strategic use of reasoning is that reasoning seems to be determined by the constraints of doctrine. Even if two possible forms of reasoning can be used in the case, the judge will usually

[24] The findings of Shachar et al. regarding per curiam decisions are that in 1948 they were about 43% of the three justices' rulings. In the next ten years they had a high percentage, reaching a record of 56% of the three justices' judgments in 1954. At the end of the 1950s, their number fell to 10% of the three justices' judgments, and since then, the rate went down steadily until those judgments disappeared completely from the database in the 1990s; see *Ibid.*, at 754. Some uniquely controversial cases were issued per curiam even later; they are discussed in Chapter 2D3 of this book.

use only one of these forms and declare it is prescribed by legal doctrine. Although doctrine may constrain the use of reasoning in many cases, there are special cases in which it is verifiable that two types of reasoning can be used equally to support either a more demanding or a less demanding judgment. If the Court uses the more constrained form of reasoning when it issues a demanding judgment and the discretionary form of reasoning when it issues a less demanding judgment, this supports the theory, although it cannot prove it. Because these cases deal with the same issue, the Court likely did not arbitrarily decide to demand more in one case, but rather matched the remedy to the type of reasoning used.

This theory is illustrated by the Court's judgments regarding exempting yeshiva students from mandatory military service. In the *Ressler* case,[25] the petitioners raised two main claims against the current exemptions of yeshiva students: that the minister of defense who issued this exemption was not authorized to do so, because such a fundamental decision must be specifically made in primary legislation, and that the decision of the minister was unreasonable.[26] Justice Barak, who issued the first opinion in this case and was joined by the other two justices regarding the result, therefore had two routes for annulling the decision. He could either apply a constrained method of deciding

[25] HCJ 910/86 *Ressler* v. *Minister of Defense* [1988] IsrSC 42(2) 441.
[26] *Ibid.*, at 453.

the minister was not authorized, or he could use his discretion to find that the decision was unreasonable. In the *Ressler* case, Justice Barak approved the decision of the minister on both grounds, deciding that he had authority and that his decision was reasonable. He also stated, however, that the reasonableness of the decision depended on the number of yeshiva students exempted – more than a certain number would render the decision unreasonable.[27] This statement exposed the discretion in Barak's judgment, because it showed he had to balance complex matters of degree to reach the result.

When the issue reached the Court again about a decade later in the *Rubinstein* case,[28] the number of yeshiva students exempted had grown substantially.[29] Barak could have annulled the exemption based on lack of reasonableness,[30] yet Barak chose to support the demanding judgment to annul the current exemption by deciding instead that the minister of defense had no authority to initiate the exemption without specific authorization by a statute.[31] This example shows that when the Court issued a judgment

[27] *Ibid.*, at 505.

[28] HCJ 3267/97 *Rubinstein* v. *Minister of Defense* [1998] IsrSC 52(5) 481, 530.

[29] See *Ibid.*, at 490 stating that when the Ressler case was decided, the number of yeshiva students exempted was 17,017, while at the time of the Rubinstein case their number was 28,772.

[30] Barak even indicates this possibility at *Ibid.*, at 530.

[31] *Ibid.*, at 529–530.

that demanded nothing in the *Ressler* case, it used the opportunity to threaten the use of the discretionary tool of reasonableness. When the Court issued a demanding judgment in a similar case, however, it opted for the use of the constrained course of reasoning – finding that the minister was unauthorized.

Different interpretations could also be applied to these judgments. Barak tried to show in his judgment in the *Rubinstein* case[32] that legal and factual conditions changed during the decade between the *Ressler* and *Rubinstein* cases. Maybe the exemption policy was both reasonable and under the authority of the minister at the time of the *Ressler* case, but failed both tests at the time of the *Rubinstein* case. Furthermore, maybe the Court's reputation increased in the interim, allowing it to issue a more demanding judgment at a later date. Nevertheless, those judgments do show that sometimes similar results may be reached by using different courses of reasoning.[33] They also suggest that the Court is more ready to threaten the use of discretionary reasoning when it does not demand significant actions from the state and will support demanding judgments with constrained reasoning.

Several years after the *Rubinstein* case, the Knesset legislated a statute meant to exempt the yeshiva students

[32] *Ibid.*, at 529–530.

[33] A fact noted with regard to these cases at Omri Yadlin, Judicial Activism and Judicial Discretion as a Strategic Game, 19 *Bar Ilan University Law Review* 665, 690 (2003) (Hebrew).

from service. Petitioners argued that this statute was unconstitutional in the *Quality of Government* case.[34] President Barak issued the majority judgment that set a precedent deciding that the right to equality is protected under the Basic Law: Human Dignity and Liberty. This judgment decided that the infringement of equality by the statute was not proportional because the statute did not fulfill the goals of increasing equality and integrating ultra orthodox men into the work market in Israel. However, the final decision was to deny the petition and to wait five years from the legislation of the statute before deciding about its constitutionality. This judgment did not order any immediate action, and it used discretionary reasoning because it presented a new and contestable interpretation of the Basic Law.[35] This serves as another example of using more discretionary reasoning in less demanding cases.

In 2012, after several years had passed and the number of yeshiva students exempted from military service continued to grow, the Court decided in the *second Ressler* case[36] that the statute that exempted the yeshiva students was unconstitutional. The Court ruled that the relevant statute could not fulfill its purpose and therefore its force

[34] HCJ 6427/02 *The Movement for Quality of Government in Israel* v. *Knesset* [2006] IsrSC 61(1) 619.

[35] Barak's reasoning is not evident from the text and is criticized by Justice Cheshin in par. 68–75 of his judgment.

[36] HCJ 6298/07 *Ressler* v. *The Knesset* (not yet published, February 21, 2012).

could not be extended further. This judgment was very demanding and its reasoning seemed relatively constrained, because it followed precisely the doctrine set in the *Quality of Government* case. Because the Court followed its own precedent, it could present its more recent decision as constrained, even if the judgment it referred to was considered innovative at the time.

Although the Court had grounded the judgment in precedent, some judges were wary of demanding such a significant change of policy. Two justices supported leaving the issue undecided and held in the Court's docket. Justice Gronis wrote a short dissent in which he supported rejecting the petition both on the ground that the policy in question favored a minority and should not call for judicial intervention, and specifically because the judgment would not be complied with and the issue would be brought again to the Court, damaging its public standing.

Another example of balancing between the remedy and the reasoning concerns the issue of detaining certain members of the militant organization Hezbollah to use them as bargaining chips for future negotiations to release captive Israeli soldiers, even though these members did not pose a direct security threat. In the first *Anonymous* case,[37] Barak decided in a majority opinion that it was permitted in extreme circumstances to detain persons due to actions or

[37] ADA 10/94 *Anonymous* v. *Minister of Defense* [1997] IsrSC 53(1) 97, 108–109.

dangers posed by others and not by themselves. The minister of defense was therefore authorized to detain the petitioners. Barak also found that the detainment in question was proportional.

In the second *Anonymous* case,[38] an enlarged panel reviewed the same issue. Barak, again issuing the majority decision, contradicted his previous decision and held that Israel's domestic law, when interpreted according to its purpose, does not allow the detainment of persons who pose no direct threat to Israel's security. Barak could have decided that detaining the captives for such long periods was not proportional – in fact, he claimed he would do so even if he found that there was authority[39] – but Barak tried to support his demanding judgment with the most constrained method of reasoning possible, finding no authority under domestic law.[40]

These examples suggest that when the Court decides to accept the executive's position, it tries to present the whole arsenal of doctrinal tools that can review the executive's

[38] Cr.A. 7048/97 *Anonymous* v. *Minister of Defense* [2000] IsrSC 54(1) 721.

[39] *Ibid.*, at 744–745.

[40] After the second *Anonymous* decision, the parliament legislated the Law for the Imprisonment of Illegal Warriors, 2002–5762, in order to allow the executive to continue and detain Dirany and Ubeid, two of the high-profile prisoners discussed in this case. Before the Court could decide on the constitutionality of the new law, these prisoners were released as a part of a bargain with Hezbollah, *see* Cr.A. 3660/03 *Ubeid* v. *Israel* (not published, September 8, 2005).

decision, openly exposing the Court's discretion. Conversely, when the Court requires the executive to take difficult measures, it tries to use constrained reasoning.

3. Incrementally progressing doctrine

When the Court tries to create a new precedent, it supports it in several cases that either repeat the same reasoning or edge it slowly forward. The next two examples suggest that the Court may be trying to issue novel judgments in close pairs that use the same reasoning; the latter judgment appears consistent by referring to a previous similar judgment issued shortly beforehand. In the *Ganimat* case, President of the Court Barak referred to his judgment given three days before in *Bank Hamizrahi* case. The relevant decision in *Ganimat* was that the Basic Law: Human Dignity and Liberty should influence the interpretation of statutes legislated prior to its inception, even if they were protected from being annulled by a clause in the Basic Law. This judgment was given on November 12, 1995.[41] It built on the groundbreaking judgment of the Court in the *Bank Hamizrahi* case that the Basic Law has a higher normative status than regular acts of parliament and that it has constitutional status, which was given on November 9, 1995.[42]

[41] CrimFH 2316/95 *Ganimat* v. *State of Israel* [1995] IsrSC 49(4) 589, 653.

[42] CA 6821/93 *Bank Hamizrahi* v. *Migdal* [1995] IsrSC 49(4) 221, 351. See also Ariel L. Bendor and Zeev Segal, *The Hat Maker: Discussions with Justice Aharon Barak*, 24 (Kinneret, Zmora-Bitan, Dvir:

Similarly, in the *Hatnua Leeichut Hashilton* case,[43] President Barak decided that when an infraction of equality contradicts aspects of the right to equality that are closely related to human dignity as expressing the autonomy of will, freedom of choice, or the freedom to act, it is protected by the Basic Law: Human Dignity and Liberty. Three days later,[44] in the *Adala* case, Barak referred to this judgment and ruled that the equal right of an Israeli citizen to establish a family in Israel was protected by the Basic Law because it was part of the right

Or Yehuda), 2009 (Hebrew). In this interview Barak is asked whether delivery of the judgment on November 9, 1995, only five days after Israeli Prime Minister Yitzhak Rabin was assassinated, was deliberately planned to lower the media coverage of the case. Barak admits the judgment did not provoke a social debate due to the prime minister's murder; however, he explains that this judgment was given at the last moment that the leaving president of the Court Meir Shamgar could give a judgment and only by chance coincided with the murder. I find Barak's answer convincing, and I do not think the murder affected the judgment, which was probably almost ready at the time of Rabin's assassination. The strategic element that was involved was the assurance that the popular leaving president Shamgar would also take part in the judgment in order to use his prestige to increase the legitimacy of this revolutionary judgment. Furthermore, the extreme length and complexity of the judgment in Bank Hamizrahi, which is almost entirely obiter dictum, made any attempt of criticism or serious discussion impossible in the short term.

[43] HCJ 6427/02 *Hatnua Leeichut Hashilton* v. *the Knesset* [2006] IsrSC 61(1) 619, par. 38–40 to the judgment of Chief Justice Barak.

[44] The *Hatnua Leeichut Hashilton* case was issued on May 11, 2006. The *Adala* case was issued on May 14, 2006.

of equality related to human dignity.[45] Barak's controversial judgment in the *Adala* case remained in the minority, yet he might have been trying to enhance the legitimacy of that judgment by referring to his own judgment accepted by the majority in the *Hatnua Leeichut Hashilton* case shortly beforehand.

The close proximity of the two pairs of cases is not surprising; justices in Israel can sign judgments for three months after they retire from the court, and they usually try to finish as many important decisions as they can in this time. The judgments in *Bank Hamizrahi* and *Ganimat* were issued in the last days President Shamgar could sign judgments, and the judgments in *Adala* and *Hatnua Leeichut Hashilton* were issued in the last days of President Barak on the Court. Nevertheless, the tendency to issue a judgment that uses the same innovative reasoning shortly after this reasoning was used for the first time lends support to the idea that the Court progresses doctrine incrementally.

The doctrines used by the Court to assess the outcome of flaws in administrative action can serve as an example for its tendency to incrementally develop new doctrinal tools – especially those that allow greater judicial discretion. The Court inherited the British doctrine that acts committed without authority are null and void and that the Court can only declare their voidness and has no discretion in

[45] HCJ 7052/03 *Adala* v. *The Minister of Interior* [2006] IsrSC 61(2) 202, par. 39–40 to the judgment of President Barak.

manipulating the remedy. The Israeli Court considered most types of flawed administrative actions, such as actions committed without observance of the rules of procedural justice – or even unreasonable actions – as equivalent to acting without authority. This meant the Court had no discretion in setting the remedy to most types of flawed administrative actions.[46] The Court then slowly reverted to the doctrine of relative voidness, declaring first that it had discretion to determine the remedy in any case where the administrative agency was authorized to act,[47] and later trying to introduce the doctrine that, even in the core case of lack of functional authority, the Court has discretion to decide on the remedy.[48] The doctrine of relative voidness increases

[46] The Court's attempt in early years to characterize flaws such as breaking the rules of procedural justice (*see* CA 183/69 *Petah Tikva Municipality* v. *Tahan*, [1969] IsrSC 23(2) 398, 403–406) or creating unreasonable secondary legislation by the administrator (*see* CA 311/57 *The Attorney General* v. *Dizengoff and Partners (SIT) Limited*, [1959] IsrSC 13 1026, 1039) as similar to the flaw of lack of authority, which leads to complete voidness without any opportunity for the exercise of judicial discretion, can be seen as attempts to reduce the Court's discretion in order to increase the legitimacy of its decisions. In later years, as the Court increased its reputation and could lower the constraints on its decisions, it chose to increase its discretion by adopting the relative voidness doctrine.

[47] HCJ 118/80 *Grinstein* v. *the Military Advocate General* [1981] IsrSC 35(1) 239, 246.

[48] See the decisions of: Justice Dorner at HCJ 2918/93 *Kiryat Gat Municipality* v. *the State of Israel* [1993] IsrSC 47(5) 832, 847–848; and Justice Zamir at CrimA 866/95 *Sosan* v. *the State of Israel* [1996] IsrSC 50(1) 793, 817. For an analysis of the evolution of the

the flexibility of the Court and allows it to shape the remedy of the case in a way that suits its strategic interest.

As the Court changes its doctrine, it shifts to new forms of reasoning, rendering older judgments obsolete. This is one possible explanation for the Court's tendency to cite mainly new judgments.[49]

4. Matching demanding precedents with nondemanding remedies

In an interview a while after his retirement, Aharon Barak openly admitted that he used the tactic of developing new doctrine in cases that did not demand immediate action by the executive. He explained that he developed a new doctrine in one case without applying it and used it only in a later case. The example Barak himself gave was the *Bank Hamizrahi* case, discussed above,[50] in which the Court decided it had the power of judicial review and could annul acts of parliament that were contrary to the two new Basic Laws: Human

doctrine of relative voidness in Israel, *see* Shai Dothan, *Elasticizing the Remedy of Voidness Due to Flawed Administrative Action: Relative Voidness* (Hebrew) (unpublished LLM thesis, Tel Aviv University 2003, on file with author).

[49] Shachar et al. show that more than 50% of the precedents cited by the Israeli Supreme Court are ten years old or less when they are cited; a similar phenomenon of citing mainly new judgments exists in older U.S. courts; see Yoram Shachar, Ron Harris, and Miron Gross, Citation Practices of the Supreme Court: Quantitative Analyses, 27 *Hebrew University Law Review* 119, 172–174 (1996).

[50] Bendor and Segal, *supra* note 42 at 25.

Dignity and Liberty and Freedom of Occupation, which enjoy constitutional status. While the Court decided that the act interfered with the right of property, it ruled that the act stood within the permitted limits of the Basic Law and was therefore not annulled.[51] Similarly, when Justice Beinisch, writing for the Court, set the precedent that allowed the Court to undertake judicial review over acts that were legislated in a defective process in the *Bird Breeders* case, the decision was to uphold the act in the case at hand.[52]

Even if the Court finds a statute is defective and must be annulled, it can try to reduce the cost of compliance for the executive and the legislature by manipulating the outcomes of the declaration of voidness. The Court applied the doctrine of relative voidness to flawed statutes: While the statute was declared void, it remained in force for a set period of time. For instance, the Court first annulled a clause in a statute in the *Investment Directors* case. President Barak ruled that the clause setting exams for investment directors damaged their freedom of occupation without abiding the limits of the Basic Law: Freedom of Occupation and was therefore void. Yet while the clause was declared unconstitutional, it was to remain in force

[51] *Bank Hamizrahi* case, *supra* note 42 at 351–352.

[52] HCJ 4885/03 *The Israeli Birds Breeders Organization Agricultural Cooperation Society Ltd* v. *The Israeli Government* [2005] IsrSC 59(2) 14, 56.

until December 31, 1997, about three months after the judgment was issued. This time period allowed the legislature time to adjust and legislate new provisions, thereby increasing the chances of ultimate compliance.[53]

In the *Tzemah* case,[54] another legislative provision, allowing for the 96-hour arrest of a soldier by a military policeman, was annulled for being unconstitutional. Again, the Court delayed the voidness of the statute for six months. This progression of cases is also an example of incrementalism, because in *Tzemah*, for the first time, the Court annulled a part of a statute that improved the conditions of human rights compared to the version of the statute that existed before the Basic Law: Human Dignity and Liberty. The original version of the statute was protected from judicial review by article 10 to the basic law. Yet the author of the majority opinion, Justice Zamir, decided that even parts of statutes improving the conditions of human rights are not immune from judicial review.[55]

C. The executive's response

Under the presidency of Aharon Barak, the Israeli Supreme Court perfected its judicial tactics and increased its

[53] HCJ 1715/97 *Israel Investments Directors Office* v. *Minister of Finance* [1997] IsrSC 51(4) 367, 414, 416–417.

[54] HCJ 6055/95 *Tzemah* v. *Minister of Defense* [1999] IsrSC 53(5) 241.

[55] *See Ibid.*, at 261.

reputation. The executive viewed with concern the Court shifting to more and more demanding judgments, and in recent years, retaliated forcefully against the Court. The primary measure of retaliation that the executive can use against the Court is to fail to comply with its judgments. The executive will usually fail to comply if the material cost of compliance is greater than the reputational loss from noncompliance. Alternatively, the executive can fail to comply even when doing so will cause it more reputational damage than the cost of compliance to lower the Court's reputation or to signal to the Court that it will not comply with future demanding judgments. It may be difficult to discern the true reason for noncompliance. Furthermore, noncompliance itself is often hidden by different evasive tactics, such as asking for repetitive delays by the executive. Despite these difficulties, it is evident that in the first decade of the 21st century, the Israeli Supreme Court began to face a substantial problem of noncompliance by the executive.

Recent examples of noncompliance by the executive in Israel are not difficult to find. Consider, for instance, the *Yasin* case.[56] In this case, the Court decided that part of the separation barrier constructed in the occupied territories had to be replaced by an alternative route, following certain guidelines, within a reasonable time. Eight months

[56] HCJ 8414/05 *Yasin* v. *The Government of Israel* [2007] IsrSC 62(2) 822.

later, following a request for a writ of contempt of court, the Court found that the new route implemented by the state digressed from the guidelines set in its original judgment, and the Court urged the state to comply swiftly with the judgment.[57] While the *Yasin* case involved a measure of discretion by the executive in constructing a new barrier (and therefore made it harder to determine the existence of intentional noncompliance), clearer instances of noncompliance also exist.

Take, for example, the *Daharia* case,[58] in which the Court gave a specific judgment to dismantle a low barrier (82 cm in height) erected near the roads in a certain part of the West Bank. This time the executive failed to comply and asked for a delay only three days before the deadline issued in the initial judgment, leading the Court to strongly condemn the government for noncompliance and demand the execution of the judgment within only 14 days.[59]

The executive failed to comply with judgments unrelated to national security, as well. Consider, for example, the *Kav Laoved* case,[60] in which the Court decided that the

[57] HCJ 8414/05 *Yasin* v. *The Government of Israel* (decision, December 15, 2008).

[58] HCJ 1748/06 *Mayor of Daharia* v. *IDF Commander in the West Bank* (not yet published, December 14, 2006).

[59] HCJ 1748/06 *Mayor of Daharia* v. *IDF Commander in the West Bank* (decision, July 24, 2007).

[60] HCJ 4542/02 *Kav Laoved Association* v. *The Government of Israel* [2006] IsrSC 61(1) 346.

policy of binding foreign employees to specific employers infringed upon the constitutional rights of workers and should be annulled. The Court gave the government six months to form a new policy. More than two years later, while discussing a request for a writ of contempt of court in the matter, the Court found that although the government was contemplating new policies, workers were still being treated according to the old policy repealed by the Court.[61]

While the previous cases might suggest that the executive fails to comply only in cases involving minorities without political power or influence, such as the Palestinians in the occupied territories or foreign employees who are not citizens, the executive failed to comply even in cases that involved Israeli citizens facing the risk of terrorist attacks. In the *Eduardo* case, discussed in Chapter 2D,[62] the Court demanded the protection of classrooms against short-range rockets fired by militants from the Gaza strip. Two weeks before the deadline set in the judgment, the executive asked for a delay. The executive claimed that

[61] HCJ 4542/02 *Kav Laoved Association* v. *The Government of Israel* (decision, November 24, 2008). In a later decision in the same case issued on December 3, 2009, the Court criticized the state again for still failing to apply new policies that are in line with its judgment. Despite the strong criticism of the state, the request for a writ of contempt of court is denied and the Court expresses the hope that new policies will resolve the problems that led to the petition.

[62] HCJ 8397/06 *Eduardo* v. *Minister of Defense* [2007] IsrSC 62(2) 198.

protecting all twenty-four relevant schools was impossible; that only seven of those schools could be protected fully, while the other seventeen would have to be rebuilt completely. In fact, the state abided to the timetables in only three schools, while in the other schools the work was delayed.[63]

This stream of cases of noncompliance, of which the cases discussed above are only a few examples, led to a letter by former long-term deputy attorney general of Israel Yehudit Karp to the current attorney general.[64] In the letter, Karp discussed at length the examples above, as well as other cases in which the executive failed to comply or complied after an unreasonable delay with judgments of the Supreme Court or with judgments of the courts for administrative issues. The letter was publicized by the Israeli media[65] and led to a detailed response from the attorney general's office, mainly stressing that the complexity of the cases justified the need for delays in complying with them.[66] The attorney general also decided to follow a

[63] HCJ 8397/06 *Eduardo* v. *Minister of Defense* (decision, November 13, 2007).

[64] For Karp's letter, see www.acri.org.il/pdf/karp1.pdf.

[65] www.haaretz.co.il/hasite/spages/1154117.html.

[66] For the response of the attorney general's office, see www.news1.co.il/RedirectToFile.aspx?FileID=2445. Karp responded by sharply criticizing the attorney general's response as one that does not show a determination to comply with future judgments of the Court; see www.acri.org.il/pdf/karp3.pdf. In a later letter, Karp criticizes the practice of not complying with intermediate decisions

suggestion in Karp's letter and publish new instructions for monitoring compliance by the state with judgments requiring specific actions other than monetary payments (judgments requiring monetary payments were already covered by previous instructions).[67]

Why did the executive start to not comply with the Court if judicial tactics used by the Court have, at least until recently, increased its reputation? The primary reason the executive decided to make its stand against the Court recently is probably the fact that the Court's public support has suffered a significant decline. If the public does not support the content of the Court's judgments, they will not criticize the executive if it fails to comply with the Court – some segments of the public may even view non-compliance positively. The executive may still lose reputation if it fails to comply with a Court that lost the support

of the Court and with promises made by the state to the Court and asks that new instructions be created to address those cases; see www.adalah.org/upfiles/2011/Karp_letter_to_the_AG_Feb_2011_Hebrew.pdf.

[67] The new instruction is Attorney General Instruction 6.1006, "Complying with Judgments of Courts against the State," see www.justice.gov.il/NR/rdonlyres/B8FF9988-D087–4765-A2D3–3B475EA534E0/21665/61006.pdf. The previous instruction regarding judgments that require monetary payments by the state is Attorney General Instruction 6.1003, "Implementing Judgments against the State," see www.justice.gov.il/NR/rdonlyres/985382CD-5B49–424B-B1C9-D32F783DB2A4/21381/61003.pdf.

of the public, but its incentive to comply is much weaker because it does not fear public criticism.

Political changes in Israel damaged the power base of the secular left and center, which was the greatest supporter of the Court.[68] The Court may have contributed to the decline in its support by its perceived left-wing political bent and its willingness to demand more and more from the executive. Some of the decline in the Court's support may indeed result from miscalculation of the tolerance of the Israeli public, but some resulted simply from the evolution of Israeli society. Some politicians and other agenda-setters helped this trend against support for the Court by criticizing it and its decisions. For example, the Finance Minister Yuval Steinitz accused the Court of issuing judgments that were economically damaging for Israel.[69]

[68] *See* Ran Hirschl, *Towards Juristocracy: The Origins and Consequences of the New Constitutionalism*, 58 (Cambridge, MA: Harvard University Press), 2004. According to Hirschl, in 1981 there were 95 Knesset members representing "a secular bourgeoisie policy agenda" and 25 members representing the preferences of "peripheral" groups. In 1999 members of the first type decreased to 58 and members of the second type increased to 62.

[69] See www.ynet.co.il/articles/0,7340,L-3819873,00.html. After this speech, which gave rise to many voices both in support and opposition, President of the Court Beinisch called Prime Minister Binyamin Netanyahu to complain about this attack on the Court. The prime minister claimed that the speech was not his instruction and that he supports the Court. He also spoke with Steinitz and instructed him to call Beinisch and assure her he does not mean to harm the Court; Steinitz called Beinisch and said he meant no harm

Besides changes in Israeli society and in the behavior of the Court and the executive, other specific reasons may account for the drop in the Court's public support. One reason may be the retirement of Barak after his extremely influential tenure as the president of the Court and his controversial replacement by President Beinisch. Another reason may be the concentrated attack of Minister of Justice Friedmann on the Court that included many suggestions for reforms that could damage the Court's independence. Whatever the reasons for the drop in public support, it seems impossible to dispute that it happened. A comparison of recent polls with polls conducted several years ago shows a significant and consistent decline in the faith that the Israeli public has in the Supreme Court.[70] The Court must

to the Court, but he did not go back on his criticism; see www.ynet.co.il/articles/0,7340,L-3821102,00.html.

[70] See Asher Arian Et Al, *Auditing Israeli Democracy: 2010 Democratic Values in Practice* (Jerusalem: The Israel Democracy Institute), 2010 (Hebrew) available at: www.idi.org.il/PublicationsCatalog/Documents/Book_7114/madad%202010%20sofi.pdf at page 78, which shows the decline in the public support for the court with 70% (2003), 79% (2004), 72% (2005), 68% (2006), 61% (2007), 49% (2008), 52% (2009), and 54% (2010) of the public having faith in the Supreme Court. Despite the decline in the support for the Court, it still has higher support then other branches of government; for instance, only 37% of the public had faith in the parliament and only 33% had faith in the executive in 2010. The support for political parties is even lower and stood at 25% in 2010; see *Ibid.*, at 77. These results are confirmed in other studies as well, for instance:

adjust to its new position in which it has little public support and is susceptible to noncompliance that damages its reputation.

D. The court's adaptation

Faced with deliberate noncompliance and other countermeasures meant to restrain it and with diminishing public support, the Court had to adapt its strategy. The theory suggests that, as the Court's reputation descends, it should lower its demands of the executive or shift to more constrained reasoning in order to avoid more cases of noncompliance that would do further damage to its reputation. It is incredibly difficult to prove that the Court lowered its

Research conducted by Rattner finds a stable trend of decline in the trust for the Court in all the major segments of Israeli society; see Arye Rattner, *Legal Culture: Law and the Legal System in the Eyes of the Israeli Public 2000–2009*, at 50–51 (Jerusalem: Sasa Center for Strategic Research) (Hebrew), available at http://public-policy.huji.ac.il/upload/shshaBook07.09.09complete.pdf. References to more data showing the trend of decreasing support for the court appears at Or Bassok, Television Coverage of the Israeli Supreme Court 1968–1992: The Persistence of the Mythical Image, 42 *Israel Law Review* 306, 307 (2009). Bassok explains the decline in support for the Court as a result of adding a commercial channel to Israeli television, which used to be controlled by one public channel that promoted a professional image of the Court. Hirschl explains the decline in support for the Court as a result of the erosion of its impartial image and the acceptance of the view that it follows a political, secular liberal agenda; see Hirschl, *supra* note 68, at 70.

demands, because the costs of judgments are very hard to quantify. It is also difficult to identify trends in reasoning over a short time frame, because the Court changes its reasoning very slowly and tends to repeat forms of reasoning used in its previous judgments.

Even if a shift in reasoning or in the demands of the Court is discernible, it may be explained in ways other than the theory presented here. Most importantly, if the Court restrains itself in a period where noncompliance is likely, this does not prove it is concerned with increasing its reputation over the long term. This motive is possible, but it is also possible that the Court may be trying to secure compliance by restraining itself without considering the effect of this behavior on its reputation. On the other hand, it is the Court's attempt to issue judgments with increasingly more discretionary reasoning when its reputation increases that supports the theory of the Court as a reputation maximizer. Restraint, however, must be gauged relative to other judgments of the Court, and if the Court practices restraint when its reputation is low compared to greater demands when its reputation is high, this supports the theory that the Court maximizes its reputation, because it shows that it shifts to more demanding judgments if it can secure compliance with them.

Another potential explanation for restraint is that judges sincerely follow their individual preferences that accidently point in the direction of restraint. Cases in which the Court's final judgment is restrained, despite the clear preference of some of the justices for a demanding judgment, can nevertheless attest to the Court's efforts to restrain itself strategically. In these unique cases, it may be that justices feel free to declare their true preferences when in the minority, but the majority ends up issuing a restrained decision to protect the Court's reputation. Cases in which the judges are evenly split may suggest that some of the judges in the majority would prefer to sign on to the views of the minority, if it were not for their concern for the Court's reputation.

One of the cases in which a close split may indicate a strategic attempt to restrain the Court's judgment is the *Adala* case.[71] This case concerned a petition against an act of parliament that prevented Palestinians from the occupied territories from acquiring Israeli citizenship if they married Israeli citizens. Eleven justices sat on the bench; five of them decided that the act should be repealed and five decided that it should remain in force. The decisive vote of Justice Levy accepted the reasoning of those who supported the annulment of the act, but eventually decided not to void it. Because the justices were so closely split, it seems reasonable to suspect that some of the justices in the majority were sympathetic to the petition, but decided to reject it out of concern for the Court's reputation. Justice Levy's judgment seems especially suspicious in this respect because he accepted most of the reasoning of the majority. This suspicion is

[71] HCJ 7052/03 *Adala* v. *The Minister of Interior* [2006] IsrSC 61(2) 202.

strengthened when a petition regarding a later transformation of this act, the *Zahava Gal-On* case[72] is considered.

In this case, again eleven justices sat on the bench, six decided to deny the petition and five supported accepting the petition and annulling the law. Justice Levy wrote a strong judgment in which he supported accepting the petition. This time, his vote was not pivotal and his position remained in the minority, so there was no need for him to restrain his judgment to save the Court's reputation. Other justices in the majority may have decided not to annul the act in order to protect the Court's reputation, although they would prefer to side with the minority. This, of course, cannot be proven unequivocally. It is possible to suspect not only that justices changed their judgments to secure restraint, but also that the decision in the case was deliberately delayed to allow a choice of justices that adopted the restrained position. Because the decision in this case was delayed, Justice Procaccia, who supported annulling the law in the earlier *Adala* case, retired from the court and was replaced on the chamber by Justice Hendel, who decided to deny the petition.[73]

There may be other signs of an attempt by the Court to restrain itself strategically, against the policy preferences of the justices, in addition to close splits between the justices on the panel. Empirical research has shown that in split

[72] HCJ 466/07 *Zahava Gal-On* v. *The Attorney General* (not yet published January 11, 2012).

[73] For this claim, see www.haaretz.co.il/news/law/1.1616390.

decisions issued by the Israeli Court, the first decision has twice the chances of a consecutive decision to be in the majority, and the president of the Court is also more likely to be in the majority.[74] When this predominant pattern (which probably reflects the most effective way to minimize friction between the justices)[75] is broken, the reason may be that at least some of the justices understand that the Court must restrain itself, even if this means they have to vote against their own preferences.

An example is the *Anonymous (a)* case.[76] This case discussed the attorney general's decision to strike a plea

[74] Shachar et al., *supra* note 22, at 775. The article finds that when the Court is split, the first opinion is in the majority in 68% of cases, compared to 32% for other opinions. Considering all cases, the first opinion has a 98% chance of being in the majority, because in most cases there is no disagreement between the justices. Presidents often write the first judgment and are only rarely left in the minority. Admittedly, Shachar et al. focus on chambers of three justices, which constitute the standard chamber of the court in Israel, while in many controversial cases the court was composed of five justices or more. The practice of leading the court may be different in judgments of more than three justices, but probably the advantage of the justice writing the first opinion will be maintained to some degree.

[75] Shachar et al. show indications of the fact that justices do not work on their opinions simultaneously. Instead, the justice who writes the first decision studies the file and writes his judgment first and then passes it on to the other justices; see *Ibid.*, at 761–763. Justices may be more inclined to be persuaded by the justice who wrote the first decision in the case.

[76] HCJ 5699/07 *Anonymous (a)* v. *The Attorney General* [2008] IsrSC 62(3) 550.

bargain with the former president of Israel, Moshe Katzav, that agreed to indict him only for minor sexual acts compared to the severe complaints issued against him and even to an indictment that was drafted by the prosecution prior to the hearing with Katzav's lawyers. Justice Levy, an expert in criminal law, who wrote the first judgment, and President Beinisch, who wrote the second judgment, both supported annulling the plea bargain, while a majority of three justices decided not to intervene. Restraint was particularly essential in this case in order to prevent noncompliance of the attorney general, who could simply sign a new plea bargain that was only superficially different.

Another example of a close split was the *Ometz* case.[77] In this case, a petition was lodged against the appointment of a weak governmental investigating committee, instead of a more potent national committee, to investigate the failures of the Israeli government and security forces during the war fought between Israel and Hezbollah in 2006. All the seven justices on the panel wrote separate opinions; three were for annulling the current committee and four decided not to intervene. Notably, the pivotal judgment of Justice Gronis specifically mentioned the need to practice self-restraint in this case.

[77] HCJ 6728/06 *"Ometz" Association (Citizens for Good Governance and Social Justice)* v. *The Prime Minister of Israel* (not yet published, November 30, 2006).

As indicated above, trends in reasoning are hard to identify over a short time period; it appears, however, that some justices are trying to reintroduce more constrained forms of reasoning that were used by the Court in the past and to criticize the discretionary doctrines used by the Court in recent years. Unless this trend is accompanied by a substantial increase in the demands of the Court – a possibility that seems unlikely – this could be a rational response to the decline in the Court's reputation.

Consider the following examples: In the *Ometz* case, Justice Gronis criticized the use of the doctrine of reasonableness in the discretionary form in which the Court used it. He stipulated that judges did not have the necessary abilities to scrutinize public policy issues that did not involve direct damage to human rights.[78] In the *Abu Safiya* case,[79] Justice Vogelman decided that closing route 443, which goes through the West Bank, to Palestinians was done without authority because the military commander was not authorized to issue a total ban (as opposed to partial limitations) on the movements of Palestinians on the route. Vogelman's majority opinion used the constrained reasoning of lack of authority, although Vogelman himself considered that the military commander's actions were not proportional and despite the fact that Justice Levy

[78] See his judgment at *Ibid*.

[79] HCJ 2150/07 *Abu Safiya* v. *Minister of Defense* (not yet published, December 29, 2009).

criticized this new legal construct that confused lack of authority and gross lack of proportionality. Out of the realm of public law, Justice Danziger challenged the Court's discretionary doctrine of contract interpretation and called on judges to look primarily to the language of the contract, when it is clear.[80]

A shift to less demanding judgments and to more constrained reasoning can decrease the chances of noncompliance. If the Court lowers its demands across all cases, however, it loses the main mechanism for increasing its reputation. Furthermore, if the Court is noticeably more restrained, this signals to the public that it believes its own reputation to be low. This can reinforce the beliefs of members of the public about the Court's low reputation and damage its reputation even further. In order to not send a signal that the Court is overly restrained, it tried to hide its restraint by continually delaying decisions, promoting compromise between the parties, and trying to defuse cases by issuing technical decisions.[81] Besides those tactics of hiding restraint, however, the Court needed to adapt and

[80] See, for instance, his judgment in CA 7379/06 *G.M.H.L Building Company 1992 Limited* v. *Issai Taholian* (not yet published, September 10, 2009).

[81] See Yoav Dotan, Pre-petitions and Constitutional Dilemmas Regarding the Role of Government Lawyers, 7 *Mishpat Umimshal* 159, 193–194 (2004) (Hebrew). Dotan shows that when the cases reach the Court, it can decide how and when to decide them by the use of postponing tactics, such as deciding that the petition is premature, demanding certain actions from the parties before

find new ways to introduce demanding judgments while minimizing the risks of noncompliance.

One of the ways to achieve that end is to issue demanding judgments in cases where noncompliance will be highly visible to the public. If noncompliance cannot be hidden from the public and the media, the executive will suffer severe criticism for noncompliance, and for that reason the executive will be more likely to comply.[82] This tactic signals that the Court is still powerful and willing to issue demanding judgments, while minimizing the risk of noncompliance. The judgment of the court in *Human Rights Division* case issued on November 19, 2009,[83] can serve as an example.

This was an extremely demanding judgment; it annulled an entire statute authorizing the use of the first private prison in Israel, and it forced the government to go back on an efficient contract with a private operator, sustaining significant material costs. Despite the cost of compliance with the judgment, the chances of noncompliance were

reaching a decision, or simply delaying the judgment, thus allowing the Court to mold its agenda.

[82] For the claim that the political branches are less likely to comply when the public is less informed about noncompliance (and is therefore less able to enforce compliance), leading to greater judicial restraint in those cases *see* Jeffrey K. Staton, *Judicial Power and Strategic Communication in Mexico*, 25 (New York: Cambridge University Press), 2010.

[83] HCJ 2605/05 *Human Rights Division* v. *The Minister of Finance* (not yet published, November 19, 2009).

minimal because the government could not hide the operation of a private prison from the eyes of the media, and it could not ask for delays or adopt creative solutions to circumvent the Court's ruling, as it did in many other cases, because the judgment was clear and precise. Because the Court annulled the statute as a violation of the Basic Law: Human Dignity and Liberty (instead of other more intuitive legal options mentioned in the judgment), the only way the legislature could override the Court was by changing the Basic Law, which would have exposed it to unacceptable public criticism. Furthermore, because the judgment seemed to suit public opinion, there was a smaller risk that the government would try to respond by criticizing the Court's decision.[84] Following public opinion may also help the Court rebuild its public support.

The Court can issue a writ of contempt of court against the government and enforce compliance with its judgments by fine or incarceration of public officials.[85] This tool was

[84] This did not stop criticism completely, as the incident discussed in *supra* note 69 (in which the finance minister referred among other judgments to this demanding judgment of the Court) shows, but might have nevertheless weakened it. A poll from December 2007 about the private prison shows that the majority of the public, and especially those with lower incomes, are against the private prison, see www.idi.org.il/events1/RoundTableDiscussion/Documents/%D7%A1%D7%A7%D7%A8.pdf. The Court may be trying to increase its support, especially with lower-income citizens who are usually its critics.

[85] Contempt of Court Order art 6(1).

never used against the government,[86] but not for lack of instances of noncompliance, as this chapter shows. The reason is probably that the use of this tool openly admits that the Court cannot rely on the force of its reputational sanction to ensure compliance by the government. The Court can threaten to issue a contempt of court writ against the government and then decide not to issue it. While this threat may be considered cheap talk because the Court cannot afford to implement it, the mere threat to issue a writ of contempt of court can damage the executive's reputation by signaling the severity of its noncompliance.

The threat of issuing a writ of contempt of court may also damage the Court's reputation, however, because it signals to the public that the executive is disobedient. Furthermore, if the Court continues to threaten to issue a writ of contempt of court and never implements this threat, the Court's credibility will be damaged. Threatening the use of the contempt of court mechanism, or even a severe criticism of the executive, may also increase the chances that the media will take interest in the case, which would expose the Court in its weakness. For these reasons, the Court will reserve even the threat of issuing a writ of contempt of court only for the most severe and unjustified cases of disobedience, and even then will try only to allude to this threat by condemning the government for noncompliance instead of openly threatening to issue a writ of contempt of court.

[86] See *supra* note 16.

When the Court has used the time since the initial judgment and before the issue was raised again by petitioners to gather more information that shows the initial judgment was too demanding, the Court will attempt to retreat and go back on its demands. Because the executive usually asks for repeated delays and does not declare its intentions of noncompliance, the Court can easily retreat by granting the executive further delays. The difference between the response of the Court to noncompliance in the *Eduardo* and *Daharia* cases discussed above is telling in this respect. In the *Eduardo* case, the Court grasped that its initial judgment was too demanding and for that reason it granted the delay requested by the government. Furthermore, the Court did not grant the applicants the remedy they requested: driving the children to other schools out of the reach of short-term rockets.[87] Faced with noncompliance that could not be similarly justified in the *Daharia* case, the Court severely condemned the state for noncompliance and granted only a very short time frame of 14 days for compliance with the initial judgment.[88]

The Court often finds new and creative tools to express its dissatisfaction with the government's behavior without

[87] HCJ 8397/06 *Eduardo* v. *Minister of Defense* (decision, November 13, 2007)

[88] HCJ 1748/06 *Mayor of Daharia* v. *IDF Commander in the West Bank* (decision, July 24, 2007).

using the ultimate weapon of a writ of contempt of court. One of those tools is for the Court to demand that the government compensate the petitioner for her legal fees for the request for a writ of contempt of court, even if the government eventually complied with the Court's judgments and prevented the need for such a writ. Because these fees are usually small, this tool is used mainly not to increase the material costs of delayed compliance for the government, but instead to signal the Court's disapproval of the government's behavior and increase the reputational sanction imposed on the government.

For example, after the *Hasin* case,[89] which stated that the route of the separation barrier was illegal, the government failed to comply with the judgment for over two years. Only after a request for a writ of contempt of court was issued by the petitioner did the government finally comply. The Court criticized the government for complying only under the imminent threat of contempt of court, and to signal the severity of this criticism, it decided that the government would face the expenses of the petitioners at a sum of 20,000 NIS.[90]

Another new tool for conveying criticism of the executive was used in the *Kav Laoved* case discussed above. Faced with

[89] HCJ 2732/05 *The Mayor of Azon, Hasin* v. *The Government of Israel* (not yet published, June 15, 2006).

[90] *See* HCJ 2732/05 *The Mayor of Azon, Hasin* v. *The Government of Israel* (decision, October 5, 2009) (at that time 1 NIS = approximately 0.25 US Dollars).

noncompliance by the executive, the Court decided that a copy of the decision would be sent to the attorney general.[91]

Another possibility open to the Court when it is faced with a significant risk of noncompliance is to only recommend a policy change with a vague threat of future intervention. If the Court only suggests a change in the executive's practices, it does not face the risk of noncompliance. If the executive does not follow the Court's suggestion, the damage to the Court's reputation will be minimal. If the justices suggest the change of policy in one of the Court's hearings, the public will almost certainly be unaware of this suggestion, and the executive's disregard of it will not cause any reputational damage to the Court. On the other hand, if the executive decides to adopt the suggestion and changes its policy, the Court may gain reputation, because the media might discover the nonbinding judicial suggestion and point to it as the source of the executive's change of heart.

A partly successful judicial suggestion occurred, for example, when the former President of the Court Barak remarked in a hearing that demolishing houses of relatives of terrorists for deterrence purposes in the occupied territories may be illegal under international law (although such demolitions were approved many times by the Court in the past).[92]

[91] HCJ 4542/02 *Kav Laoved Association* v. *The Government of Israel* (decision, November 24, 2008).

[92] See Yossi Wolfson, Punitive House Demolitions: HCJ 1730/96 *Sabih* v. *Major General Ilan Biran commander of IDF Forces in the Judea and Samaria Region* (judgment dated March 19, 1996) available at

After this hearing, the IDF created a think-tank that recommended stopping the use of demolitions. The IDF accepted this recommendation and stopped the policy of house demolitions for the sake of deterrence. This case was not a complete success story, however: Four years later, the IDF decided to change its policy again and to authorize more house demolitions. The Court approved the policy change, stating that it was within the government's discretion to change its policy as the circumstances changed.[93] This illustrates the problem with judicial suggestions: Although they may help to change policy in the short run, they do not constrain the executive from changing its policy back again.[94]

www.hamoked.org/Document.aspx?dID=Documents1272 Wolfson claims this remark was made by Barak in a hearing of the case of HCJ 7733/04 *Nasser* v. *Commander of IDF Forces in the West Bank* (not yet published, June 20, 2005). Indeed, in this judgment the Court describes the decision to stop the policy of house demolitions and accordingly rejects the petition. But see Eyal Benvenisti, Judicial Review and Democratic Failures: Minimizing Asymmetric information Through Adjudication, 32 *Tel Aviv University Law Review* 277, 298–299 (2010) (Hebrew). Benvenisti describes the IDF's policy change as a response to another subtle hint by Justice Or that the house demolition policy must be reconsidered. This hint appeared in HCJ 8575/03 *Azadin* v. *The Commander of the IDF Forces in the West Bank* [2003] IsrSC 58(1) 210, 213.

[93] HCJ 9353/08 *Abu Dheim* v. *GOC Home Front Command* (not yet published, January 5, 2009).

[94] Putting informal pressures on the government is beyond the scope of this book, which is focused on the way judgments affect policy. It is worth mentioning, however, that this is not a new tool, and it was used by the Court extensively during the first Intifada; see Yoav

Because of the decline in the Court's public support, it can find greater value in organizations that petition it or join petitions as a friend of the court (*amicus curiae*). Those organizations can increase the support for the Court by their willingness to appear before it, which signals their respect for the Court's decisions. Their participation also increases the Court's reputation, because it signals their expectation that the Court's judgments will be compiled with and are therefore worth their effort. Those organizations also increase the exposure the Court's judgments receive and their potential effect on the Court's reputation. Organizations expose the Court to all the relevant issues on the nation's agenda, allowing it to pick and decide the cases that are best suited to improve its reputation. Furthermore, organizations supply information about the views of interest groups or segments of the public, and this information can assist the Court in developing expectations about the chances of compliance and the effect its judgments will have on its public support, thereby allowing it to make better strategic choices. In exchange for these benefits, the Court allows the petitioners a forum to proclaim their views and obtain valuable media exposure and a chance to affect the Court's decisions and consequently to shape government policy.

Dotan, Judicial Rhetoric, Government Lawyers, and Human Rights: The Case of the Israeli High Court of Justice during the Intifada, 33 *Law & Society Review* 319 (1999).

Albert Hirschman's theoretical framework of exit and voice can help explain the way the Court's decision making is affected by petitioners that appear before it repeatedly.[95] Under this framework, petitioners have two methods for influencing the Court: either through their voice (the contents of their petitions) or through committing exit (withholding or withdrawing their petitions and denying their benefits from the Court).

Such a dynamic was illustrated in March 2009 when three public petitioners decided to withdraw a petition against a statute dealing with the detention of persons suspected of security offenses and allowing, among other provisions, hearing of the case in Court without the presence of the suspect. The petition was withdrawn in protest of the Court's preliminary decision to decide the case based on classified material hidden from the petitioners.[96] Those petitioners were aware, however, that a similar petition by a private person, joined in the same case by the Court, was still pending. The Court decided in that petition unanimously, by nine justices, that the relevant article of the statute was void because it contradicted the Basic Law:

[95] Albert O. Hirschman, *Exit, Voice, and Loyalty: Responses to Decline in Firms, Organizations, and States* (Cambridge, MA: Harvard University Press), 1970.

[96] See HCJ 2028/08 *Public Committee Against Torture* v. *Israel* (decision, March 24, 2009). See www.stoptorture.org.il/he/node/1404. I thank Avinoam Cohen and Sigal Shahav for our discussions of this incident.

Human Dignity and Liberty.[97] While it is hard to assess whether the strategic withdrawal of the petition affected the final result, it was certainly considered by the justices: Justice Rubinstein opened his judgment by criticizing the public petitioners for withdrawing their petition.

Even before cases are withdrawn or not filed at all, significant public petitioners, such as the Adala organization, use the public threat of considering such withdrawal to signal their discontent with the Court's judgments, thereby using the threat of exit as a potent form of voice.[98]

The Court can also use the threat of foreign or international intervention to improve its position vis-à-vis the executive. The executive can force the Court to restrain itself if the Court cannot commit not to yield to the executive's pressure. If the Court can commit credibly not to restrain itself, however, by proving to the executive that this restraint will lead to unacceptable damage to its international standing, the Court can significantly improve its bargaining power and be able to issue more demanding judgments.[99]

[97] CrimA 8823/07 *Anonymous* v. *Israel* (not yet published, February 11, 2010). The court voided article 5 to the Criminal Procedure Law (Detainees suspected of security offences) (temporary order) 5766–2006. Eight justices decided that the article was void immediately; Justice Naor wrote a minority opinion that also voided the article but suggested delaying its nullity for six months.

[98] See www.adalah.org/newsletter/heb/feb08/roundtable/roundtable.html.

[99] The concept of commitment was first investigated at Thomas C. Schelling, *The Strategy of Conflict*, 28 (Cambridge, MA: Harvard

Foreign intervention can also cast an effect on the executive that is favorable for the national court. International courts can damage the executive's international legitimacy. This increases the executive's willingness to comply with the national court that may help it rebuild some of its international legitimacy.

For example, in the cases of *Beit Sourik*[100] and *Mara'abe*[101] the Court issued major judgments that demanded changes to the route of the separation barrier in the West Bank shortly before and after the advisory opinion of the International Court of Justice (ICJ), which stated that the entire barrier constructed beyond the green line was illegal.[102] The Court could commit to issuing those demanding decisions because it was constrained to maintain its international standing. At the same time, the executive had a strong interest to comply because that was the only way to partly legitimize its actions despite the ICJ's advisory opinion.

University Press), 1960. A similar negotiation scenario to the one described here, where a principal (here the international court) constrains the agent (here the national court) and in doing so increases its bargaining power, is discussed at Robert D. Putnam, Diplomacy and Domestic Politics: The Logic of Two-Level Games, 42 *International Organization* 427, 440 (1988).

[100] HCJ 2056/04 *Beit Sourik Village Council* v. *The Government of Israel* [2004] IsrSC 58(5) 807.

[101] HCJ 7957/04 *Mara'abe* v. *The Prime Minister of Israel* [2005] IsrSC 60(2) 477.

[102] Legal Consequences of the Construction of a Wall in the Occupied Palestinian Territory, Advisory Opinion (9 July 2004).

The retiring president of the Court and its chief strategist, Barak, may have argued that Israel should ratify the Rome Statute and join the jurisdiction of the International Criminal Court (ICC), a step Israel still did not take, because foreign intervention could improve the court's position vis-à-vis the executive.[103] According to the complementarity principle in the Rome Statute, the ICC can prosecute for war crimes only when the same person is not being tried and was not tried for the same crimes by another court in a fair trial. If Israel were under the ICC's jurisdiction, the Court could therefore protect Israeli officials from international prosecution, which would improve its bargaining power against the executive.[104]

[103] www.haaretz.co.il/hasite/spages/1 990.html. Even before ratifying the Rome Statute, there is a possible threat of prosecution of Israelis by the ICC; see Yuval Shany, The Entry into Force of the Rome Statute: What Are the Implications for the State of Israel? 9 *Hamishpat* 51, 64–76 (2004) (Hebrew). Nevertheless, if Israel were to ratify the Rome Statute, this may make prosecution by the Court more likely.

[104] See articles 17(1)(c) and 20(3) to the Rome Statute of the International Criminal Court. Even before joining the ICC, the threat of prosecution may have improved the Court's position. Amichai Cohen claimed that the application of international law by the Court in cases regarding the occupied territories after 2002 may be a result of the establishment of the International Criminal Court; *see* Amichai Cohen, The Supreme Court and the Israel-Arab Conflict: An International Law Perspective 6 *Ono Academic College Law Journal* 263, 331–332 (2006) (Hebrew).

E. Conclusion

This chapter demonstrates that the Israeli Supreme Court acts strategically to increase its reputation. The Court used various judicial tactics to issue demanding judgments and judgments that used discretionary reasoning and to lead the executive to comply with these judgments. The executive, however, responded strategically to the Court's attempt to increase its reputation. When public support for the Court declined, the executive seized the opportunity to fail to comply with the Court's judgments. These instances of noncompliance lowered the Court's reputation and forced it to show greater restraint. They also made the Court take more sophisticated steps to ensure compliance, including cooperation with public petitioners and international courts.

Because of the numerous factors that affect judicial strategy and the behavior of the executive, the future of the Israeli Supreme Court remains a mystery. A lot will depend on the preferences and character of the key individuals involved in this political game, factors that are outside the scope of the institutional analysis attempted here. Nevertheless, the experience of Israel's Supreme Court can serve as a valuable lesson to many other national courts when they issue judgments against the executive.

6 International court case study: European Court of Human Rights

This book develops a theory to explain the behavior of both national and international courts. This chapter will analyze the behavior of the European Court of Human Rights (ECHR) as the main case study of an international court. The ECHR is different from the classical model of an international court, whose main representative is the International Court of Justice (ICJ). The ICJ deals with disputes between states. In contrast, the ECHR deals mainly with petitions lodged by individuals against states. For that reason, some term the ECHR a "supranational court" to distinguish it from courts such as the ICJ. The ECHR's jurisdiction also does not cover the entire world; it is a regional court that deals with violations of the Convention for the Protection of Human Rights and Fundamental Freedoms (the Convention) within the states that signed the Convention, which together form the European Council. Nevertheless, lessons learned from the analysis of the ECHR can serve to explain the behavior of many other influential courts.

One court whose behavior can be illuminated by lessons learned from the ECHR is the European Court of Justice (ECJ). While the ECJ deals with European Union Law and its procedures are very different from those of the ECHR, it is also a regional court, because its jurisdiction is limited to the European Union. It also built its power gradually and incrementally in a way that resembles the behavior of the ECHR.

The ECHR also served as an inspiration for the creation of similar regional human rights regimes and tribunals such as the Inter-American Court of Human Rights and the African Court of Human Rights. These courts have failed so far to acquire the reputation and the usage rates of the ECHR, and they display very different behavior; some of these behaviors will be discussed in the next chapter. The comparison between the ECHR and these courts may change in the future, however. If there is anything that the history of the ECHR shows, it is that international courts can change quickly and unpredictably. Lessons learned from the ECHR may therefore be applicable in the future to courts that were created in its image.[1]

[1] For an attempt to learn from the success of the ECJ and the ECHR and use the lessons to improve other courts, see Laurence R. Helfer

This chapter shows that the ECHR uses similar tactics to the ones used by national courts of last resort that decide constitutional cases. This concurs with the intuition that the purpose of the ECHR, just like Supreme Courts and Constitutional Courts, is not only to resolve individual disputes, but primarily to protect rights and to influence the behavior of states. The ECHR is concerned about the long-term implications of its judgments and about its long-term ability to affect future policy, just like national courts. Therefore, lessons learned from the analysis of the ECHR can be applied to the domestic arena.

The ECHR is also an important court in its own right, a court that issued thousands of judgments, many of them tremendously influential. The doctrines developed by the ECHR shaped, to a great extent, human rights protection in Europe and beyond. The large case load of the ECHR, the many states under its jurisdiction, and its surprisingly high compliance rates, despite the lack of a strong enforcement mechanism, make it a perfect case study to test the theory described in this book and to demonstrate the use of judicial tactics in practice.

This chapter will start by introducing the main attributes of the ECHR and the conditions under which it

and Anne-Marie Slaughter, Toward a Theory of Effective Supranational Adjudication, 107 *Yale Law Journal* 273 (1997). The exercise attempted in this book is to study the behavior of the court instead of the background conditions that led to its success, which is what Helfer and Slaughter study.

operates. Then the analysis will turn to the strategy of the ECHR to increase its reputation and the tactics that it used: the trend of shifting to more demanding judgments and the incremental changes to doctrine. Finally, the chapter will discuss the way the ECHR issued more or less demanding judgments to states, conditioned on their ability to harm it, and will raise a controversial argument – the ECHR demands more from low-reputation states than it demands from high-reputation states.

A. Background

The ECHR is a regional human rights court located in Strasburg, France. The jurisdiction of the ECHR covers the forty-seven states (state parties) that are members of the European Council and signatories to the Convention.[2] The Convention protects core human rights such as the right to life (art. 2), the right not to be subjected to torture (art. 3), the right to liberty (art. 5), the right to a fair trial (art. 6), and the right to respect for private and family life (art. 8).

Any individual, nongovernmental organization (NGO), or group of individuals that claim they were a victim of a violation by one of the state parties to the Convention may

[2] For the list of signatories and ratifications to the convention, see http://conventions.coe.int/Treaty/Commun/ChercheSig.asp?NT=005&CM=&DF=&CL=ENG

submit an application to the ECHR.[3] The ability of the ECHR to receive applications from individuals was termed *individual petition*. Individual petition is responsible for the ECHR's large and rapidly increasing caseload. This rule became a condition all state parties had to agree to after the acceptance of protocol 11 in 1998, but was accepted by most state parties long before that time. The Convention allows every state party to refer a violation of the Convention by another state party to the ECHR,[4] even if the referring state is not a victim of the violation, but this provision was almost never used.[5]

The number of applications that reach the ECHR has grown from a few every year to incredible proportions that strain the ECHR's processing abilities. In 2011 alone 64,500 new applications were allocated to the judges and the number of pending applications surpassed 150,000.[6] State parties are constantly considering reforms to the ECHR that will make it more efficient and make processing this flood of cases possible. The main reforms to the ECHR were Protocol 11, which abolished the European

[3] The Convention, art. 34.

[4] The Convention, art. 33.

[5] See Dragoljub Popovic, Prevailing of Judicial Activism over Self-Restraint in the Jurisprudence of the European Court of Human Rights, 42 *Creighton Law Review* 361, 372 (2009).

[6] See *ECHR Analysis of Statistics 2011*, available at: www.echr.coe.int/NR/rdonlyres/11CE0BB3-9386-48DC-B012-AB2C046FEC7C/0/STATS_EN_2011.PDF at p. 4.

Commission that had been used to screen cases before they reached the court, and Protocol 14, which made many procedural changes, including allowing smaller panels to make technical decisions and decisions regarding admissibility. Approximately 60% of the applications that reach the ECHR are "repetitive cases" – cases where the violation found by the court affects many individuals, and because the state fails to remedy the violation, more and more individuals bring separate cases to the ECHR. To address the problem of repetitive cases the ECHR began to issue the so-called *Pilot Judgments* – judgments that do not only find a violation, they also demand specific actions from the state to remedy the violation. Another factor burdening the ECHR's caseload is the cases that the court decides are inadmissible. These cases comprise more than 90% of the cases where a decision was made. The simplified procedures accepted in protocol 14 try to address this problem.[7]

The ECHR does not have an internal enforcement mechanism; the Committee of Ministers of the Council of Europe (the Committee) is tasked with monitoring the enforcement of ECHR judgments. The Committee can issue decisions and declarations against states that fail to comply and may also expel states from the Council of Europe

[7] See *Fact Sheet – Protocol 14 – The Reform of the ECHR*, available at: www.echr.coe.int/NR/rdonlyres/57211BCC-C88A-43C6-B540-AF0642E81D2C/0/CPProtocole14EN.pdf at p. 1.

(but this measure has never been used).[8] Despite this very weak enforcement mechanism, most ECHR judgments were complied with, by most accounts.[9]

The ECHR is not formally bound by its previous judgments. However, it often refers to its previous judgments, and even ruled in the *Goodwin* case that it would not digress from its judgments without good reason. In the same judgment, the ECHR ruled that it will also respond to changing conditions within state parties and effectively protect the

[8] The Committee came close to expelling Greece, where a military dictatorship ruled at the time, in 1970. Greece denounced the Convention before the Committee had a chance to use this rare tool. This affair and the circumstances leading to it are described in section C1.

[9] The exact compliance rates are difficult to establish both because data on compliance is imperfect and because of the problems with addressing partial compliance and delayed compliance (see Chapter 2F). Nevertheless, most of the sources that dealt with this issue claim compliance rates are very high. For instance, Ryssdal claims that compliance is perfect; while some instances of delayed or partial compliance occurred, there were no cases of noncompliance. See R. Ryssdal, The Enforcement System set up under the European Convention on Human Rights, in *Compliance with Judgments of International Courts*, 49,67 (M.K. Bulterman and M. Kuijer, eds., 1996). For other sources that claim compliance is high, see Helfer and Slaughter, *supra* note 1 at 296; Andrew Moravcsik, Explaining International Human Rights Regimes: Liberal Theory and Western Europe, 1 *European Journal of International. Relations* 157, 171 (1995). However, Posner and Yoo claim to use more systemic means to measure compliance and fail to reach a conclusive result; see Eric A. Posner and John C. Yoo, Judicial Independence in International Tribunals, 93 California Law Review 1, 65–66 (2005).

rights enshrined in the Convention.[10] The judgments of the ECHR, as well as its decisions and press releases that contain information about the ECHR and its activities, are published online at the HUDOC database.[11]

There are currently forty-seven permanent judges in the ECHR, one for every state in the council of Europe. One judge is elected from a list of three candidates submitted by each state to the European Parliamentary Assembly.[12] The ECHR can sit in several different panels: in a single-judge formation, in Committees of three judges, in Chambers of seven judges, or in a Grand Chamber of seventeen judges.[13] Most of the important judgments of the ECHR are issued either by a Chamber or by a Grand Chamber. If a Chamber finds a case poses a serious question of interpretation or a potential for digression from past judgments, it can relinquish jurisdiction in favor of the Grand Chamber.[14] The parties can also ask for a referral of a case to the Grand Chamber within three months after a Chamber decides the case. A panel of five Grand Chamber judges will allow the referral if the case raises a significant issue of interpretation or an issue of great importance.[15]

[10] See *Christine Goodwin* v. *The United Kingdom*, judgment of July 11, 2002, 2002-VI EUR. Ct. H.R. 1 at 26.
[11] www.echr.coe.int/echr/en/hudoc.
[12] The Convention, art. 20, 22.
[13] *Ibid.*, art. 26.
[14] *Ibid.*, at art. 30–31.
[15] *Ibid.*, at art. 31, 42–42.

Judgments of the Grand Chamber are final, but judgments of Chambers will become final three months after they were issued if the parties did not request a referral to the Grand Chamber, if the parties declare they will not make such a request, or if the request is denied by the Grand Chamber.[16]

Scholars found that while ECHR judges tend to support their countries of origin more than other judges, this tendency changed the result in very few cases, due to the size of panels.[17] Protocol 14 further increased the independence of judges by instituting a nine-year nonrenewable term instead of the previous renewable term of six years. This change prevented states from rewarding or punishing their respective judges for their behavior on the bench. The registrar of the ECHR supervises the entire staff of legal advisers. Legal advisers are not subordinate to individual judges.[18]

B. The court's strategy

This chapter argues that the ECHR tried to increase its reputation by walking on the brink of noncompliance and matching the remedies and the reasoning used in its judgments to the level of its reputation. The first challenge

[16] *Ibid.*, at art. 44.

[17] See Erik Voeten, The Impartiality of International Judges: Evidence from the European Court of Human Rights, 102 *American Political Science Review* 417, 426 (2008).

[18] See the analysis in Chapter 3B6.

for supporting this argument is to determine the demands of each judgment and compare it to other judgments of different periods. This challenge is common to every attempt to evaluate trends in the demands of courts, although it may be more difficult to meet concerning the ECHR, because of the different states it faces. Different states have different abilities to pay and to undertake actions prescribed by the ECHR, and therefore a similar judgment may be considered demanding on certain states and less demanding on other states.

The argument that the ECHR shifted to more demanding judgments is also uniquely difficult to support, due to the special history of the ECHR and the changes to its structure, procedural rules, jurisdiction, and caseload. Before Protocol 11 took effect in 1998, the ECHR received cases that were prescreened by the European Commission of Human Rights. Protocol 11 abolished the European Commission and allowed the ECHR to hear cases directly. This may have changed the nature of the cases, for instance, by opening the court's doors to cases of less severe violations that could naturally lead to less demanding judgments.

Protocol 11 also made the rules of individual petition and compulsory jurisdiction mandatory for all states, which may have changed the nature of cases that reach the ECHR.[19] Over the years, the ECHR's jurisdiction expanded

[19] The change may not have been dramatic, however, because states were widely expected to accept individual petition and compulsory

to include many new states, some of which had frequent and gross human rights violations. It is fair to intuit that these more severe violations called for more demanding judgments to remedy them.

The number of cases that reach the ECHR has increased tremendously over the years, which may also have changed the demands of the ECHR's judgments due to selection effects. The proliferation of cases means that the ECHR is sometimes forced to decide which cases to decide and which cases will be continuously delayed, or even dismissed, on technical grounds. The ECHR may choose to decide mostly cases of the most severe violations, mostly cases where noncompliance is unlikely, or mostly cases that can help it build its reputation. All these hypotheses are extremely challenging to prove.

Complicating matters further is the possibility that individuals may respond to the ECHR's strategy of selecting cases by deciding to petition according to their chances of success at the ECHR and based on their own litigation costs. States may also change their litigation strategy and be more or less inclined to settle in response to the ECHR's policies and to the behavior of individuals.

This chapter will not attempt a quantitative study of the nature of the ECHR's judgments. Conventional quantitative

jurisdiction even before Protocol 11; *see* Clare Ovey and Robin C.A. White, in Jacobs and White, *The European Convention on Human Rights*, 8–9 (New York: Oxford University Press), 4th ed., 2006.

measures such as the amount of reparations granted, the costs of compliance with the judgment, the levels of dissent among judges, or the length of judgments are all rendered nearly useless because of the problems presented above. Instead of these measures, what follows is an attempt to study the evolution of the doctrine of the ECHR. The findings of scholars, the interpretive tools used by the ECHR, and an analysis of key judgments are used here to assess the trends in the ECHR's judgments. The ECHR is committed to its precedents, even if it is not legally bound to follow them. Therefore, even a small number of judgments, especially if they are important and well-known judgments, can be used to demonstrate a shift in the demands of the ECHR from the states under its jurisdiction.

1. Increasing the demands from the states

As section A suggests, most accounts argue that the ECHR has very high compliance rates. If the ECHR's judgments are generally complied with, the theory presented in this book will deduce that the ECHR's reputation has continuously increased over the years. As the ECHR's reputation increased, it should have shifted to issuing increasingly demanding judgments. If the ECHR heightened the human rights standards demanded from the states, this would have resulted in more demanding judgments regarding similar issues. Therefore, any indication that the ECHR has required states to comply with increasingly stricter standards of human rights protection over the years will be consistent with the theory presented here.

In a classical paper that surveys the court's behavior, Paul Mahoney, who served for many years as a senior administrator in the ECHR and was recently appointed as a judge on this court, claimed that the ECHR is heightening the required human rights standards in Europe.[20] More recent papers have corroborated this claim and indicated that the judgments of the ECHR are forming a clear trend toward increasing the obligations of states.[21]

Erik Voeten applied quantitative methods to assess the tendency of ECHR judges to find states in violation of the convention. While his study cannot show whether individual judges have changed their propensity to find states in violation, it does find strong evidence that judges appointed in later years are more likely to find states in violation. In other words, the pool of judges serving on the court is becoming increasingly more likely to find violations. This tendency indicates an overall trend of the ECHR to increase its demands from states, exemplified by the court finding more violations in states' behavior. Voeten finds alternative explanations for this trend by pointing out that members of the European Council who support European

[20] See Paul Mahoney, Judicial Activism and Judicial Self-Restraint in the European Court of Human Rights: Two Sides of the Same Coin, 11 *Human Rights Law Journal* 57, 67 (1990).

[21] See Alastair Mowbray, The Creativity of the European Court of Human Rights, 5 *Human Rights Law Review* 57, 57–58 (2005).

integration or who want to join the European Union attempt to appoint activist judges. However, these explanations do not exclude the possibility that the institutional dynamics described here are at least partly responsible for the increasing tendency of ECHR judges to find violations.[22]

The ECHR uses a variety of doctrines of interpretation, which can be analyzed to determine the level of discretion the ECHR professes to use, but some can also indicate ECHR judges' perspective of the trend in the demands of the court's judgments over the years. The ECHR has consistently adopted the doctrine of evolutionary interpretation. According to this doctrine, the Convention is a living instrument and its interpretation should change over time.[23] The direction of this progress, however, is not arbitrary and is greatly influenced by another doctrine of interpretation used by the ECHR – the principle of effectiveness. This doctrine directs the ECHR to interpret the Convention in a way that renders its safeguards of human rights practical and effective.[24] The combination of these two doctrines of interpretation was used by the ECHR to change its doctrine gradually in a way that increasingly protects human rights in Europe,

[22] See Erik Voeten, The Politics of International Judicial Appointments: Evidence from the European Court of Human Rights, 61 *International Organization* 669, 690–691, 697 (2007).

[23] See *Tyrer* case, judgment of April 25, 1978 EUR. Ct. H.R. (ser. A) 26, at 15–16.

[24] See *Soering* case, judgment of July 7, 1989, EUR. Ct. H.R (ser. A) 161 at 34.

a trend that is consistent with the theory that the ECHR should slowly ratchet up its demands from states.[25]

The ECHR often interpreted the Convention according to the teleological method of interpretation, which directs the judge to look to the object and the purpose of the Convention it interprets.[26] This method of interpretation facilitated the progression of the ECHR's judgments toward greater human rights protection and concurred with the prescriptions of the doctrine of evolutionary interpretation and the principle of effectiveness.

The object and purpose of the Convention can change over time as conditions change, while the text of the Convention and the original intentions of the parties remain fixed. For that reason, teleological interpretation can be used to interpret the Convention in an evolutionary manner more than other schools of interpretation that direct the judge to the text of the treaty or the intentions of the signatories.

Teleological interpretation allows the ECHR to interpret the duties of states expansively and the exceptions from these duties restrictively,[27] a level of flexibility that is

[25] For many examples, see Mowbray, *supra* note 21.

[26] See François Ost, The Original Canons of Interpretation of the European Court of Human Rights, in *The European Convention for the Protection of Human Rights: International Protection Versus National Restrictions*, 283, 292 (Mireille Delmas-Marty, ed.), 1992.

[27] About expansive interpretation by the ECHR, see Shai Dothan, In Defence of Expansive Interpretation in the European Court of Human Rights, 3 *Cambridge Journal of International and Comparative Law* 508 (2014). P. Van Dijk and G.J.H. Van Hoof,

harder to reach by other schools of interpretation. Therefore, the use of teleological interpretation allows the ECHR to ensure the effective protections of human rights from transgressions by the states.

These methods of interpretation reveal substantial judicial discretion. It seems that the ECHR opted for the use of discretionary reasoning even in relatively early judgments

Theory and Practice of the European Convention on Human Rights, 74–76 (The Hague: Kluwer Law International), 3rd ed., 1998; G. Merrills, *The Development of International Law by the European Court of Human Rights*, 98–124 (Manchester: Manchester University Press), 2nd edn.,1993.

The ECHR employed many methods of interpretation to expand states' obligations: It stressed the importance of interpreting the Convention in a way that fulfills the purpose of the rights protected by it (see *Golder* v. *The United Kingdom* judgment of February 21, 1975, EUR. Ct. H.R. (ser. A) 18 at 34; the *Minelli* case, judgment of March 25, 1983, EUR. Ct. H.R. (ser. A) 62, and even of rights not mentioned specifically in the text (see *Soering* case, *supra* note 24); it required states to provide practical safeguards to ensure the protection of rights (see *Artico* v. *Italy*, judgment of May 13, 1980, EUR. Ct. H.R. (ser. A)37; *Airey* case, judgment of October 9, 1979, EUR. Ct. H.R. (ser. A)32; and it read articles that provide protection from state actions as creating positive obligations on states (see *Marckx* case, judgment of June 13, 1979, EUR. Ct. H.R. (ser. A)31, *Mehemi* v. *France* (No. 2), judgment of April 10, 2003, 2003-IV EUR. Ct. H.R. 311, 325, and even as creating an obligation on the state to protect individuals from other individuals (see *X and Y* v. *The Netherlands*, judgment of March 26, 1985, EUR. Ct. H.R. (ser. A) 91. At the same time, exceptions and derogations from the rights protected by the Convention were interpreted narrowly (*see Klass and Others* judgment of September 6, 1978 EUR. Ct. H.R. (ser. A)28 at 21.

and continued to do so in its later judgments, as Dragoljub Popovic, who serves as a judge on the ECHR, highlighted in a recent paper.[28] Because even early ECHR judgments exposed the judges' extreme discretion, it is difficult to point to a trend toward exposing greater discretion over the years, which, under the theory, is another possible response to increasing the court's reputation. This is why this chapter focuses on the increased demands of the ECHR from states instead of on changes in its reasoning.

Demonstrating a trend toward increasingly demanding judgments is difficult due to the great number of ECHR judgments and the different issues they discuss. It is possible, however, to look at the development of doctrine on a certain issue that can serve as an example of this trend. An important issue that the ECHR dealt with over the years involves the rights of individuals with minority sexual orientations and gender identities; an analysis of the judgments pertaining to this issue exposes a clear progression towards stricter human rights standards.

Mahoney supports his claim that the ECHR is increasing human rights protection by referring to the *Dudgeon* case.[29] The judgment in this case decided that criminal laws in Northern Ireland that proscribed homosexual practices between consenting adults violated the right to

[28] Popovic, *supra* note 5 at 382.

[29] *Dudgeon* v. *The United Kingdom*, judgment of October 22, 1981, EUR. Ct. H.R. (ser. A)45.

respect for private life protected by the Convention. Mahoney showed that similar complaints of similar violations were dismissed at a preliminary stage in previous decades.[30]

The ECHR's judgments regarding the rights of transsexuals show a clear trend towards greater protection of human rights. In the *Rees* case[31] the ECHR decided that the refusal of the United Kingdom to change the registration of sex in the birth certificate of transsexuals and its refusal to allow transsexuals to marry a person of their opposite current sex do not violate the Convention. Fifteen years later the ECHR decided in the *Goodwin* case[32] that these practices do violate the Convention.

The ECHR was slowly setting the ground for this shift towards greater human rights protection with the reasoning used in a series of judgments issued between the *Rees* case and the *Goodwin* case. In the *Cossey* case,[33] the ECHR emphasized the seriousness of the problems facing transsexuals and the need to keep the issue under review. In the *Sheffield* case,[34] the ECHR stressed its

[30] See Mahoney, *supra* note 20 at 61–62.

[31] *Rees* v. *The United Kingdom*, judgment of October 17, 1986, EUR. Ct. H.R. (ser. A)106.

[32] *Christine Goodwin* v. *The United Kingdom*, judgment of July 11, 2002, 2002-VI EUR. Ct. H.R. 1.

[33] *Cossey* case, judgment of September 27, 1990, EUR. Ct. H.R. (ser. A) 184, at 17.

[34] *Sheffield and Horsham* v. *The United Kingdom*, judgment of July 30, 1998, 1998-V EUR. Ct. H.R. 2011, 2029.

growing displeasure with the practices of the United Kingdom in this respect.[35]

Laurence Helfer and Erik Voeten recently conducted a comprehensive empirical study of the ECHR rulings regarding lesbian, gay, bisexual, and transgender (LGBT) issues that confirms the existence of a clear pattern toward incrementally increasing protection of their rights.[36]

The trend toward greater protection of the rights of homosexuals and transsexuals is consistent with the theory that the ECHR increased its demands from states as its reputation improved. However, this trend is also consistent with the claim that the ECHR is following a change in public opinion in Europe, a so-called "emerging consensus." If the European public is becoming more tolerant toward people with different sexual inclinations and identities, the ECHR may be following this emerging consensus as it often declares it will do.[37]

This alternative explanation is problematic, however, because the ECHR does not prove a European consensus actually exists. In the *Dudgeon* case, the majority opinion

[35] See Beate Rudolf, Constitutional Developments: European Court of Human Rights: Legal Status of Postoperative Transsexuals, 1.4 *International Journal of Constitutional Law* 716 (2003).

[36] Laurence R. Helfer and Eric Voeten, International Courts as Agents of Legal Change: Evidence from LGBT Rights in Europe, 68 *International Organization* 77, 88 (2014)

[37] See Laurence R. Helfer, Consensus, Coherence and the European Convention on Human Rights, 26 *Cornell International Law Journal* 133, 134 (1993).

referred to the increasing tolerance toward homosexuals in European states, but this argument was resisted by the dissenting judges. The Cypriot judge Zekia referred to the criminalization of similar homosexual practices in Cyprus to deny the existence of a true European consensus. Judge Walsh attacked the argument of an emerging consensus by referring to the extreme diversity of the states within the Council of Europe.

The attempt to refer to a norm that evolves in different legal systems is often susceptible to the criticism that the judges are choosing to refer only to the systems that support their initial intention.[38] It is entirely possible, therefore, that the ECHR makes its decision based on its strategic interest and masks this decision by referring only to states that share the same value judgments and ignoring states that adopt other value judgments. In the study mentioned above, Helfer and Voeten showed that the ECHR does not necessarily follow only rules adopted by almost all the states. Instead, the court follows policies supported by at least a majority of the states – a policy they call *majoritarian*

[38] Justice Scalia of the U.S. Supreme Court raises this important point in his dissenting opinion in the case of *Lawrence* v. *Texas* under similar circumstances; see *Lawrence* v. *Texas*, 539 U.S. 558, 598 (2003). In this case the U.S. Supreme Court repealed the laws against sodomy in Texas. The majority judgment, delivered by Justice Kennedy, referred to foreign legal systems and decisions (including the *Dudgeon* judgment) to indicate that the protections of the rights of homosexuals is not uncommon in other Western systems.

activism. This policy gives the ECHR a substantial degree of flexibility. They also demonstrated that states change their practices following an ECHR judgment that protects LGBT rights, and therefore sometimes it is the ECHR that pushes European consensus forward.[39]

The argument that the ECHR is following an emerging consensus, even one supported by only a majority of the states in Europe, can serve as an alternative explanation for the court's tendency to increase its demands only if such a consensus actually exists. As suggested above, this may not be the case in some LGBT cases, but in another area of the ECHR's judgments, prisoners' right to vote, the ECHR showed that even without the support of a European consensus, it was willing to increase its demands from states. In *Hirst* v. *United Kingdom*, the Grand Chamber of the ECHR decided that a blanket ban on the right of prisoners to vote violated article 3 of Protocol 1 of the Convention, which protects the right to free elections.[40] Five judges wrote a joint dissenting opinion in this judgment and criticized this decision as digressing from the ECHR's consistent case law,

[39] Helfer and Voeten, *supra* note 36 at 106. See Shai Dothan, The Optimal Use of Comparative Law, Forthcoming *Denver Journal of International Law & Policy* (providing a normative justification for interpreting the emerging consensus doctrine as directing the ECHR to follow policies adopted by the majority of the states in Europe).

[40] *Hirst* v. *The United Kingdom* (No. 2), judgment of October 6, 2005, 2005-IX EUR. Ct. H.R. 187.

which left wide discretion to states to determine their own electoral system. The dissenting judges specifically called attention to the fact that there is no European consensus that supports this judgment, because many European states restrict prisoners' right to vote. While the majority's judgment indicated that only a minority of the states in Europe indiscriminately prevent all prisoners from voting, as the United Kingdom does, it acknowledges that many states actually have harsher laws than the United Kingdom – for example, these states prevent prisoners from voting even after their release. The majority specifically states that a violation exists even if there is no common European approach on the issue. This judgment led to strong criticism of the ECHR in the United Kingdom, which refused to amend its laws to comply with the judgment.[41]

Five years later, the ECHR issued a Pilot Judgment in the *Greens* case[42] against the United Kingdom that allowed it a period of six months to introduce legislative proposals to amend its laws to conform to the *Hirst* judgment. This period was extended to accommodate proceedings in a later case, *Scoppola* v. *Italy*,[43] where the United Kingdom submitted arguments as a third party.

[41] See Erik Voeten, Public Opinion and the Legitimacy of International Courts, 14 *Theoretical Inquiries in Law* 411, 418–419 (2013).

[42] *Greens and MT* v. *United Kingdom*, judgment of November 23, 2010, Reports of Judgments and Decisions 2010.

[43] *Scoppola* v. *Italy* (No. 3), judgment of May 22, 2012, App. No. 126/05.

In *Scoppola* v. *Italy* the ECHR reiterated its previous decision that an indiscriminate ban on prisoners' right to vote violated the Convention. But the ECHR also indicated that a ban that was not automatic, general, and indiscriminate may be permitted even if it is applied by a statute, without the need for intervention by a judge.[44] The ECHR approved the partial voting ban in Italy, despite the criticism of the dissenting judge Bjorgvinsson, who argued that the judgment digressed from the principles mentioned in the *Hirst* case. Importantly, following this judgment and a proposal to change legislation in the United Kingdom that could limit the ban on prisoners' right to vote, the ECHR decided to adjourn the consideration of 2,354 pending applications against violations of the right to vote by the United Kingdom until as late as September 30, 2013.[45]

This development indicates an attempt by the ECHR to gradually increase its demands from states, but when a powerful state responds to this trend by noncompliance and severe criticism, the ECHR may commit a partial retreat and change its doctrine to make it more acceptable to this state. Section C1 in this chapter argues that there is a great difference between the willingness of the ECHR to retreat following criticism of its judgments by low-reputation

[44] *Ibid.* at par. 99.

[45] See Press Release, issued by the Registrar of the Court, ECHR 091 (2013), 26.03.2013.

states and by high-reputation states. The ECHR is far more ready to compromise in the face of criticism and to accommodate the interests of high-reputation states. The trend in the ECHR's judgments is to increase its demands from both low-reputation states and high-reputation states. But because high-reputation states can cause great damage to the ECHR by noncompliance or criticism, the ECHR may partially retreat from its demanding judgment if it is met by resistance from a high-reputation state.

The human rights that the ECHR is charged with protecting can conflict with each other, and in some cases a greater protection of one right would necessarily mean a lesser protection of another right. Therefore, progress toward greater human rights protection is very hard to prove. The examples brought here certainly do not cover the whole breadth of the ECHR judgments, and in some issues, other trends toward allowing the states greater leeway to act may be observed. Nevertheless, the quantitative and qualitative scholarly attempts to assess ECHR judgments seem to support the claim that it is moving toward greater protection of human rights. This claim is also supported by the doctrines the ECHR uses and by the examples mentioned here. This trend is consistent with the argument that the ECHR increases its demands from states over the years. Further examples supporting this trend are presented in the next section, because they demonstrate the incremental nature of some doctrinal changes.

2. *Progressing incrementally*

Until recently, the ECHR issued only judgments declaring that certain state actions violated the Convention, without specifying how the state should remedy these violations. The states were granted the discretion to choose the means of remediation. The ECHR can now issue Pilot Judgments – judgments that require the state to undertake specific actions to comply. This doctrinal shift allowed the ECHR to increase its demands from states over time. The shift was undertaken incrementally in a series of ECHR's judgments. By introducing this new doctrinal tool in several judgments that refer to each other, the ECHR was able to reduce resistance to this revolutionary move by appearing consistent.

Joshua Jackson described the series of cases that introduced the tool of Pilot Judgments.[46] The court first moved toward a doctrine requiring the state to undertake specific actions in the case of *Assanidze* v. *Georgia*.[47] In this case, the ECHR demanded that the applicant be released from prison "at the earliest possible date." This judgment was complied with almost immediately, and the prisoner was released a day after the judgment was issued. The second move was undertaken in the case of *Ilascu* v.

[46] Joshua L. Jackson, *Broniowski* v. *Poland:* A Recipe for Increased Legitimacy of the European Court of Human Rights as a Supranational Constitutional Court, 39 *Connecticut Law Review* 759, 783–784 (2006).

[47] *Assanidze* v. *Georgia*, judgment of April 8, 2004, 2004-II EUR. Ct. H.R. 221.

Moldova and Russia,[48] discussed in Chapter 2D1. In this case, the court demanded the "immediate release" of prisoners. The discretion left to the violating state was more limited in this case, because no discretion was allowed regarding the date of the release. This time the prisoners were not released until the end of their illegitimate trials. Jackson explained that while these judgments required the states to undertake specific actions, at the time, this was the only reasonable way to end the violation. Therefore, these judgments were inherently different from the most revolutionary judgment that introduced the Pilot Judgment procedure – *Broniowski* v. *Poland*.[49]

In *Broniowski* v. *Poland*, the applicant was one of a group of tens of thousands of Polish citizens who lost their property when territories were taken from Poland at the end of World War II. The ECHR decided that the arrangements made to compensate the applicant for his property loss made him shoulder a disproportionate burden compared to the rest of Polish society, and therefore violated article 1 of Protocol 1 to the Convention. The ECHR did not just declare the violation in the case of the applicant, however. The judgment required Poland to take the appropriate legal and administrative measures to secure the property rights

[48] *Ilascu and others* v. *Moldova and Russia*, judgment of July 8, 2004, 2004-VII EUR. Ct. H.R. 179.

[49] *Broniowski* v. *Poland*, judgment of June 22, 2004, 2004-V EUR. Ct. H.R. 1, at 79.

of other Polish citizens affected by this violation. In this judgment, the ECHR therefore required a state to take specific actions to remedy a violation, even when there was more than one possible route to do so.[50]

An even more important revolutionary aspect of this judgment was that the steps required from the states were not needed to remedy the situation of the applicant himself, but were needed to protect the rights of thousands of others.[51] *Broniowski* v. *Poland* was the first time the ECHR issued a real Pilot Judgment that required a state to take specific actions to remedy a systemic problem that violated the rights of numerous individuals. The ECHR was following a recommendation of the Committee of Ministers that called on it to identify such systemic problems.[52] This doctrinal tool proved essential to allowing the ECHR to address violations more efficiently, and has been used since in several other important ECHR judgments.[53]

[50] See Jackson, *supra* note 46 at 791.

[51] This aspect is highlighted by Judge Zupancic in this concurring opinion; see *Broniowski* v. *Poland, supra* note 49 at 82.

[52] Committee of Ministers of the Council of Europe, Res(2004)3 (May 12, 2004).

[53] See *Supervision of the Execution of Judgments and Decisions of the European Court of Human Rights – Annual Report 2011*, available at www.coe.int/t/dghl/monitoring/execution/Source/Publications/CM_annreport2011_en.pdf, at pp. 9–10 (arguing that in 2011 the effective use of Pilot Judgments helped reduce the number of repetitive cases transmitted to the Committee for the first time in years).

C. Facing the states' strategy

The theoretical analysis in Chapter 4G suggests that international courts should issue more demanding judgments against low-reputation states compared to the judgments they issue against high-reputation states. High-reputation states can respond to demanding judgments by failing to comply with them, even when noncompliance goes against their reputational interest. This strategic noncompliance can signal to the court that the state will fail to comply with future demanding judgments and will cause great damage to the court's reputation. High-reputation states can also criticize international courts, and this criticism will cause significant damage to the court's reputation and public support.

High-reputation states are expected by the international community to comply more often with the court's judgments than low-reputation states. The international community can assess the probability that different states will comply based on their past behavior. States that complied in the past will be expected to comply in the future and will therefore have a high reputation. Accurate data about the level of compliance of different states with the ECHR is hard to find. Often, states comply only with a part of the requirements of the judgment or delay their compliance. However, if states continuously delay their compliance, this may indicate that they are less likely to comply at all.

The Committee of Ministers monitors the compliance of states with ECHR judgments, and keeps cases pending on its agenda as long as the state fails to comply. States with many pending cases are therefore more likely to be low-reputation states than states with fewer pending cases. In 2011, the five states with the highest number of pending cases were Italy (2,522), Turkey (1,780), Russia (1,087), Poland (924), and Ukraine (819). To get a better estimate of whether the number of pending cases on the Committee of Ministers represents many fundamentally different violations that were not remedied or repetitive cases that address the same issue, the ECHR defined *leading cases* as cases that raise a new and distinct problem. The number of leading cases that were pending on the Committee's agenda may therefore give a better sense of the number of violations the state did not remedy, despite an ECHR judgment, than the aggregate number of pending cases. The five states with the most leading pending cases on the Committee's agenda as of 2011 were Turkey (164), Russia (134), Bulgaria (116), Romania (88), and Ukraine (85).[54]

Another possible proxy for the willingness of states to comply is the number of judgments issued concerning it. If the state continues to commit violations, more cases will be brought to the court against it, and more judgments will be issued concerning it. Many of these judgments are actually addressing the same or similar violations that were not redressed by the state after failing to comply with previous judgments. A substantial number of the cases

[54] See *Ibid.* at 37–39.

before the ECHR are repetitive cases that deal with nonredressed violations. Furthermore, if a state intends to comply with the judgments of the ECHR, it will generally avoid committing violations in the first place to avoid the reputational cost of the judgment against it. Therefore, states that commit many violations will usually also comply with fewer judgments against them and have a low reputation as a result.

In 2011, 59% of ECHR judgments were directed against seven states that lead the list in terms of the number of judgments issued against them. The states were Turkey, Russia, Ukraine, Greece, Poland, Romania, and Bulgaria.[55] Russia, Turkey, Italy, and Romania were collectively responsible for over half of the pending cases on the ECHR's docket in 2011.[56] The identity of the states that were responsible for the largest number of applications and judgments remained relatively stable over time. Russia, Poland, Turkey, and Romania were nicknamed the "Big Four" due to their consistent responsibility for the highest number of cases before the ECHR.[57]

[55] *Annual Report 2011 of the European Court of Human rights, Council of Europe*, available at www.echr.coe.int/NR/rdonlyres/77FF4249-96E5-4D1F-BE71-42867A469225/0/2011_Rapport_Annuel_EN.pdf, at p. 14.

[56] *Ibid.* at 13.

[57] See Luzius Wildhaber, The European Court of Human Rights: The Past, The Present, The Future, 22 *American University International Law Review* 521, 527 (2007).

The data point to very big differences in the proportions of pending cases of delayed compliance monitored by the Committee of Ministers, pending cases awaiting decision by the ECHR, and ECHR judgments with respect to different states. These figures can, therefore, be used as an accurate proxy to assess the reputation of states. Russia, Turkey, and several Eastern European states are typical low-reputation states. Many of the states of Western Europe are typical high-reputation states. Some states, such as Italy, may lie somewhere in the middle between these two camps, but several states can be categorized as having either a high or a low reputation.

1. Demanding more from low-reputation states

Any attempt to prove that the ECHR issues more demanding judgments against low-reputation states than it does against high-reputation states must address the inherent differences between these states. High-reputation states usually have better human rights practices than low-reputation states. Thus, if the ECHR requires both types of states to apply the same human rights standards to their citizens, it will be forced to find more violations with respect to low-reputation states. In order to redress these violations and reach the human rights standards required by the ECHR, low-reputation states will be required to undertake more difficult and expensive measures, rendering the judgments issued against them more demanding. For that reason, a comparison of the number of violations found with respect to the two different types of states, and even of the costs of redressing these violations, will not prove that the ECHR treats high-reputation states and low-reputation states differently.

In order to maintain its public support, the ECHR must prove that it is impartial and treats different states equally. If the ECHR is suspected of bias against a certain state, this state and its allies may retaliate by criticizing the court, failing to comply with its judgments, or other steps intended to harm the court's interests. For example, Russian representatives have claimed that the ECHR is politicized and biased against Russia, and Russia responded by refusing for a long time to ratify Protocol 14 to the Convention.[58] Russia was the last state in Europe to ratify this protocol, which was an essential tool for addressing the ECHR's mounting caseload. Russia's refusal to ratify the protocol delayed its entry into force for several years. The former president of the ECHR, Luzius Wildhaber, accused Russia of a far less traditional method of retaliation – he claimed he was poisoned by the Russians.[59]

[58] In an interview on January 11, 2007, Russian President Putin explained the Russian State Duma (lower house of parliament) decision not to ratify Protocol 14 on its December 20, 2006 vote as a response to the ECHR political decision in the *Ilascu* case. See Bill Bowring, Russia's relations with the Council of Europe under Increasing Strain at www.eu-russiacentre.org/articles.asp?id=1884&Ing=ru. Russia agreed to ratify Protocol 14 only on January 15, 2010.

[59] Luke Harding, I Was Poisoned by the Russians, Human Rights Judge Says, *The Guardian*, 1 February 2007. www.guardian.co.uk/world/2007/feb/01/russia.topstories3.

To fend off such accusations of bias and hostile responses, the ECHR must try to distinguish between the judgments addressing different states on legal grounds and hide any evidence of double standards. Furthermore, if the ECHR decides strategically, as this book claims, it may also try to hide its biases strategically, for instance, by deliberately issuing demanding judgments against high-reputation states and mild judgments against low-reputation states in some cases.

The problems presented above suggest that the best way to demonstrate the ECHR's bias in favor of high-reputation states is to carefully compare specific instances where different legal standards were applied to different types of states. Several authors have argued that the ECHR issues less demanding judgments toward states that generally have good human rights practices compared to states with worse practices.[60] These authors drew attention to the contrast between the

[60] Brendan Mangan, Protecting Human Rights in National Emergencies: Shortcomings in the European System and a Proposal for Reform, 10 *Human Rights Quarterly* 372, 383 (1988); Fionnuala Ni Aolain, The Emergence of Diversity: Differences in Human Rights Jurisprudence, 19 *Fordham International Law Journal* 101, 114 (1995); Frede Castberg, *The European Convention on Human Rights*, 169 (Dobbs Ferry, NY: Oceana Publications), 1974; Joan F. Hartman, Derogation from Human Rights Treaties in Public Emergencies, 22 *Harvard International Law Journal* 1 (1981).

decisions in the *Lawless* case[61] and the *Greek* case[62] as evidence for this claim.

The *Lawless* case discussed the detention without trial of G. R. Lawless, a former member of the Irish Republican Army (IRA), as a part of the attempts of the Irish government to suppress the activities of the IRA in Northern Ireland. The ECHR ruled that the detention of Lawless contradicted the rights to liberty and to a fair trial protected by articles 5 and 6 of the Convention. The ECHR also ruled, however, that a public emergency existed in Ireland at the time, and that as a result, article 15 of the Convention allowed the Irish government to take measures that derogated from the rights protected by the Convention. The judgment decided that the derogation in this case was legitimate, and therefore, the Convention was not violated.

In contrast, in the *Greek* case, the European Commission of Human Rights (which served as the first tier of the ECHR structure until it was abolished by Protocol 11) decided that the situation in Greece did not constitute a public emergency, and therefore derogation from the rights protected in the Convention was impossible, and the Greek military government had violated the Convention. This decision was

[61] *Lawless* v. *Ireland* (No. 3) judgment of July 1, 1961, EUR. Ct. H.R. (ser. A) 3.

[62] "Greek case" [1969] Eur. Comm. on Human Rights (report) at *Yearbook of the European Convention on Human Rights* 1969.

followed by the Committee of Ministers, which decided that Greece committed numerous violations of the Convention.

It is difficult to compare the conditions in Greece and in Ireland in the 1960s. It is also important to note that the commission itself may have been uncertain about the conditions in Greece and did not believe the statements of the military government there.[63] These differences may have been responsible for the different results in these two cases. Another important difference is that the *Lawless* case was the first case decided by the ECHR, which may have led it to take greater caution, according to the theory described in this book that recommends greater restraint for low-reputation courts. It is also important to note that the *Greek* case never reached the court itself. The Commission referred its report directly to the Committee of Ministers.[64] Despite these differences, the contrast between the doctrines adopted in the two cases raises the suspicion that the ECHR system, including the court, the commission, and the Committee of Ministers, were applying double standards to states based on their reputation.

[63] See Hartman, *supra* note 60 at 29.

[64] If the Commission's report was not referred to the court within three months, the Committee of Ministers was authorized to decide the case with a two-thirds majority. In previous years, when the court decided much fewer cases, some important issues, such as the *Greek* case, were referred directly to the Committee of Ministers; *see* Mark W. Janis, Richard S. Kay, Anthony W. Bradley, *European Human Rights Law: Text and Materials*, 27 (New York: Oxford University Press), 3rd edn., 2008.

This suspicion is strengthened when the aftermath of the *Greek* case is considered. Following the commission's report, the Greek government denounced the Convention system on December 12, 1969 and refused to take part in the discussions in the Committee of Ministers. Had a high-reputation state taken such a dramatic step, especially in this early period of the ECHR's life, the result may have been very detrimental to the entire Convention system. The commission and the Committee of Ministers may have taken into account the fact that the damage Greece, at the time a very low-reputation state, could cause to the convention system by criticism, noncompliance, and even withdrawal was sustainable. This may have led them to apply a stricter standard to Greece than the one applied to Ireland in the *Lawless* case.

Another example of the restraint the ECHR exercises toward high-reputation states can be found in the *Bankovic* case.[65] In this case, Bankovic and several other citizens of the Federal Republic of Yugoslavia claimed that seventeen member states of NATO[66] were responsible for the killing of several people in a NATO airstrike, and therefore violated the Convention. This application accused all the high-reputation, powerful nations of Western Europe of a severe

[65] *Bankovic and Others* v. *Belgium and Others*, decision of December 12, 2001, EUR. Ct. H.R. 2001-XII 333.

[66] Belgium, the Czech Republic, Denmark, France, Germany, Greece, Hungary, Iceland, Italy, Luxembourg, the Netherlands, Norway, Poland, Portugal, Spain, Turkey, and the United Kingdom.

violation of the right to life. If the ECHR were to have found such a violation, it would have had to face formidable resistance by these powerful nations. The ECHR decided that the case was inadmissible, because the injured persons were not under the jurisdiction of the respondent states, and by this, the court avoided the potentially dangerous conflict with those states.

In the *Bankovic* case, the ECHR adopted an extremely narrow reading of the concept of state jurisdiction. This narrow reading can be contrasted with the expansive jurisdictional standards that were adopted in other cases concerning low-reputation states and allowed for demanding judgments against them.

In the *Loizidou* v. *Turkey* case,[67] for instance, a Cypriot national claimed that Turkey violated the Convention by preventing her from enjoying her property, which included plots of land located in northern Cyprus. The ECHR ruled that Turkey had jurisdiction over the area, which lay outside its territory, because it exercised effective control over it. Scholars criticized the ECHR's ruling in *Bankovic* as a digression from the precedent set in *Loizidou* v. *Turkey*.[68]

[67] *Loizidou* v. *Turkey* (Preliminary Objections), judgment of March 23, 1995, EUR. Ct. H.R. (ser. A)310 at page 23–24 par. 62; *Loizidou* v. *Turkey*, judgment of December 18, 1996 (merits), *Reports of Judgments and Decisions* 1996-VI at pages 2234–2235 par. 52.

[68] Alexander Orakhelashvili, Restrictive Interpretation of Human Rights Treaties in the Recent Jurisprudence of the European

The ECHR tried to distinguish the two cases by arguing that the decision in *Loizidou* v. *Turkey* was meant to prevent the inapplicability of the Convention in a territory owned by one member state but controlled by another member state, both of whom were obligated by the Convention. In contrast, in the *Bankovic* case, the territory was owned by Yugoslavia, which was not a member state, so the court was not required, in this case, to prevent the rise of a vacuum from Convention protection where it previously had applied. Commentators found this argument unconvincing and argued that the court introduced the idea of a need to close a vacuum in *Loizidou* v. *Turkey* only as a way to expand the state's extraterritorial jurisdiction; in the *Bankovic* case, the ECHR used this argument as a way to limit the state's jurisdiction.[69]

In another case against a low-reputation state, *Ilascu* v. *Moldova and Russia*, which was discussed at length in Chapter 2D1, the ECHR found Moldova responsible for actions in a territory it did not, in fact, control. In his partly dissenting judgment in this case, Judge Loucaides strongly criticized the inconsistency between this judgment and the judgment in the case of *Bankovic*.

Court of Human Rights, 14 *European Journal of International Law* 529, 545–546 (2003).

[69] Alexandra Ruth and Mirja Trilsch, *Bankovic v. Belgium* (Admissibility), 97 *American Journal of International Law* 168, 172 (2003).

Finally, in 2011 the ECHR set a clear precedent that member states can be responsible for actions they commit outside their territory, even if this territory never belonged to a state party to the Convention. The *Al-Skeini*[70] judgment found the United Kingdom violated article 2 protecting the right to life because it failed to properly investigate the killing of civilians in occupied Iraq by British forces. In the *Al-Jedda*[71] judgment, the court decided that the United Kingdom violated article 5 of the Convention by administratively detaining a British-Iraqi citizen in British-occupied Iraq. The United Kingdom is a high-reputation state, which should lead the ECHR to greater restraint, according to the theory described here. At the same time, the ECHR also increased its reputation between 2001, when the *Bankovic* case was issued, and 2011. As the ECHR's reputation increased, it could shift to issuing demanding judgments that adopted a wide definition of jurisdiction, even against high-reputation states.

Section B in this chapter describes how, as the ECHR increases its reputation, it can shift to issuing more demanding judgments against the states under its jurisdiction. As the ECHR's reputation increases, it can also issue demanding judgments against high-reputation states

[70] *Al-Skeini and Others* v. *The United Kingdom*, judgment of July 7, 2011 (Application. No. 55721/07).

[71] *Al-Jedda* v. *The United Kingdom*, judgment of July 7, 2011 (Application No. 27021/08).

that it previously issued only against low-reputation states, because it is increasingly certain that its judgments will be complied with. Furthermore, once the ECHR issues a judgment against a low-reputation state, it becomes an accepted doctrine, and the ECHR can more legitimately use the same doctrine against high-reputation states while it still appears constrained by the law. This is how the ECHR developed its doctrine of Pilot Judgments.

As section B demonstrates, the ECHR developed the doctrine of Pilot Judgments incrementally. The ECHR first introduced the possibility of judgments that require specific actions instead of merely declaring a violation in the cases of *Assanidze* v. *Georgia* and *Ilascu* v. *Moldova and Russia*. Those cases were issued against low-reputation states and legitimized the future use of specific requirements from states. These judgments, however, do not qualify as real Pilot Judgments because they do not deal with a structural problem, and they require actions that are clearly necessary to remedy a specific violation.

The next big step forward in terms of developing this doctrine is the case of *Broniowski* v. *Poland*, which for the first time introduced the Pilot Judgment procedure. The fact that this case was issued against Poland, which is a low-reputation state, was again instrumental in allowing the ECHR to undertake this important development in its doctrine. A similar judgment against a high-reputation state would have exposed the ECHR to criticism that could seriously damage its reputation.

Pilot Judgments are used to remedy structural problems. It could well be argued that low-reputation states usually suffer from greater structural problems than high-reputation states, which could justify the more frequent use of this tool against low-reputation states. But, this argument cannot account by itself for the differences in the use of Pilot Judgments against low-reputation and high-reputation states.

Wojciech Sadurski shows that systemic problems used to exist in the United Kingdom regarding the issue of granting widow benefits for men. The ECHR, however, failed to identify this problem in the United Kingdom, probably because the court feared retaliation from this state, which I define as having a high reputation.[72]

Sadurski also shows that even when the ECHR identified a systemic problem in Italy in the case of *Sejdovic* v. *Italy*, it accorded Italy a favored treatment compared to its treatment of Poland. The Chamber judgment in *Sejdovic* v. *Italy* found that Italy failed to effectively protect the rights of persons convicted in absentia.[73] The Grand Chamber judgment that followed this judgment, however, did not include any finding of violation in the operative part of the

[72] Wojciech Sadurski, Partnering with Strasburg: Constitutionalisation of the European Court of Human Rights, The Accession of Central and East European States to the Council of Europe and the Idea of Pilot Judgments, 9 *Human Rights Law Review* 397, 430 (2009).

[73] *Sejdovic* v. *Italy*, judgment of November 10, 2004.

judgment.[74] It should be noted, on the other hand, that Italy instituted a reform in the meantime, which might have changed the conditions of some applicants, and the ECHR indicated that an assessment of violations after the reform was premature. The contrast with the specific requirements in the Pilot Judgments issued against low-reputation states is still illustrative.

Another example for such a case is *Hutten-Czapska* v. *Poland*.[75] In this case, the ECHR decided that the legal situation in Poland imposed restrictions on landlords' rights and did not allow them to recover the losses they incurred by maintaining the property. The operative part of the judgment clearly found a systemic problem and instructed Poland to remedy this by securing a mechanism to maintain a fair balance between the interests of landlords and general community interests.

Sadurski noted that the ECHR tries to use Pilot Judgments when there is a fair chance that the state will cooperate with its judgment and comply. The fear of non-compliance is a problem when the ECHR addresses low-reputation states, and this may have affected the ECHR's choice of cases.[76] Nevertheless, the fear of retaliation from high-reputation states, which can cause the

[74] *Sejdovic* v. *Italy*, judgment of March 1, 2006, 2006-II EUR. Ct. H.R. 241., *see* Sadurski, *supra* note 72 at 427.

[75] *Hutten-Czapska* v. *Poland*, judgment of June 19, 2006, 2006-VIII EUR. Ct. H.R. 57

[76] See Sadurski, *supra* note 72 at 429.

ECHR a much greater damage than low-reputation states, made the ECHR avoid the use of Pilot Judgments against high-reputation states until this doctrine matured and was generally accepted as legitimate.

In recent years, the doctrine of Pilot Judgments became accepted as one of the regular tools in the arsenal of the ECHR and a main way to battle the court's mounting case-load. The legitimacy that this doctrine acquired allowed the ECHR to use Pilot Judgments even against high-reputation states. For example, in the *Greens* case discussed above, the ECHR required the United Kingdom to change its laws and lift the blanket ban on prisoners' right to vote.[77] Yet, the ECHR's partial retreat from this judgment in the *Scoppola* case indicated its continuing deference to the interests of high-reputation states.

More generally, the different standards the ECHR applies to high-reputation and low-reputation states are illustrated by the ECHR's willingness to retreat from judgments issued against high-reputation states once those judgments are criticized. Similar criticism voiced in low-reputation states does not seem to threaten the ECHR so much and will generally not lead it to backtrack on its decisions. In fact, when the ECHR faces a low-reputation state that fails to comply with its judgments consistently and criticizes its decisions, it may try to prove that it is

[77] See *supra* note 42 and the text near it.

immune to the influence of such criticism and deliberately keep its course.

The ECHR displayed its willingness to sustain criticism by low-reputation states without changing its judgments with its position toward Russia regarding its military operation in Chechnya in 1999–2000. By May 2009, the ECHR had issued its hundredth judgment regarding the Russian military operation. In many judgments, for instance in *Magomed Musayev and Others* v. *Russia*,[78] the ECHR accused Russia of severe violations of the Convention, including extra-judicial killings. Russian criticism of the ECHR has been severe, and many methods of retaliation, some of which are discussed in this chapter, were used in an attempt to deter the ECHR. Yet, the ECHR did not surrender and instead continued to issue these judgments against Russia.

In contrast, even much milder criticism voiced by a high-reputation state proved in the past to be enough to make the ECHR change its doctrine. An even more illustrative example than the ECHR's partial retreat from its decision that a ban on prisoners' right to vote violated the Convention is the ECHR's willingness to retreat from the doctrine it had set in the case of *Osman* v. *United Kingdom*.[79]

[78] *Magomed Musayev and Others* v. *Russia*, judgment of October 23, 2008 (application no. 8979/02).

[79] *Osman* v. *The United Kingdom*, judgment of October 28, 1998, Reports of Judgments and Decisions 1998-VIII 3124.

A retreat committed in the later case of *Z and Others* v. *United Kingdom*, following criticism voiced in the United Kingdom.[80] In the case of *Osman* v. *United Kingdom*, the victims of an obsessive killer claimed that they were not properly protected by the police although they warned the police of the danger posed to them. The United Kingdom's domestic courts rejected the suit of the applicants against the police without deciding the issue on its merits. The ECHR decided that article 2 of the Convention, which protects the right to life, was not violated in this case, but that article 6, which protects the right to access to a court, was violated.

The decision of the ECHR that the right to access the court was violated was criticized in an article published in the *Modern Law Review*, a prominent law journal based in the United Kingdom.[81] The case of *Z and Others* v. *United Kingdom* discussed children who were mistreated by their parents but were not removed from their control by the state for several years and suffered severe psychological damage as a result. The suit of the children against the authorities was dismissed in a similar way as the conduct of the United Kingdom legal system in the *Osman case*. The ECHR decided that article 3 protecting against

[80] *Z and Others* v. *The United Kingdom*, judgment of May 10, 2001, EUR. Ct. H.R. 2001-V 1.

[81] Conor Gearty, Unravelling Osman, 64 *Modern Law Review* 159 (2001).

inhuman and degrading treatment and article 13 protecting the right to an effective remedy for violations of the convention were violated in this case. Strikingly, the ECHR found no violation of the right to access to a court, despite the similarity of the facts to the ones discussed in the *Osman case*. Within the court's judgment five judges in two separate dissents criticized the ECHR's decision in this case as contrary to its own judgment in the *Osman* case. The ECHR's retreat from its decision in *Osman* was explained by Wright as a response to the arguments in the scholarly paper that criticized this decision.[82]

In conclusion, it seems that the ECHR is deterred by the ability of high-reputation states to retaliate against it with criticism or noncompliance. This fact makes the ECHR issue less demanding judgments against high-reputation states compared to low-reputation states. It also makes the ECHR less willing to try out new doctrines in its judgments against high-reputation states and ready to retreat from its own judgments when they come under attack from these states.

D. Conclusion and the falsifiability of conflicting tendencies

This chapter demonstrates several trends in the judgments of the ECHR that correlate with the judicial tactics

[82] Jane Wright, The Retreat from Osman: *Z* v. *United Kingdom* in the European Court of Human Rights and Beyond in *Tort Liability of Public Authorities in Comparative Perspective*, 55, 63 (Duncan Fairgrieve, Mads Andenas, and John Bell, ed. 2002).

discussed in this book. Two main regularities are identified in the ECHR's judgments: It issues increasingly demanding judgments over the years, and it issues more demanding judgments against low-reputation states than against high-reputation states. When two judgments of the ECHR are compared to each other, two factors are therefore relevant: the period when the judgment was issued and the state the judgment was issued against. Sometimes these factors pull in opposite directions. For instance, if one judgment is both later in time than another and issued against a state with a higher reputation, it is impossible to predict whether the judgment will be more or less demanding.

For example, the recent *Greens* case led to a demanding Pilot Judgment against the United Kingdom, and the recent *Al-Skeini* and *Al-Jedda* judgments expanded jurisdiction over the United Kingdom's actions. The theory would account for these cases by explaining that, although the United Kingdom is a high-reputation state, the ECHR has increased its reputation enough over the years to make these judgments possible. While these judgments may be more demanding than judgments issued in the past against low-reputation states, this does not refute the claim that the ECHR is more restrained when facing high-reputation states, but instead it concurs with the claim that the ECHR raises its demands of all states over time.

There are several other reasons that make it difficult to demonstrate trends in the ECHR's behavior. The

ECHR will try to hide any sign of bias against certain states in order to maintain its public support. In order to refute accusations of bias, the ECHR can carefully distinguish between cases in ways that make their comparison nearly inscrutable. Furthermore, the ECHR may even strategically decide cases in ways that contradict the theory described here primarily to resist accusations of bias. For instance, the ECHR may deliberately demand more from a high-reputation state or deliberately reduce its demands from a low-reputation state in order to appear impartial. Comparing cases is also very difficult because cases always present different factual situations that call for different legal solutions. The doctrine of the ECHR itself changes over time and is different from case to case, which makes the comparison of cases even more problematic. In different cases, there are also political factors that can shape the strategy of the ECHR. For example, support from the national judiciary or the actions of NGOs may affect the ECHR's behavior. Finally, the reasoning the ECHR uses affects the remedies it can issue while expecting compliance and makes the analysis of reasoning and remedy inseparable.

Karl Popper, the great philosopher of science, emphasized that in order for a theory to have scientific value it must set conditions under which it can be falsified. In other words, if no possible empirical observation can contradict the theory, it does not have real predictive value.[83] The many possible factors mentioned above that determine the behavior of the ECHR render it difficult for any specific observation to falsify the theory described in this book. This difficulty should not be exaggerated, however. While a single judgment may not falsify the theory, certain patterns of behavior certainly can. If the ECHR incrementally reduced its demands from states over the years, despite very high compliance rates, this would have certainly falsified the theory. If the ECHR consistently demanded more from high-reputation states than from low-reputation states, this would falsify the theory as well. Trends in the judgments of courts are always difficult to describe, but this description is possible and often fruitful. Trends that contradict the theory presented in this book are certainly possible and could be described if they existed. This chapter, however, found that major trends in the ECHR's judgments concur with the theory and thus lend the theory some additional support.

While trends that contradict the theory can be easily imagined, they cannot be carefully analyzed as long as they remain abstract counterfactuals. The theory described in this book applies only to certain courts that operate under certain conditions. Other courts, or the same courts

[83] See Karl Popper, *Conjectures and Refutations*, 43–48 (London and New York: Routledge Classics), reprinted, 2006. See also Jeffrey A. Segal and Harold J. Spaeth, *The Supreme Court and the Attitudinal Model Revisited*, 47–48 (Cambridge, UK: Cambridge University Press), 2002.

operating under different conditions, may behave differently from the prescriptions of the theory. These behavior patterns can be analyzed to expose how they differ from the trends explained by the theory. This analysis will illustrate and demonstrate the conditions for the falsification of the theory. This is the purpose of the next chapter.

7 When compliance is irrelevant

The previous chapters described the behavior of courts that try to maximize their reputation by walking on the brink of noncompliance. These chapters argued that courts take calculated risks; they risk a certain probability of noncompliance by issuing demanding judgments or using discretionary reasoning, but can potentially increase their reputation as a result. Courts would behave in this manner under certain conditions that are detailed in Chapter 2G. When different conditions hold, courts would not necessarily behave differently; in fact, many judicial tactics mentioned in this book are intuitively applicable to courts in other conditions as well. However, under different conditions, courts might behave differently and practice other forms of strategic behavior.

The main condition for courts to practice a strategy of walking on the brink of noncompliance is that a risk of noncompliance is possible but not likely. If compliance is certain, the court does not take a risk of noncompliance and may behave differently from a court that has to consider the risk of noncompliance in its calculations. If the court expects a very high probability of noncompliance, either with all its judgments or with a specific judgment, its reputational calculations are fundamentally different from a court that expects compliance with most of its judgments, and it may behave differently. If the court's judgment does not require any act of compliance, the court does not have to consider the possibility of noncompliance at all and may behave differently than a court that requires certain actions to comply with its judgment. Finally, judges may stray from the strategy presented here in a host of other unique situations in which they take into account other considerations as more important than maximizing their reputation over the long term. These different conditions and the different forms of behavior they lead to are described in the next sections.

The examples in this chapter are not meant to provide a comprehensive theory of how courts act when they do not act as reputational maximizers. The purpose of this chapter is rather to demonstrate that forms of behavior that contradict the judicial tactics mentioned here are possible. By presenting and analyzing different forms of courts' behavior, this chapter demonstrates that the strategy presented in the previous chapters does not cover all possible forms of judicial behavior. This suggests that the theory of how courts act when they do act as reputation maximizers is falsifiable, and the conditions for its falsification are not far-fetched or imaginary.

Chapter 2G describes other conditions for the applicability of the theory to different courts that do not relate directly to compliance. They pertain to other issues such as the institutional structure of the court, the parties it faces, and the size of its caseload. If these conditions do not apply, courts may also behave differently than the theory prescribes, but these other conditions and the behaviors they lead to will not be discussed in this book.

A. Almost certain compliance

Even high-reputation courts usually face some risk of noncompliance. This is why walking on the brink of noncompliance is risky. The court may miscalculate and issue a judgment that would not be complied with and will damage its reputation. Parties usually comply with courts because they fear a reputational sanction in case of noncompliance. If the judgment is too demanding, parties may decide not to comply because the reputational sanction is lower than the costs of compliance. In some situations, however, parties may have other reasons to comply in addition to the fear of a reputational sanction. Alternatively, facts relating to the judgment may render any act of noncompliance especially damaging for the reputation of the party subject to the judgment. In these situations, the court may be able to issue especially demanding judgments even though other judgments that require actions of similar magnitude would result in noncompliance. The following are several examples of such situations that demonstrate behavior contrary to the tactics discussed in this book.

Chapter 4B argued that when the court's reputation is low, it should issue less demanding judgments than when its reputation is high. In the beginning of the new millennium, the Israeli Supreme Court came under attack by the executive and suffered instances of noncompliance that lowered its reputation. The court responded by shifting to less-demanding judgments in an effort to ensure compliance, as described in Chapter 5. In this regard, the court's practice concurred with the theory that low-reputation courts should issue less-demanding judgments than high-reputation courts. Yet in 2009 the court issued one of its most demanding judgments in the *Human Rights Division* case.[1] This judgment annulled the statute that authorized the operation of the first private prison in Israel. Nevertheless, the analysis of this judgment in Chapter 5 suggests that noncompliance was not a viable option. It is impossible to hide the operation of a new prison from the media and the public, and the only way to override the judgment is to

[1] HCJ 2605/05 *Human Rights Division* v. *The Minister of Finance* (not yet published, November 19, 2009).

change the Basic Law: Human Dignity and Liberty. Although the Israeli executive proved willing to repeatedly delay compliance in other cases, or to ignore judgments when this could be done quietly and secretly, it was not prepared to openly admit to noncompliance with the court in such a salient issue. The executive also could not afford to change or annul Israel's most important Basic Law. This case therefore presented the court with a golden opportunity. It allowed the court to issue a very demanding judgment that was almost certain to lead to compliance because noncompliance could not be hidden from the public. Furthermore, because the majority of the public resisted the idea of a public prison, the chances of noncompliance were even smaller, and the court could use its decision to rebuild its damaged public support. This case demonstrates that even when the court's reputation is relatively low and the theory recommends the court should shift to less-demanding judgments, the court may behave differently if it does not face the risk of noncompliance. If compliance is assured because of unique attributes of the case, the court may use the case to issue especially demanding judgments.

Chapter 4D suggested that courts should match very demanding judgments with constrained reasoning – for instance, by suppressing dissent and referring to sources that seem to constrain judicial discretion. The decision of the U.S. Supreme Court in *Lawrence* v. *Texas*[2] seems to

[2] *Lawrence* v. *Texas*, 539 U.S. 558 (2003).

contradict this judicial tactic. This judgment found the Texas law forbidding sodomy between members of the same sex unconstitutional because it violated the right to liberty under the due process clause. The judgment overruled a precedent of the Supreme Court in the *Bowers* v. *Hardwick* case[3] issued only seventeen years before, and because the Texas statute was annulled on constitutional grounds, all states had to conform to the new decision. Therefore, the judgment was certainly demanding. However, the judgment contained a strong dissenting opinion by Justice Scalia that exposed the fact that the judgment was not constrained by the law. Chief Justice Rehnquist joined the dissenting opinion. Even Justice Thomas joined the dissent, although he argued that the law was "uncommonly silly" and that if he were a member of the Texas Legislature, he would vote to repeal it. Thomas noted that he had to decide cases according to the Constitution and found no general right of privacy that justified an annulment of the law, thus exposing the majority's decision as either wrong or discretionary. Why did the justices in the majority not suppress these dissents, either by compromising on the final result, delaying their judgment, or negotiating with the justices in the minority? In similarly demanding judgments in the past, such as *Brown*, great efforts to suppress dissents were used, and the Court presented a united front, as Chapter 2D3 demonstrates.

[3] *Bowers* v. *Hardwick*, 478 U.S. 186 (1986).

Besides the issue of dissent, *Lawrence* refers to a judgment of the ECHR in the *Dudgeon* v. *United Kingdom case*,[4] which ruled that laws proscribing homosexual conduct between consenting adults violated the European Convention. The reference was used to disprove the claim in *Bowers* that protecting the rights of homosexuals was foreign to Western civilization. The reference to a judgment of a foreign court in a case of the U.S. Supreme Court that dealt with constitutional interpretation was extremely rare and problematic.[5] It was criticized by Scalia, who argued the Court chose only the legal systems that suited its wishes and ignored those that contradicted its decision;[6] in other words, the justices used their discretion and did not hide it.

A possible explanation for the use of discretionary reasoning in this demanding judgment is the substantial public support for the decision to decriminalize private homosexual conduct.[7] The majority opinion deliberately stressed that the judgment did not support same-sex marriages, which were still not endorsed by the consensus,[8] even though Scalia tried to suggest that the logic of the

[4] *Dudgeon* v. *The United Kingdom*, judgment of October 22, 1981 EUR. Ct. H.R. (ser. A)45.

[5] Michael J. Klarman, *Brown* and *Lawrence* (and *Goodridge*), 104 *Michigan Law Review* 431, 439 (2005).

[6] *Lawrence*, *supra* note 2 at 598.

[7] See Klarman, *supra* note 5 at 478.

[8] See *Ibid*. at 450; *Lawrence* at 578, 585.

judgment would necessitate this further step.[9] The Court was therefore certain that the public was on its side and supported the decision on the merits. It did not have to rely on reputational sanctions to ensure compliance and knew the public would not tolerate noncompliance with the decision it considered just and correct. For this reason, the Court could neglect the practice prescribed by the theory of supporting demanding judgments with constrained reasoning. Instead the Court acted contrary to the theory that explains cases where noncompliance is possible and supported a very demanding decision with a reasoning that exposed its discretion.

Chapter 4G suggests that international courts should issue less-demanding judgments against high-reputation states than they do against low-reputation states. Noncompliance by a high-reputation state can cause the court a substantial damage, and the court should usually restrain itself to avoid this result. However, if a high-reputation state is almost certain to comply for another reason not related to the court, and is also unlikely to criticize the court or damage it in other ways, then the court may behave differently. Without a real risk of noncompliance, the court can issue demanding judgments with impunity. This is an opportunity for the court to change the behavior of high-reputation states to suit its preferences. It is also an opportunity to improve its reputation by showing

[9] See *Lawrence* at 604–605.

compliance with demanding judgments and to refute any accusations of bias in favor of high-reputation states.

Chapter 3E gives the example of the ECHR case *A* v. *United Kingdom*. This case ruled that it was a violation of liberty to detain foreign nationals suspected of terrorism who could not be deported for fear they would be abused in their home countries. The court could mount this attack on a policy of the United Kingdom in the sensitive issue of national security with relative safety because it followed a decision of the British House of Lords on exactly the same issue that also condemned the British policy. This case demonstrates that international courts can shed the restraint they adopt when they face high-reputation states when they are certain they will not suffer noncompliance or criticism.

The examples above do not even begin to outline a theory of how courts act when compliance is assured. Instead, they try to trace the borders of the applicability of the strategy of walking on the brink of noncompliance. When the brink is guarded by some other actor, such as public opinion or another powerful court, courts do not have to practice caution and can put aside the judicial tactics described in Chapter 4 in favor of other forms of behavior.

B. Almost certain noncompliance

The theory presented in this book applies only to courts that are usually complied with. Low-reputation courts as they are defined here are complied with less often than high-reputation courts, but even in low-reputation courts compliance is the norm. If a court expects noncompliance in most or even many of its cases, the theory will not apply because the incentives of this very-low-reputation court are fundamentally different than the incentives of the courts discussed in this book. The theory rests on the assumption that courts lose more reputation for every instance of noncompliance than the reputation they gain for every instance of compliance, because noncompliance is far less expected than compliance and therefore serves as a more potent signal. This assumption leads to the strategy of walking on the brink; courts try to ensure compliance with their judgments by requiring states to undertake actions they perceive to be slightly less costly than the reputational cost of noncompliance for the state.

If the norm is that the court's judgments are not complied with, however, in every instance compliance is less expected than noncompliance. This means the court would gain more reputation for compliance than it would lose for noncompliance. In this case, the court may find it profitable to take wild risks and issue demanding judgments that have only a small chance of compliance. Even if many of these judgments do lead to noncompliance, as the court expects, perhaps one or two would result in compliance and attract attention that would improve the court's reputation significantly. If compliance leads to a higher benefit than the cost of noncompliance, the expected utility of a demanding judgment that would be complied with only at a low probability may still be positive and prove to be the best strategy for the court. It may prove a better course than to minimize the requirements of the judgments to the point where compliance, which is still uncertain, does not help the court's reputation at all, because it does not signal a real ability to affect the conduct of other parties. Strategies of issuing restrained judgments by very-low-reputation courts are certainly possible, however. This book does not try to provide a full theory of how these courts act. It only stresses that their fear of noncompliance is not as great as that of the courts discussed in this book, and they have very much to gain from a salient case of compliance with a demanding judgment. This inverse incentive structure can lead to many different forms of behavior; only some are discussed here.

The Inter American Court of Human Rights (IACHR) is a clear example of a court where noncompliance is the norm. The court was conceived in 1969 when the Organization of American States adopted the American Convention of Human Rights, and the first set of judges was elected to the court in 1979, making it a relatively young court. Besides its youth, the court had to face other enormous challenges, including the complex issues arising from atrocities committed by dictatorial regimes, severe resistance by states under its jurisdiction, and an extremely low budget.[10]

[10] See Alexandra Huneeus, Courts Resisting Courts: Lessons from the Inter-American Court's Struggle to Enforce Human Rights, 44 *Cornell International Law Journal* 493, 499–500 (2011).

It may come as no surprise that the IACHR has a very low compliance rate. Exact compliance rates are hard to calculate and to agree upon, but the data is unambiguous. Some scholars claim that states fully implemented only one out of ten judgments.[11] Others assess the chances of full compliance as 11.57%[12] or estimate a compliance rate of 5%.[13] What is far more surprising is that despite these great obstacles, the IACHR issues incredibly demanding judgments and does so at an increasing intensity.

In many of its judgments, the IACHR issues specific and detailed orders to the states under its jurisdiction, increasingly requiring actions from national judiciaries.[14] In many cases the IACHR calls for prosecution of criminals that involves the state's executive, judiciary, and public ministry in charge of prosecution – only one out of fifty such orders was complied with.[15] Why would the IACHR deliberately issue judgments it knows face a 2% chance of compliance instead of restraining itself as much as possible, for instance by requiring actions only from the executive or even settling

[11] *Ibid.* at 504.

[12] See James L. Cavallaro and Stephanie Erin Brewer, Reevaluating Regional Human Rights Litigation in the Twenty-First Century: The Case of the Inter-American Court, 102 *American Journal of International Law* 768, 786 (2008).

[13] See Eric A. Posner & John C. Yoo, Judicial Independence in International Tribunals, 93 *California Law Review* 1, 43 (2005).

[14] Huneeus, *supra* note 10 at 501–502.

[15] See *Ibid.* at 509.

for monetary compensation when these actions may well result in compliance in one out of two or one out of three judgments? One reason may be purely ideological: The IACHR refuses to settle for bland remedies for fear it would betray its purpose and sticks to the right course no matter the consequences.[16] Another reason may be strategic: The IACHR must adopt a different strategy than the courts discussed in this book. It cannot focus on maximizing the chances of compliance if this means that its judgments will be so restrained that compliance would not signal any judicial power. Besides, even in these judgments, apparently the best chances of compliance it can hope for are less than 50%. Instead, the IACHR adopted the mentality of a gambler. It continues to issue demanding judgments and hopes to obtain compliance once in a while, which would greatly boost its reputation.

The entire theory of courts as reputation maximizers rests on the assumption that courts try to promote their preferences through their judgments, an assumption that is shared by much of the literature on judicial behavior. Reputation is a tool to ensure compliance with the court's future judgments. If the court's judgments are complied with, the court can change the behavior of the parties under its jurisdiction to suit its policy preferences. However, courts may have other aspirations besides shaping policy by ensuring compliance with their

[16] See *Ibid.* at 519–520.

judgments.[17] For example, an international court may want to expose information that can lead to long-term changes in public opinion and to acceptance of certain norms and values in the distant future. If this international court knows that its ability to shape policy by issuing judgments that are complied with is questionable, it may rationally decide to put less emphasis on increasing its reputation. The court may instead try to serve as a tool to disseminate information that may change the world for the better, even if this practice results in damage to its reputation.

The conduct of the IACHR may be inspired by this rational calculation as illustrated by the unique way the IACHR treats states in its jurisdiction that are attempting to acknowledge their guilt and admit responsibility for their actions. The IACHR often follows an acceptance of responsibility by the state with days of hearings, the collection of evidence from witnesses, and a presentation of a comprehensive analysis of the facts. This conduct suits the court's goal of exposing information to shape long-term processes within the states. It prevents the state from preempting this exposure of information that can damage its interests by

[17] See Yuval Shany, Assessing the Effectiveness of International Courts: A Goal-Based Approach, 106 *American Journal of International Law* 225, 244–247 (2012) (presenting four different goals of international courts: promoting compliance with the governing norms, resolving disputes and problems, supporting related regimes, and legitimizing norms and institutions).

admitting responsibility before the facts have been presented to the public.[18] Scholars urge the IACHR to invest even more of its resources in studying and presenting the facts and to court media attention by holding frequent public hearings.

These actions may not suit other courts that can rely on compliance with their judgments.[19] If a court usually expects compliance, it may accept any acknowledgment of guilt as an easy opportunity to shape the behavior of states at very little cost and decide to close the case as quickly as possible. It may economize on the resources necessary to expose information or gain media attention and instead focus on shaping its reasoning and its remedies in ways that help its reputation, or it can try to increase the volume of the cases it processes. The IACHR's behavior reflects an understanding that because its reputation is very low to begin with, it should prioritize other issues.

Sometimes even a court with a relatively high reputation may be certain that one of its judgments will not be complied with. Courts are constrained by doctrine and by political factors and cannot always bend the remedies of their judgments to suit the interests of the parties in order to ensure compliance. If the court is forced to issue a certain remedy, noncompliance may be certain or very likely, but the court may still have a way out. Courts are often tasked

[18] See Cavallaro and Brewer, *supra* note 12 at 808–816.
[19] *Ibid.* at 792–795.

with determining their own jurisdiction. If the court decides that it does not have jurisdiction to decide the case, it prevents the possibility of noncompliance. Even if the court decides it has jurisdiction, it may find the case inadmissible and avoid it in this fashion. The rules of admissibility usually give courts greater discretion than the rules on jurisdiction and therefore an even greater opportunity to strategically avoid cases.[20] Authors have claimed that the ICJ deliberately avoided cases that it was certain would result in noncompliance by finding that it had no jurisdiction, even contrary to its own established doctrines of jurisdictional competence.[21]

As an easy way out of a case, a court can decide it has no jurisdiction, but sometimes this escape route is closed or has its own risks. Decisions regarding jurisdiction are also

[20] Yuval Shany, Jurisdiction and Admissibility, in *The Oxford Handbook of International Adjudication* (Cesare P.R. Romano, Karen J. Alter, and Yuval Shany, eds.), 2013.

[21] See W. Michael Reisman, *Nullity and Revision: The Review and Enforcement of International Judgments and Awards*, 641–642 (New Haven: Yale University Press), 1971. Reisman provides two examples for this strategy: The Anglo-Iranian Oil Company case (Preliminary Objections), [1952] ICJ Rep 93, where the ICJ uses a very restrictive interpretation, which markedly differs from the interpretation it employed only days earlier to decline jurisdiction, knowing that Iran would fail to comply, and the Case Concerning the Aerial Incident of 27 July 1955 (Preliminary Objections), [1959] ICJ Rep. 127, where the court uses a reasoning it overruled in succeeding cases knowing that communist Bulgaria would fail to comply.

constrained by the law and by the political pressures on the court. In some cases, the court may be forced to find jurisdiction because the relevant norms are clear, and in others it may acknowledge that abdicating this case may lead to criticism or expose its fear of noncompliance to all states involved, thus lowering its reputation. In these cases, the court may be forced to decide the case and issue a judgment it knows will almost certainly lead to noncompliance. A court stuck in this difficult position may adopt a unique strategy: It may decide to deliberately issue a very demanding judgment and by this minimize the reputational costs of noncompliance. Noncompliance with a very demanding judgment does not damage the court's reputation as much as noncompliance with a less-demanding judgment, because even high-reputation courts are likely to suffer noncompliance when their demands are extreme. This move is very dangerous, however. The party against which this especially demanding judgment is issued may respond by damaging the court in other ways besides noncompliance. It may criticize the court, curtail its budget, or even exit its jurisdiction; actions it would not take if the judgment was milder and took its interest into account. The ICJ *Nicaragua* case may serve as an example for this unique gambit.

The ICJ is not a perfect example for the theory because it always faces two states at the same time. However, it often embodies the theory because it tries to ensure compliance with its current and future judgments. If one state that appears before the ICJ is far more powerful than the other, the ICJ may prudently consider mainly the interests of this powerful state and act in a similar fashion to a supranational court, which faces one state at a time.

The ICJ *Nicaragua* case pitted the United States against a small and powerless state and may therefore have called for a cautious strategy targeted at ensuring American compliance. However, the circumstances of the case prevented the ICJ from practicing this standard strategy, and instead led it to exaggerate its demands from the United States. The ICJ first decided that it had jurisdiction, thus leaving it little possibility to retreat. This decision was made despite an effort by the United States to leave the court's jurisdiction by sending a notification that excluded disputes with Central American states or disputes related to events in Central America from its agreement to compulsory jurisdiction. The United States intended to make these reservations effective immediately.[22] When its efforts to escape jurisdiction proved futile and before the judgment on the merits, which was issued separately, the United States responded with a series of actions that made it clear it would not comply with a judgment against it, at least one that required any substantial action. It decided not to

[22] Case Concerning Military and Paramilitary Activities in and Against Nicaragua (jurisdiction of the court and admissibility of the application) [1984] ICJ Rep 392, 398 (judgment of November 26, 1984).

participate in the case and made no appearances in the merits stage. Later it withdrew its general agreement to the ICJ's compulsory jurisdiction.[23]

Faced with the imminent prospect of noncompliance, the ICJ decided not to retreat. Instead of minimizing its requirements from the United States, it issued a very demanding judgment. The judgment found that the United States breached its duty under customary international law not to intervene in the affairs of other states or to use force against them. It ordered the United States to cease its violations and to compensate Nicaragua for the injuries caused by its actions.[24] This strategy may have minimized the damage to the ICJ's reputation when the United States failed to comply, because noncompliance to such a judgment was anything but unexpected. This judgment may have provoked the ire of the United States, however, and fueled its long-term hostility to the ICJ.[25]

It is important to reiterate that a decision by a state to comply or fail to comply does not end the strategic interaction between it and the court. States can continue to exert

[23] Robert J. Delahunty and John Yoo, Executive Power v. International Law, 30 *Harvard Journal of Law & Public Policy* 73, 110 (2006–2007).

[24] Case Concerning Military and Paramilitary Activities in and Against Nicaragua (Merits) [1986] ICJ Rep 14, 146–149 (*Nicaragua* v. *U.S.*).

[25] See Eric A. Posner, *The Perils of Global Legalism*, 147–148 (Chicago: The University of Chicago Press), 2009.

pressure or punish the court in a variety of ways, some of which are discussed in Chapter 3. The court may also consider that although it lost the battle for compliance, it may yet win the war and bend the state to its will by shaping public opinion. Chapter 3E argues that this may have been the ICJ's intention in its decision in the *Avena* case.[26] Although the United States expectedly failed to comply with the requirement to review convictions and death sentences of Mexican nationals who were denied their rights under the Vienna Convention on Consular Relations, the ICJ may have won important support for the legal considerations mentioned in its judgment. To the extent that international and national courts consider their ability to shape public opinion in the long run as important, this is a consideration that can shape the remedies and reasoning of their judgments. If compliance is viewed as unlikely in any case, this consideration would assume priority.

C. No tangible compliance required

The main tool parties can use to retaliate against a court that issues a judgment against them is to fail to comply. The court can try to prevent this behavior using several tactics. For instance, Chapter 4F discussed the ability of courts to prevent noncompliance with a judgment that sets

[26] Case Concerning Avena and Other Mexican Nationals (*Mexico* v. *U.S.*), [2004] ICJ Rep. 12.

an important precedent by actually accepting the arguments of the party whose interests are damaged by this precedent regarding the case at hand. Chapter 4H discussed ways to appease the party who lost the case by taking its interests into account. There is another possibility, however: The court can decide against a party, but require no remedy, and therefore no action of compliance. If the court does not require any action from the party whose conduct it considers a violation of the law, this party cannot fail to comply and is thus denied its key method of retaliation against the court. The losing party also cannot comply with such a judgment, and this judgment therefore cannot serve to increase the court's reputation.

Yet such a judgment may help the court serve another goal such as to progress doctrine in a certain direction. If the court does not face the possibilities of either compliance or noncompliance, it may shape legal reasoning in ways that differ from the bulk of its judgments. For example, the court may use reasoning less carefully and preserve only a thin veneer of legality to disguise its policy making.

An example is the judgment of the ICJ against the United Kingdom in the *Corfu Channel* case.[27] This case discussed an incident in which two British warships struck mines in the Corfu Channel near the coast of Albania. The United Kingdom reacted by issuing a mine sweeping operation in the channel. The United Kingdom blamed

[27] Corfu Channel Case [1949] ICJ Rep. 4.

Albania for mining the channel and demanded compensation, while Albania argued that the mine sweeping operation violated international law. The case against Albania was decided on factual grounds; the court decided based on expert opinion that Albania knew that mines were laid in the channel. Because even the Albanian council conceded in advance that if Albania knew about the mines, it was responsible to notify the British ships, there was no legal question that Albania was guilty of the damage. The court required Albania to pay for the damage to the ships, but Albania failed to comply for more than forty years. Only in 1992 was a settlement on compensation between the United Kingdom and Albania eventually reached.

The judgment against the United Kingdom was a completely different story. The United Kingdom argued that it had a right to conduct the mine sweeping operation in order to secure evidence according to the rule of self-help. Instead of engaging with this legal argument, the court simply decided that in order to ensure respect for international law, it must find the British actions as violating Albanian sovereignty. However, this legal declaration served by itself as appropriate satisfaction, and no remedy was issued against the United Kingdom.[28] In making its decision, the court simply assumed the very thing that is had to prove, namely that British actions illegally violated Albania's sovereignty. If the United Kingdom's argument that it had

[28] *Ibid.* at 35.

a right to act under the rule of self-help was true, it served as an exception to Albania's right to preserve its sovereignty. This argument had to be fully addressed to reach the legal conclusion adopted by the court. The judgment against the United Kingdom therefore made a controversial policy decision that masqueraded as a legal one by using deliberate rhetoric.

The use of rhetoric to disguise policy decisions as legal ones is certainly not a unique phenomenon. Many would argue that judges make new laws all the time, while they dishonestly mask their policy decisions by referencing legal sources.[29] Nevertheless, this book draws attention to the fact that the willingness of judges to risk the exposure of their arguments as legally flawed varies according to the risk of retaliation they face.

If the court issues a demanding judgment and fears noncompliance as a result, it will be extra cautious to use constrained legal reasoning, as Chapter 4D argues. In the unique situation described above, the court does not face any prospect of noncompliance. It can therefore make law more freely and pay little heed to the need to mask its actions as legal. While some façade of legality is still necessary to preserve the court's public support, the court can risk flaws in reasoning that would be easily exposed by a careful lawyer or an ardent party whose interests were damaged.

[29] Martin Shapiro, Judges as Liars, 17 *Harvard Journal of Law & Public Policy* 155, 156 (1994).

In the *Corfu Channel* case the ICJ probably calculated that the United Kingdom could not fail to comply because it was required to do nothing and would be unlikely to criticize a judgment that partly serves its interests by granting it compensation from Albania. This gave the court an opportunity to develop the law without hiding its policy choices.

The same caveat that appears in the preceding sections applies also here. The arguments raised here do not try to present a theory of how courts act when they do not require any compliance. Different forms of behavior are certainly possible in this situation. Instead, the example brought here highlights that this is a unique situation that can lead to different behaviors than the ones described in the rest of the book.

D. Other unique situations

Chapter 4 stressed that courts do not practice the strategy of walking on the brink in all or even most of their cases. Courts may be constrained by doctrine, swayed by the fear of hostile responses, or may serve immediate policy goals instead of trying to increase their reputation. Moreover, there are other situations, some of which will now be addressed, in which courts would view certain cases as unique and therefore suitable for special types of strategic behavior, either directed at increasing their reputation or at serving other goals.

Reputation is a public perception of the court, and this public perception does not view all cases equally. Some cases are particularly salient, and the public would view compliance or noncompliance with them as more impactful on the court's reputation than other cases. A case may be salient because of the issue it deals with or because of the remedy the court issues.[30] However, some cases can also draw their salience from their timing and their place among other cases the court deals with. For instance, if a judgment is issued very early in the life of the court, it would naturally draw greater attention by the public. New courts should be aware of the harmful potential of noncompliance with their early judgments and practice greater caution. Even more veteran courts should ascribe different importance to cases according to their timing. For instance, if parties failed to comply with a series of the court's judgments, the court may try to break this pattern by issuing a very mild judgment that is likely to induce these parties to comply. Such an act of compliance can help the court's reputation, which may be fatally damaged by a pattern of persistent noncompliance.

Courts may also try to prevent a pattern of restrained judgments from emerging in the eyes of the public. If the court issues a series of restrained judgments, the public may deduce that it has a low reputation. In order to prevent that,

[30] See Frederick Schauer, Forward: The Court's Agenda and the Nation's, 120 *Harvard Law Review* 4, 34, 44–46 (2006).

the court can try to manipulate public perceptions by issuing a few demanding judgments. If these few judgments are salient enough, they may change the public perception of the court and improve its reputation. For example, some authors have argued that the Israeli Supreme Court usually served the interests of the Israeli government in the occupied territories, but has ruled against the government in a few highly publicized cases.[31] The court may have calculated that although serving the government's interests should be its primary strategy, it should sometimes change a strategy to avoid appearing too restrained.

It is important to stress that the final judgments of courts are only the tip of the iceberg in the legal and political drama of judicial decision making. Judges do much more than write final judgments. Before a case is decided, judges can pressure parties to settle and prevent the need for a judgment. This renders the set of judgments that are issued an inaccurate picture of the actual influence of the court on policy.[32] Judges may also affect the political arena by offering their views on legislation and reforms or through their activity as scholars. These activities have a bearing on the court's judgments because judges may change the

[31] Ronen Shamir, "Landmark Cases" and the Reproduction of Legitimacy: The Case of Israel's High Court of Justice, 24 *Law & Society Review* 781 (1990).

[32] Yoav Dotan, Judicial Rhetoric, Government Lawyers, and Human Rights: The Case of the Israeli High Court of Justice during the Intifada, 33 *Law & Society Review* 319, 346–347 (1999).

reasoning they use in their judgments to foster the success of these practices. Therefore, the political circumstances that are not covered in this book may change judgments in ways that may conflict with the theory presented here.

Chapter 4I discussed the possibility that courts would behave in ways that could harm their reputation to serve other goals and, in a sense, spend their reputational capital. In some cases judges may behave in ways that do not serve their reputation but do not necessarily damage it. In these cases, judges may use their legal position to affect the behavior of other branches of government in ways that serve their policy ends. Courts may realize that their ability to affect policy is limited by the legal tools they possess and by their political power. Some policy changes necessitate a reliance on another branch of government, such as the legislature, which can issue statutes and set a more general and a less vulnerable policy.

William Eskridge provides an example for such a strategy. He argues that the U.S. Supreme Court decided in the *Alyeska Pipeline Services* case[33] that attorney's fees for enforcing important rights were unrecoverable, in order to force Congress to settle fee shifting in a statute, as they eventually did.[34]

[33] *Alyeska Pipeline Service Co.* v. *Wilderness Society*, 421 U.S. 240 (1975).

[34] William N. Eskridge, Jr., Reneging on History? Playing the Court/Congress/President Civil Rights Game, 79 *California Law Review* 613, 625–626 (1991). For a similar strategy, see also William

Similarly, the Israeli Supreme Court sometimes forced the parliament to set the policy it deemed appropriate in legislation. For example, in the *Neiman* case[35] the court decided to repeal the decision of the election committee not to allow the racist party Kach to participate in the upcoming election. The justices made it abundantly clear they would rather Kach was not allowed to participate, but wanted the conditions for preventing parties from participating in elections to be set in legislation. After this decision, the parliament amended the Basic Law: The Knesset and added to it article 7A, which prevents the participation in elections of parties that deny the Jewish or democratic nature of Israel or that incite racism. Therefore, while the legislature was content to let the court pull its chestnuts out of the fire for years prior to the *Neiman* case,[36] the court's strategic response eventually pushed it to amend a legal situation described by Justice Ben Porat in the *Neiman* case as "intolerable." To complete the story, in the next elections Kach was again denied participation by the election committee, but under the new legal situation, the decision was affirmed by the court in the *Neiman II* case.[37]

N. Eskridge Jr., Overriding Supreme Court Statutory Interpretation Decisions, 101 *Yale Law Journal* 331, 388–389 (1991).

[35] EA 2/84 *Neiman* v. *Chairman of the Central Election Committee for the 11th Knesset* [1985] IsrSC 39 (2) 225.

[36] As an example, consider the *Yardor* case discussed in Chapter 2D3.

[37] EA 1/88 *Neiman* v. *Chairman of the Central Election Committee for the 12th Knesset* [1988] IsrSC 42 (4) 177.

This section provided a few scattered examples of conditions under which courts might issue judgments that do not fit a simplistic description of the strategy presented in this book. Many more situations may occur in which judgments cannot be easily explained by the theory, and a richer picture of the institutional and legal context is necessary to make sense of them. It is not the purpose of this chapter to detail all these conditions, only to highlight the fact that they are possible.

E. Conclusion

This chapter presented some of the situations where courts behave in ways that contradict or do not concur with the prescriptions of the theory presented in this book. This exercise served two goals: It circumscribed the boundaries of the theory's applicability, and it demonstrated behaviors that can falsify the theory under reasonable conditions. These goals, in turn, serve the purpose of demonstrating that under the conditions described in this book, a theory is presented that can fruitfully explain the behavior of courts. Admittedly, many times judgments and political situations are ambiguous and susceptible to many interpretations, so no theory of how courts behave is going to be conclusive. Nevertheless, to the extent that the arguments brought here are convincing, this book fulfilled its aim of providing a useful new way to interpret the behavior of courts.

8 Conclusions

A. Summary

In essence, this book tries to answer two questions: What do courts want, and how do they get it? The preceding chapters attempted to answer these two questions by providing a theory of courts as reputation maximizers. According to this theory, courts want to improve their judgment compliance reputation – the expectation of the public that parties would comply with the court's future judgments. This theory explains the interaction between national courts and the domestic executive as well as the interaction between international courts and states. In these interactions, the higher the court's reputation, the higher the reputational sanction against a party that fails to comply with its judgment and, consequently, the higher the chances that parties would comply with the court's judgments. A high reputation ensures the court that parties would comply with more of its judgments and would comply even with more demanding judgments than they would if the court had a low reputation. A high reputation therefore gives the court a greater ability to shape the behavior of parties according to its policy preferences. The theory of court's reputation was elaborated in Chapter 2.

The book argues that courts increase their reputation by issuing, in some cases, demanding judgments and judgments that use discretionary reasoning, which they expect parties to comply with. Courts try to "walk on the brink of noncompliance"– they issue judgments that, because of their demanding remedy or discretionary reasoning, would not be complied with if they were issued by a lower-reputation court. If such judgments are complied with, this signals that the court has a high reputation and leads the public to adjust their expectations upward that parties would comply with the court in the future, thus increasing the court's reputation.

Walking on the brink of noncompliance is risky, because parties may choose not to comply with the court's judgments, damaging the court's reputation. To minimize the risk and maximize the benefit to their reputations, courts use a variety of judicial tactics that are described in Chapter 4: Courts issue more demanding judgments and judgments with more discretionary reasoning when their reputation is higher, courts match demanding judgments with more constrained reasoning and less demanding judgments with more discretionary reasoning, and courts introduce new doctrines and shift to more demanding judgments incrementally while trying to minimize the chances of noncompliance. States that have an iterated interaction with the court may respond strategically to its judgments, forcing the court to use counter strategies. For example, courts can issue less demanding judgments against high-reputation states than against low-reputation states, knowing that high-reputation states can significantly damage the court's reputation by noncompliance, whereas low-reputation states can cause the court only limited damage.

National and international courts operate under several constraints as they try to increase their reputation. These were described in Chapter 3. Some constraints are internal: They circumscribe the discretion that doctrine and the legal system allow the judges. Other constraints are external: They include harmful responses that an executive can use against a national court and that states can use against an international court. These responses include criticizing the court, damaging its budget, and restricting its jurisdiction. As courts try to increase their reputations, internal and external constraints limit their ability to manipulate their judgments strategically. Courts must also be cautious to preserve their public support – the views of the public about the content and quality of their judgments. If courts lose public support, parties can more easily fail to comply with their judgments and damage their reputation.

This theory can explain the behavior of both international courts and national courts, but it does not apply to all courts under all conditions. In terms of international courts, the theory mainly explains the behavior of supranational courts. These are courts that deal with disputes between a single state and an individual, allowing the court to focus its strategic behavior on one state at a time. The behavior of national courts, on the other hand, is explained mainly in cases directed against the executive, a party that can fail to comply with the court.

Under the conditions described above, courts usually do not have strong enforcement mechanisms and must therefore rely on reputational sanctions to ensure compliance. The theory applies mainly to courts that have the following characteristics: They are courts of last resort, their judgments are regularly complied with, they deal with complex legal issues that give rise to judicial discretion, and they have a caseload large enough to allow for long-term strategic considerations.

Chapters 5 and 6 presented two case studies: one of a national court and one of a supranational court – the Israeli Supreme Court and the European Court of Human Rights, respectively. These two courts match the conditions for the applicability of the theory, and their judgments demonstrate the judicial tactics described in this book. These courts also share many characteristics with other major national and supranational courts. The analysis of their judgments exposes conditions that regularly occur in judicial decision making and can therefore help to explain the behavior of other courts operating under similar conditions. The theory can therefore shed new light on other supranational courts, such as the European Court of Justice, and national courts, such as the U.S. Supreme Court. By juxtaposing national and supranational courts, the theory also highlights the similarity of their judicial practices.

Some courts do not match the conditions for the applicability of the theory, because, for instance, their judgments are rarely complied with, as is the case with the Inter-American Court of Human Rights. If compliance with a certain judgment is either certain, almost impossible, or simply irrelevant, even courts that usually match the conditions for the applicability of the theory may behave differently than what the theory suggests. Chapter 7 investigated these conditions in the hope of both defining the boundaries of the theory and demonstrating that outside these boundaries different judicial behaviors are possible, making the theory falsifiable.

B. Normative implications

This book deliberately does not raise normative arguments. It does not take sides in the vibrant debate on whether judicial power is good or bad. Yet the analysis presented here has important normative implications that bear on this debate. The book explains how courts acquire reputation, which translates into power to shape policy and affect the behavior of other institutions. Those interested in the implications of judicial power should definitely find this book's analysis of the ways to increase, or alternatively to limit, this power fruitful.

Recent years have been marked by the proliferation of international courts. States who wish to construct a new functional international court can learn from the insights in this book. An important lesson from the book is that the reputation that the court has at its inception can significantly affect its ability to build its future reputation. If the court starts out with a low reputation, which means the community of states expects states would not comply with its judgments, states may indeed fail to comply, lowering the court's reputation even further and rendering it irrelevant. It is therefore important to give the court the highest possible reputation at the start. This can be accomplished by nominating high-quality and respected judges that parties are likely to defer to, by this increasing the expectation of compliance with the court's first judgments. The court should also be embedded within a strong treaty system, with an effective method of shaming or even coercing states into compliance. This may mean that the community of states subject to the court's jurisdiction should be limited at first only to a few states that are committed to the success of the treaty system, thus preventing rogue states from blemishing the court's reputation in its critical first years. Only if the founding states develop the habit of compliance with the court and increase its reputation over a certain point can it be profitable to extend the court's jurisdiction to other less disciplined states.

Another lesson from the book is that courts should behave differently when their reputation is high than when their reputation is low. Even a court that is constructed according to the prescription above would have a relatively low reputation at its inception, because no cases of compliance exist yet, and states' expectations of future compliance are not yet entrenched. This suggests that courts should begin their active life cautiously by issuing restrained judgments that do not require costly measures from the states and by using constrained reasoning that hides their discretion. The states that founded the court can guide the court toward the path of caution, by, for instance, setting clear rules within the treaty that prevent the need to use judicial discretion, limiting the ability of judges to dissent, or showing a preference for short and concise judgments. After the court has gathered enough reputation, it could relax these guidelines by interpreting them differently and expose more judicial discretion in an effort to further increase its reputation.

If an international court loses the support of the international public, because the public views its judgments as legally wrong or as biased, states may fail to comply with the court without subjecting themselves to criticism from the public. This increases the chances of noncompliance and therefore poses a danger to the court's reputation. If the international public do not know much about the court, they would not form a clear expectation that parties would comply with it and create no pressure on parties to comply, preventing the court from forming a stable reputation. In order to address these dangers, the states that construct an international court should invest in the court's public relations. They should invest in facilities that allow for the timely and accessible publication of the court's judgments, for the translation of these judgments to multiple languages, and for press releases that deliver the gist of the court's decision to a wide audience. They should encourage cooperation with academics and public officials within the states subject to the court's jurisdiction, for instance, by promoting clerkships and research periods at the court. This cooperation will educate knowledgeable individuals who will spread the word about the court in their own countries.

The procedures that regulate the ability of parties to serve as applicants or as friends of the court should have the long-term interests of the court in mind. For example, by drawing NGOs to bring cases or to submit briefs to the court, the court gains an opportunity to discuss important cases and earns free legal research. The court can also gain the cooperation of these NGOs: They could help to publicize the court and its judgments and may assist in exposing and shaming states who fail to comply, by this improving the chances of compliance. The interaction of the international court with national courts can also be regulated in a way that gives national courts an interest in enforcing the judgments of the international court in their states.

In some cases, it may be profitable to separate certain functions of the judicial processes, such as monitoring compliance, from the institution of the court. The court should focus its limited resources on issuing judgments that can improve its reputation. It may also be important for the court to distance itself from cases of noncompliance by associating these failures with other specialized institutions instead of with its own limitations.

Insights from this book could also serve new states or states that change their judicial systems, which may create new national courts of last resort or constitutional courts. If the government that creates one of these courts wishes the court to grow in power and influence, the government should follow similar guidelines to the ones suggested to states creating new international courts: The government should create mechanisms that help form an initial expectation of compliance by shaping the authoritative image of the court. It should also allow the court to proceed cautiously in its first years by legislating doctrines and procedures that would allow judges to hide their discretion.

The docket of the court should be calculated to allow the court to increase its reputation. This would prevent a flood of cases from reaching the court but allow it to decide enough cases to be relevant, and it would also give the court an opportunity to make meaningful decisions while at the same time closing the court's doors to certain politically sensitive cases that can harm its public support or that may lead to noncompliance. Preferably, the court should be allowed some control of its docket, allowing it to decide only cases that suit its strategic interests.

Governments who seek to empower their courts should allow the court to preserve high public support. They should give the court the proper facilities and resources to be well known and respected by the public. They should avoid criticizing the court in ways that can shift public opinion against the court by presenting the court as biased or unprofessional.

On the other hand, some governments may view judicial power with doubts and suspicion. They may want to prevent the court from garnering a high reputation from fear that a high-reputation court may force them to change their policies against their will. Such governments should do the opposite of what governments who want to serve the court's interests should do. Governments who fear judicial power may also try to constrain the court by the use of the harmful response mechanisms described in this book. But these governments should avoid giving the impression that the court is dependent on them and meekly serves their interests. If the public perceives the court as dependent on the executive, it may view the court's judgments as restrained even when they are in fact demanding. Consequently, when the executive fails to comply with a demanding judgment, it would be judged as if it failed to comply with a restrained judgment, and the executive's reputation would be severely damaged as a result. This counterintuitive dynamic gives courts that are perceived as dependent license to require more effort from the executive than courts perceived as independent, contrary to the executive's intention of constraining the court.

Judges on national and international courts who seek to increase their courts' reputation can shape their court's judgments to concur with the judicial tactics mentioned in this book. As judges seek to navigate the behavior of their court to improve its reputation, they may have to confront and bargain with other judges on the court and convince them to serve the court's interest instead of their own individual interests. If the court has a high reputation, the judges collectively gain a greater ability to serve their policy preferences. But improving the court's reputation may require judges to limit their bargaining power vis-à-vis other judges or to forgo other individual interests such as their personal prestige.

Judges can do much more than write judgments to help the court's reputation. They can increase support for the court by academic writing and lectures. They can often directly influence politicians and legislatures in their conversations and public activities outside the courtroom, even after they retire. This influence can be used to create legal and political conditions that are conducive to the court's reputation. Yet such activities were not investigated in this book.

Lawyers stand to benefit much from understanding the motivation of courts, because this understanding allows them to foresee potential judgments and to shape their litigation strategy accordingly. For example, if lawyers realize that the court has a low reputation, they should avoid petitioning for a demanding remedy, because the court may have no choice but to deny the petition in order not to generate noncompliance. Even lawyers approaching a high-reputation court with a request for a demanding remedy may want to supply the court with arguments that are well-grounded in the doctrine, because the court would need to use such arguments in its reasoning if it were to issue the requested judgment. Perhaps counterintuitively, lawyers who petition a high-reputation court for a relatively mild remedy may actually increase their chances if they supply the court with arguments that do not seem constrained by doctrine. The court may grant the requested remedy and grasp the opportunity to use the unconstrained arguments and render its reasoning discretionary, by this increasing its potential reputational gain.

As courts strategically increase their reputations, they produce judgments and precedents, and they create legal doctrines. These doctrines are followed and copied by the court that adopted them and transported to other courts through many complex routes. In this way, the laws of today are shaped by the strategies used by courts in the past. This should affect the way law is studied and understood – but that is a subject for an altogether different book.

Bibliography

Books

Arian, Asher et al., *Auditing Israeli Democracy: 2010 Democratic Values in Practice* (Jerusalem: The Israel Democracy Institute), 2010 (Hebrew).

Atiyah, P. S., and Summers, Roberts, *Form and Substance in Anglo-American Law: A Comparative Study of Legal Reasoning, Legal Theory and Legal Institutions* (Oxford: Clarendon), 1987.

Barak, Aharon, *Judicial Discretion* (Tel Aviv: Papyrus), 1987 (Hebrew).

Barak, Aharon, *The Judge in a Democracy* (Jerusalem: Keter), 2004 (Hebrew).

Bendor, Ariel L., and Segal, Zeev, *The Hat Maker: Discussions with Justice Aharon Barak* (Kinneret, Zmora-Bitan, Dvir: Or Yehuda), 2009 (Hebrew).

Boller, Paul F., Jr., and George, John, *They Never Said It: A Book of Fake Quotes, Misquotes & Misleading Attributions* (New York: Oxford University Press), 1989.

Cardozo, Benjamin N., *The Nature of the Judicial Process* (New Haven: Yale University Press), 1921.

Castberg, Frede, *The European Convention on Human Rights* (Dobbs Ferry, NY: Oceana Publications), 1974.

Dershowitz, Alan M., *Supreme Injustice: How the High Court Hijacked Election 2000* (New York: Oxford University Press), 2001.

Dijk, P. Van, and Hoof, G. J. H. Van, *Theory and Practice of the European Convention on Human Rights* (The Hague: Kluwer Law International), 3rd ed., 1998.

Dworkin, Ronald, *Taking Rights Seriously* (Cambridge, MA: Harvard University Press), 1978.

Ely, John Hart, *Democracy and Distrust: A Theory of Judicial Review* (Cambridge, MA: Harvard University Press), 1980.

Friedmann, Daniel, *The Purse and the Sword: The Trials of the Israeli Legal Revolution* (Tel Aviv: Miskal – Yedioth Ahronoth Books and Chemed Books), 2013 (Hebrew).

Gavison, Ruth, Kremnitzer, Mordechai, and Dotan, Yoav, *Judicial Activism: For and Against: The Role of the High Court of Justice in Israeli Society* (Jerusalem: Magnes Press), 2000 (Hebrew).

Guzman, Andrew, *How International Law Works: A Rational Choice Theory* (New York: Oxford University Press), 2008.

Hart, H. L. A., *The Concept of Law* (London: Oxford, Clarendon Press), 1961.

Hirschl, Ran, *Towards Juristocracy: The Origins and Consequences of the New Constitutionalism* (Cambridge, MA: Harvard University Press), 2004.

Hirschman, Albert O., *Exit, Voice, and Loyalty: Responses to Decline in Firms, Organizations, and States* (Cambridge, MA: Harvard University Press), 1970.

Janis, Mark W., Kay, Richard S., and Bradley, Anthony W., *European Human Rights Law: Text and Materials* (New York: Oxford University Press), 3rd ed., 2008.

Lahav, Pnina, *Judgment in Jerusalem: Chief Justice Simon Agranat and the Zionist Century* (Tel Aviv: Am Oved Publishers Ltd), 1999 (Hebrew).

Levitsky, Nomi, *Your Honor* (Jerusalem: Keter), 2001 (Hebrew).

Mautner, Menachem, *The Decline of Formalism and the Rise of Values in Israeli Law* (Tel Aviv: Ma'agalay Da'at Publishing House), 1993 (Hebrew).

Merrills, G., *The Development of International Law by the European Court of Human Rights* (Manchester, UK: Manchester University Press), 2nd ed., 1993.

Murphy, Walter F., *Elements of Judicial Strategy* (Chicago: The University of Chicago Press), 1964.

Ovey, Clare, and White, Robin C. A., *Jacobs & White: The European Convention on Human Rights* (New York: Oxford University Press), 4th ed., 2006.

Paul, Prucha Francis, *The Great Father: The United States Government and the American Indians* (Lincoln: University of Nebraska Press), 1984.

Popper, Karl, *Conjectures and Refutations* (London and New York: Routledge Classics), Reprinted, 2006.

Posner, Eric A., *The Perils of Global Legalism* (Chicago: The University of Chicago Press), 2009.

Posner, Richard A., *How Judges Think* (Cambridge, MA: Harvard University Press), 2008.

Rattner, Arye, *Legal Culture: Law and the Legal System in the Eyes of the Israeli Public 2000–2009* (Jerusalem: Sasa Center for Strategic Research) (Hebrew), 2009.

Reisman, W. Michael, *Nullity and Revision: The Review and Enforcement of International Judgments and Awards 641–642* (New Haven: Yale University Press), 1971.

Rosenberg, Gerald N., *The Hollow Hope: Can Courts Bring About Social Change?* (Chicago: The University of Chicago Press), 2nd edn., 2008.

Schelling, Thomas C., *The Strategy of Conflict* (Cambridge, MA: Harvard University Press), 1960.

Segal, Jeffrey A., and Spaeth, Harold J., *The Supreme Court and the Attitudinal Model Revisited* (Cambridge, UK: Cambridge University Press), 2002.

Shapiro, Martin, *The Supreme Court and Administrative Agencies* (New York: Free Press), 1968.

Smith, Jean Edward, *John Marshall: Definer of a Nation* (New York: Henry Holt and Company), 1996.

Spence, Michael, *Market Signaling: Informational Transfer in Hiring and Related Screening Processes* (Cambridge, MA: Harvard University Press), 1974.

Staton, Jeffrey K., *Judicial Power and Strategic Communication in Mexico* (New York: Cambridge University Press), 2010.

Sunstein, Cass R., *One Case at a Time: Judicial Minimalism on the Supreme Court* (Cambridge, MA: Harvard University Press), 1999.

Walker, Thomas G., and Epstein, Lee, *The Supreme Court of the United States: An Introduction* (New York: St. Martin's Press), 1993.

Zahavi, Amotz, and Zahavi, Avishag, *The Handicap Principle: A Missing Piece of Darwin's Puzzle* (New York: Oxford University Press), 1997.

Articles

Aolain, Fionnuala Ni, The Emergence of Diversity: Differences in Human Rights Jurisprudence, 19 *Fordham International Law Journal* 101 (1995).

Bassok, Or, Television Coverage of the Israeli Supreme Court 1968–1992: The Persistence of the Mythical Image, 42 *Israel Law Review* 306, 307 (2009).

Benvenisti, Eyal, Judicially Sponsored Checks and Balances, 31 *Hebrew University Law Review* 797 (2001) (Hebrew).

Benvenisti, Eyal, Judicial Review and Democratic Failures: Minimizing Asymmetric Information Through Adjudication, 32 *Tel Aviv University Law Review* 277 (2010) (Hebrew).

Benvenisti, Eyal, Reclaiming Democracy: The Strategic Uses of Foreign and International Law by National Courts, 102 *American Journal of International Law* 241 (2008).

Benvenisti, Eyal, and Downs, George W., The Empire's New Clothes: Political Economy and the Fragmentation of International Law, 60 *Stanford Law Review* 595 (2007).

Berutti, Ronald A., The Cherokee Cases: The Fight to Save the Supreme Court and the Cherokee Indians, 17 *American Indian Law Review* 291 (1992).

Brewster, Rachel, Unpacking the State's Reputation, 50 *Harvard International Law Journal* 231 (2009).

Cavallaro, James L., and Brewer, Stephanie Erin, Reevaluating Regional Human Rights Litigation in the Twenty-First Century: The Case of the Inter-American Court, 102 *American Journal of International Law* 768 (2008).

Cohen, Amichai, The Supreme Court and the Israel-Arab Conflict: An International Law Perspective 6 *Ono Academic College Law Journal* 263 (2006) (Hebrew).

Cooter, Robert D., The Objectives of Private and Public Judges, 41 *Public Choice* 107 (1983).

Cross, Frank B., and Nelson, Blake J., Strategic Institutional Effects on Supreme Court Decisionmaking, 95 *Northwestern University Law Review* 1437 (2001).

Cross, Frank B., and Tiller, Emerson H., Judicial Partisanship and Obedience to Legal Doctrine: Whistleblowing on the Federal Courts of Appeals, 107 *Yale Law Journal* 2155 (1998).

Dagan, Hanoch, The Realist Conception of Law, 57 *University of Toronto Law Journal* 607 (2007).

Delahunty, Robert J., and Yoo, John, Executive Power v. International Law, 30 *Harvard Journal of Law & Public Policy* 73 (2006–2007).

Dotan, Yoav, Judicial Rhetoric, Government Lawyers, and Human Rights: The Case of the Israeli High Court of Justice during the Intifada, 33 *Law & Society Review* 319 (1999).

Dotan, Yoav, Pre-petitions and Constitutional Dilemmas Regarding the Role of Government Lawyers, 7 *Mishpat Umimshal* 159 (2004) (Hebrew).

Dothan, Shai, *Elasticizing the Remedy of Voidness Due to Flawed Administrative Action – Relative Voidness* (Hebrew) (unpublished LLM thesis, Tel Aviv University 2003, on file with author).

Dothan, Shai, In Defence of Expansive Interpretation in the European Court of Human Rights, 3 *Cambridge Journal of International and Comparative Law* 508 (2014).

Dothan, Shai, How International Courts Enhance their Legitimacy, 14 *Theoretical Inquiries in Law* 455 (2013).

Dothan, Shai, Judicial Tactics in the European Court of Human Rights, 12 *Chicago Journal of International Law* 115 (2011).

Dothan, Shai, *Luring NGOs to International Courts* (unpublished draft).

Dothan, Shai, The Optimal Use of Comparative Law, forthcoming *Denver Journal of International Law and Policy*.

Eskridge Jr., William N., Overriding Supreme Court Statutory Interpretation Decisions, 101 *Yale Law Journal* 331 (1991).

Eskridge, Jr., William N., Reneging on History? Playing the Court/Congress/President Civil Rights Game, 79 *California Law Review* 613 (1991).

Farber, Daniel A., Rights as Signals, 31 *Journal of Legal Studies* 83 (2002).

Fuld, Stanley H., The Voices of Dissent, 62 *Columbia Law Review* 923 (1962).

Garoupa, Nuno, and Ginsburg, Tom, Reputation, Information and the Organization of the Judiciary, 4 *Journal of Comparative Law* 228 (2009).

Garrett, Geoffrey, R. Kelemen, Daniel, and Schulz, Heiner, The European Court of Justice, National Governments, and Legal Integration in the European Union, 52 *International Organization* 149 (1998).

Gearty, Conor, Unravelling Osman, 64 *Modern Law Review* 159 (2001).

Geisinger, Alex, and Stein, Michael Ashley, A Theory of Expressive International Law, 60 *Vanderbilt Law Review* 77 (2007).

Gibson, James, L., Caldeira, Gregory A., and Spence, Lester Kenyatta, Why Do People Accept Public Policies They Oppose? Testing Legitimacy Theory with a Survey-Based Experiment, 58 *Political Research Quarterly* 187 (2005).

Tom Ginsburg, Bounded Discretion in International Judicial Lawmaking, 45 *Virginia Journal of International Law* 631, 658 (2005).

Gneezy, Uri, and Rustichini, Aldo, A Fine Is a Price, 29 *Journal of Legal Studies* 1 (2000).

Goutal, Jean Louis, Characteristics of Judicial Style in France, Britain and the U.S.A, 24 *American Journal of Comparative Law* 43 (1976).

Gross, Miron, and Shachar, Yoram, Searching for Methods in Bench Selection in the Israeli Supreme Court: Quantitative Analysis, 29 *Hebrew University Law Review* 567 (1998).

Harel, Alon, The Courts and Homosexuality: Dignity or Tolerance? 4 *Mishpat Umimshal* 785 (1998) (Hebrew).

Hartman, Joan F., Derogation from Human Rights Treaties in Public Emergencies, 22 *Harvard International Law Journal* 1 (1981).

Hathaway, Oona A., Do Human Rights Treaties Make a Difference?, 111 *Yale Law Journal* 1935 (2002).

Helfer, Laurence R., Consensus, Coherence and the European Convention on Human Rights, 26 *Cornell International Law Journal* 133, 134 (1993).

Helfer, Laurence R., and Slaughter, Anne-Marie, Toward a Theory of Effective Supranational Adjudication, 107 *Yale Law Journal* 273 (1997).

Helfer, Laurence R., and Voeten, Eric, International Courts as Agents of Legal Change: Evidence from LGBT Rights in Europe, Forthcoming 68 *International Organization* 77 (2014)

Holmes, Oliver Wendell, The Path of the Law, 10 *Harvard Law Review* 457 (1897).

Huneeus, Alexandra, Courts Resisting Courts: Lessons from the Inter-American Court's Struggle to Enforce Human Rights, 44 *Cornell International Law Journal* 493 (2011).

Jackson, Joshua L., *Broniowski* v. *Poland*: A Recipe for Increased Legitimacy of the European Court of Human Rights as a Supranational Constitutional Court, 39 *Connecticut Law Review* 759 (2006).

Klarman, Michael J., *Brown* and *Lawrence* (and *Goodridge*), 104 *Michigan Law Review* 431 (2005).

Klarman, Michael J., *Brown* v. *Board of Education*: Law or Politics? (research paper No. 02–11 December 2002) available at http://ssrn.com/abstract_id=353361

Law, David S., A Theory of Judicial Power and Judicial Review, 97 *Georgetown Law Journal* 723 (2009).

Lindblom, Charles E., The Science of "Muddling Through," 19 *Public Administration Review* 79 (1959).

Lupu, Yonatan, International Judicial Legitimacy: Lessons from National Courts, 14 *Theoretical Inquiries in Law* 437 (2013).

Lupu, Yonatan, and Voeten, Erik, Precedent in International Courts: A Network Analysis of Case Citations by the European Court of Human Rights, 42 *British Journal of Political Science* 413 (2011).

Mahoney, Paul, Judicial Activism and Judicial Self-Restraint in the European Court of Human Rights: Two Sides of the Same Coin, 11 *Human Rights Law Journal* 57 (1990).

Mangan, Brendan, Protecting Human Rights in National Emergencies: Shortcomings in the European System and a Proposal for Reform, 10 *Human Rights Quarterly* 372 (1988).

McKaskle, Paul L., The European Court of Human Rights: What It Is, How It Works, and Its Future, 40 *University of San Francisco Law Review* 1 (2005).

McNollgast, Politics and the Courts: A Positive Theory of Judicial Doctrine and the Rule of Law, 68 *Southern California Law Review* 1631 (1995).

Miller, Gregory D., Hypotheses on Reputation: Alliance Choices and the Shadow of the Past, 12 *Security Studies* 40 (2003).

Moravcsik, Andrew, Explaining International Human Rights Regimes: Liberal Theory and Western Europe, 1 *European Journal of International Relations* 157 (1995).

Mowbray, Alastair, The Creativity of the European Court of Human Rights, 5 *Human Rights Law Review* 57 (2005).

Orakhelashvili, Alexander, Restrictive Interpretation of Human Rights Treaties in the Recent Jurisprudence of the European Court of Human Rights, 14 *European Journal of International Law* 529 (2003).

Ost, François, The Original Canons of Interpretation of the European Court of Human Rights, in *The European Convention for the Protection of Human Rights: International Protection Versus National Restrictions* 283 (Mireille Delmas-Marty, ed.). (Dordrecht: Kluwer Academic Publishers), 1992.

Popovic, Dragoljub, Prevailing of Judicial Activism over Self-Restraint in the Jurisprudence of the European Court of Human Rights, 42 *Creighton Law Review* 361, 372 (2009).

Posner, Eric A., and Figueiredo, Miguel F. P. de, Is the International Court of Justice Biased?, 34 *Journal of Legal Studies* 599 (2005).

Posner, Eric A., and Yoo, John C., Judicial Independence in International Tribunals, 93 *California Law Review* 1 (2005).

Post, Robert, The Supreme Court Opinion as Institutional Practice: Dissent, Legal Scholarship, and Decisionmaking in the Taft Court, 85 *Minnesota Law Review* 1267 (2001).

Priest, George L., and Klein, Benjamin, The Selection of Disputes for Litigation, 13 *Journal of Legal Studies* 1 (1984).

Putnam, Robert D., Diplomacy and Domestic Politics: The Logic of Two-Level Games, 42 *International Organization* 427 (1988).

Ramseyer, J. Mark, The Puzzling (In)Dependence of Courts: A Comparative Approach, 23 *Journal of Legal Studies* 721 (1994).

Rudolf, Beate, Constitutional Developments: European Court of Human Rights: Legal Status of Postoperative Transsexuals, 1.4 *International Journal of Constitutional Law* 716 (2003).

Ruth, Alexandra, and Trilsch, Mirja, *Bankovic* v. *Belgium* (Admissibility), 97 *American Journal of International Law* 168 (2003).

Ryssdal, R., The Enforcement System Set up under the European Convention on Human Rights, *in Compliance with Judgments of International Courts*, 49 (M.K. Bulterman and M. Kuijer eds.). (The Hague: Brill Academic Publishing), 1996.

Sadurski, Wojciech, Partnering with Strasburg: Constitutionalisation of the European Court of Human Rights, The Accession of Central and East European States to the Council of Europe and the Idea of Pilot judgments, 9 *Human Rights Law Review* 397 (2009).

Schauer, Frederick, Forward: The Court's Agenda and the Nation's, 120 *Harvard Law Review* 4 (2006).

Schulz, Heiner, The Political Foundations of Decision Making by the European Court of Justice, 99 *ASIL Proceedings* 132 (2005).

Shachar, Yoram, Solidarity and Generational Sequencing in the Israeli Supreme Court, 16 *Bar Ilan University Law Review* 161 (2000).

Shachar, Yoram, The Citation Space of the Supreme Court 1950–2004, 50 *Hapraklit* 29 (2008).

Shachar, Yoram, Gross, Miron, and Harris, Ron, Anatomy of Discourse and Dissent in the Supreme Court: Quantitative Analyses, 20 *Tel Aviv University Law Review* 749 (1997) (Hebrew).

Shachar, Yoram, Harris, Ron, and Gross, Miron, Citation Practices of the Supreme Court: Quantitative Analyses, 27 *Hebrew University Law Review* 119 (1996).

Shamir, Ronen, "Landmark Cases" and the Reproduction of Legitimacy: The Case of Israel's High Court of Justice, 24 *Law & Society Review* 781 (1990).

Shany, Yuval, Assessing the Effectiveness of International Courts: A Goal-Based Approach, 106 *American Journal of International Law* 225 (2012).

Shany, Yuval, Bosnia, Serbia and the Politics of International Adjudication, 45 *Justice* 21 (2008).

Shany, Yuval, Jurisdiction and Admissibility, in *The Oxford Handbook of International Adjudication* (Cesare P.R. Romano, Karen J. Alter, and Yuval Shany, eds.) (New York: Oxford University Press), 2013.

Shany, Yuval, The Entry into Force of the Rome Statute: What Are the Implications for the State of Israel? 9 *Hamishpat* 51 (2004) (Hebrew).

Shapiro, Martin, Judges as Liars, 17 *Harvard Journal of Law & Public Policy* 155, 156 (1994).

Spence, Michael, Job Market Signaling, 87 *The Quarterly Journal of Economics* 355 (1973).

Strauss, Peter L., One Hundred Fifty Cases per Year: Some Implications of the Supreme Court's Limited Resources for Judicial Review of Agency Action, 87 *Columbia Law Review* 1093 (1987).

Swindler, William F., Politics as Law: The Cherokee Cases, 3 *American Indian Law Review* 7 (1975).

Tamir, Michal, Sunk Cost and Stare Decisis, 1 *Haifa Law Review* 211, 285–286 (2004) (Hebrew).

Voeten, Erik, Public Opinion and the Legitimacy of International Courts, 14 *Theoretical Inquiries in Law* 411 (2013).

Voeten, Erik, The Impartiality of International Judges: Evidence from the European Court of Human Rights, 102 *American Political Science Review* 417 (2008).

Voeten, Erik, The Politics of International Judicial Appointments: Evidence from the European Court of Human Rights, 61 *International Organization* 669 (2007).

Weiler, J. H. H., The Transformation of Europe, 100 *Yale Law Journal* 2403 (1991).

Wildhaber, Luzius, The European Court of Human Rights: The Past, The Present, The Future, 22 *American University International Law Review* 521 (2007).

Wolfson, Yossi, *Punitive House Demolitions: HCJ 1730/96 Sabih v. Major General Ilan Biran commander of IDF Forces in the Judea and Samaria Region* (judgment dated March 19, 1996) available at www.hamoked.org/Document.aspx?dID=Documents1272

Wright, Jane, The Retreat from Osman: *Z* v. *United Kingdom* in the European Court of Human Rights and Beyond in *Tort Liability of Public Authorities in Comparative Perspective* 55 (Duncan Fairgrieve, Mads Andenas, and John Bell, eds.).

(London: British Institute of International and Comparative Law), 2002.

Yadlin, Omri, Judicial Activism and Judicial Discretion as a Strategic Game, 19 *Bar Ilan University Law Review* 665 (2003) (Hebrew).

Zamir, Itzhak, On Justice Zvi Berenson, 2 *Mishpat Umimshal* 325 (1994) (Hebrew).

Judgments

Israeli Supreme Court

HCJ 9353/08 *Abu Dheim* v. *GOC Home Front Command* (not yet published, January 5, 2009).

HCJ 2150/07 *Abu Safiya* v. *Minister of Defense* (not yet published, December 29, 2009).

HCJ 7052/03 *Adala* v. *The Minister of Interior* [2006] IsrSC 61(2) 202.

HCJ 5699/07 *Anonymous (a)* v. *The Attorney General* [2008] IsrSC 62(3) 550.

CrimA 8823/07 *Anonymous* v. *Israel* (not yet published, February 11, 2010).

ADA 10/94 *Anonymous* v. *Minister of Defense* [1997] IsrSC 53(1) 97.

Cr.A. 7048/97 *Anonymous* v. *Minister of Defense* [2000] IsrSC 54(1) 721.

HCJ 5973/92 *Association for Civil Rights in Israel* v. *Minister of Defense* [1993] IsrSC 47(1) 267.

HCJ 8575/03 *Azadin* v. *The Commander of the IDF Forces in the West Bank* [2003] IsrSC 58(1) 210.

CA 6821/93 *Bank Hamizrahi* v. *Migdal* [1995] IsrSC 49(4) 221.

HCJ 2056/04 *Beit Sourik Village Council* v. *The Government of Israel* [2004] IsrSC 58(5) 807.

CrimA 347/88 *Demjanjuk* v. *The State of Israel* [1993] IsrSC 47(4) 221.

HCJ 8397/06 *Eduardo* v. *Minister of Defense* [2007] IsrSC 62(2) 198.

CrimFH 2316/95 *Ganimat* v. *State of Israel*, [1995] IsrSC 49(4) 589.

CA 7379/06 *G.M.H.L Building Company 1992 limited* v. *Issai Taholian* (not yet published September 10, 2009).

HCJ 118/80 *Grinstein* v. *The Military Advocate General* [1981] IsrSC 35(1) 239.

HCJ 6427/02 *Hatnua Leeichut Hashilton* v. *The Knesset* [2006] IsrSC 61(1) 619.

HCJ 2605/05 *Human Rights Division* v. *The Minister of Finance* (not yet published, November 19, 2009).

HCJ 1715/97 *Israel Investments Directors Office* v. *Minister of Finance*, [1997] IsrSC 51(4) 367.

HCJ 241/60 *Kardosh* v. *Registrar of Companies* [1961] IsrSC 15(2) 1151.

HCJ 4542/02 *Kav Laoved Association* v. *The Government of Israel* [2006] IsrSC 61(1) 346.

HCJ 2918/93 *Kiryat Gat Municipality* v. *The State of Israel* [1993] IsrSC 47(5) 832.

HCJ 7957/04 *Mara'abe* v. *The Prime Minister of Israel* [2005] IsrSC 60(2) 477.

HCJ 1748/06 *Mayor of Daharia* v. *IDF Commander in the West Bank* (not yet published, December 14, 2006).

HCJ 7733/04 *Nasser* v. *Commander of IDF Forces in the West Bank* (not yet published, June 20, 2005).

EA 2/84 *Neiman* v. *Chairman of the Central Election Committee for the 11th Knesset* [1985] IsrSC 39 (2) 225.

EA 1/88 *Neiman* v. *Chairman of the Central Election committee for the 12th Knesset* [1988] IsrSC 42 (4) 177.

HCJ 6728/06 *"Ometz" Association (Citizens for Good Governance and Social Justice)* v. *The Prime Minister of Israel* (not yet published, November 30, 2006).

CA 183/69 *Petah Tikva Municipality* v. *Tahan* [1969] IsrSC 23(2) 398.

HCJ 2028/08 *Public Committee Against Torture* v. *Israel* (decision, March 24, 2009).

HCJ 1661/05 *Regional Council, Coast of Gaza* v. Knesset of Israel [2005] IsrSC 59(2) 481.

HCJ 910/86 *Ressler* v. *Minister of Defense* [1988] IsrSC 42(2) 441.

HCJ 6298/07 *Ressler* v. *The Knesset* (not yet published February 21, 2012).

HCJ 3267/97 *Rubinstein* v. *Minister of Defense* [1998] IsrSC 52(5) 481.

CrimA 866/95 *Sosan* v. *the State of Israel* [1996] IsrSC 50(1) 793, 817.

CA 311/57 *The Attorney General* v. *Dizengoff and Partners (SIT) limited* [1959] IsrSC 13 1026.

HCJ 4885/03 *The Israeli Birds Breeders Organization Agricultural Cooperation Society Ltd* v. The Israeli Government [2005] IsrSC 59(2) 14.

HCJ 2732/05 *The Mayor of Azon, Hasin* v. *The Government of Israel* (not yet published, June 15, 2006).

HCJ 6427/02 *The Movement for Quality of Government in Israel* v. *Knesset* [2006] IsrSC 61(1) 619.

HCJ 6055/95 *Tzemah* v. *Minister of Defense* [1999] IsrSC 53(5) 241.

Cr.A. 3660/03 *Ubeid* v. *Israel* (not published, September 8, 2005).

EA 1/65 *Yardor* v. *The Chair of the Electoral Committee of the 6th Knesset* [1965] IsrSC 19(3) 365.

HCJ 8414/05 *Yasin* v. *The Government of Israel* [2007] IsrSC 62(2) 822.

HCJ 466/07 *Zahava Gal-On* v. *The Attorney General* (not yet published January 11, 2012).

European Court of Human Rights

A and Others v. *The United Kingdom*, judgment of February 19, 2009, *Reports of Judgments and Decisions* 2009.

Airey case, judgment of October 9, 1979, EUR. Ct. H.R. (ser. A) 32.

Al-Jedda v. *The United Kingdom*, judgment of July 7, 2011 (Application No. 27021/08).

Al-Skeini and Others v. *The United Kingdom*, judgment of July 7, 2011 (Application. No. 55721/07).

Artico v. *Italy*, judgment of May 13, 1980 EUR. Ct. H.R. (ser. A) 37.

Assanidze v. *Georgia*, judgment of April 8, 2004, 2004-II EUR. Ct. H.R. 221.

Bankovic and Others v. *Belgium and Others*, decision of December 12, 2001, EUR. Ct. H.R. 2001-XII 333.

Broniowski v. *Poland*, judgment of June 22, 2004, 2004-V EUR. Ct. H.R. 1.

Christine Goodwin v. *The United Kingdom*, judgment of July 11, 2002, 2002-VI EUR. Ct. H.R. 1.

Cossey case, judgment of September 27, 1990 EUR. Ct. H.R. (ser. A)184.

Dudgeon v. *The United Kingdom*, judgment of October 22, 1981 EUR. Ct. H.R. (ser. A)45.

Golder v. *The United Kingdom*, judgment of February 21, 1975 EUR. Ct. H.R. (ser. A)18.

"Greek case" [1969], Eur. Comm. on Human Rights (report) at *Yearbook of the European Convention on Human Rights* 1969.

Greens and MT v. *United Kingdom*, judgment of November 23, 2010, *Reports of Judgments and Decisions* 2010.

Hirst v. *The United Kingdom* (No. 2), judgment of October 6, 2005, 2005-IX EUR. Ct. H.R. 187.

Hutten-Czapska v. *Poland*, judgment of June 19, 2006, 2006-VIII EUR. Ct. H.R. 57.

Ilascu and Others v. *Moldova and Russia*, judgment of July 8, 2004, 2004-VII EUR. Ct. H.R. 179.

Case of *Klass and Others*, judgment of September 6, 1978 EUR. Ct. H.R. (ser. A)28.

Lawless v. *Ireland* (No. 3), judgment of July 1, 1961, EUR. Ct. H.R. (ser. A)3.

Loizidou v. *Turkey* (Preliminary Objections), judgment of March 23, 1995, EUR. Ct. H.R. (ser. A)310.

Loizidou v. *Turkey*, judgment of December 18, 1996 (Merits), *Reports of Judgments and Decisions* 1996-VI.

Magomed Musayev and Others v. *Russia*, judgment of October 23, 2008 (application no. 8979/02).

Marckx case, judgment of June 13, 1979 EUR. Ct. H.R. (ser. A) 31.

Mehemi v. *France* (No. 2), judgment of April 10, 2003, 2003-IV EUR. Ct. H.R. 311.

Minelli case, judgment of March 25, 1983, EUR. Ct. H.R. (ser. A)62.

Osman v. *The United Kingdom*, judgment of October 28, 1998, *Reports of Judgments and Decisions* 1998-VIII 3124.

Rees v. *The United Kingdom*, judgment of October 17, 1986 EUR. Ct. H.R. (ser. A)106.

Scoppola v. *Italy* (No. 3), judgment of May 22, 2012, App. No. 126/05.

Scozzari and Giunta v. *Italy*, 2000-VIII EUR. Ct. H.R. 471.

Sejdovic v. *Italy*, judgment of November 10, 2004.

Sejdovic v. *Italy*, judgment of March 1, 2006, 2006-II EUR. Ct. H.R. 241.

Sheffield and Horsham v. *The United Kingdom*, judgment of July 30, 1998, 1998-V EUR. Ct. H.R. 2011.

Soering case, judgment of July 7, 1989, EUR. Ct. H.R (ser. A) 161.

Tyrer case, judgment of April 25, 1978 EUR. Ct. H.R. (ser. A)26.

X and Y v. *The Netherlands*, judgment of March 26, 1985 EUR. Ct. H.R. (ser. A)91.

Z and Others v. *The United Kingdom*, judgment of May 10, 2001, EUR. Ct. H.R. 2001-V 1.

U.S. Supreme Court

Alyeska Pipeline Service Co. v. *Wilderness Society*, 421 U.S. 240 (1975).

Bowers v. *Hardwick*, 478 U.S. 186 (1986).

Brown v. *Board of Education*, 347 U.S. 483 (1954).

Brown v. *Board of Education*, 349 U.S. 294 (1955).

Bush v. *Gore*, 531 U.S. 98 (2000).

Chevron U.S.A. INC v. *Natural Resources Defense Council Inc et al.*, 467 U.S. 837 (1984).

Cooper v. *Aaron*, 358 U.S. 1 (1958).

Fairfax's Devisee v. *Hunter's Lessee*, 11 U.S. 603 (1813).

Lawrence v. *Texas*, 539 U.S. 558 (2003).

Marbury v. *Madison*, 5 U.S. 137 (1803).

Martin v. *Hunter's Lessee*, 14 U.S. 304 (1816).

Medellin v. *Texas*, 552 U.S. 491 (2008).

United States v. *Nixon*, 418 U.S. 683 (1974).

Worcester v. *Georgia*, 31 U.S. 515 (1832).

International Court of Justice

Case Concerning the Aerial Incident of 27 July 1955 (Preliminary Objections), [1959] ICJ Rep. 127.

The Anglo-Iranian Oil Company Case (Preliminary Objections), [1952] ICJ Rep 93.

Case Concerning Avena and Other Mexican Nationals (*Mexico* v. *US*), [2004] ICJ Rep. 12.

Corfu Channel Case [1949] ICJ Rep 4.

Legal Consequences of the Construction of a Wall in the Occupied Palestinian Territory, Advisory Opinion (July 9, 2004).

Case Concerning Military and Paramilitary Activities in and Against Nicaragua (jurisdiction of the court and admissibility of the application) [1984] ICJ Rep. 392 (judgment of November 26, 1984).

Case Concerning Military and Paramilitary Activities in and Against Nicaragua (Merits) 1986 ICJ Rep 14, 146–149 (*Nicaragua* v. *US*).

Case Concerning Oil Platforms (*Iran* v. *US*) [2003] ICJ Rep. 161.

European Court of Justice

Case 48/74 *Mr. Charmasson* v. *Minister for Economic Affairs and Finance*, 1974 E.C.R II-1383.

Index

Index

Index